WE BELIEVE

A SIMPLE COMMENTARY ON

The Catechism of Christian Doctrine approved by the Archbishops and Bishops of England and Wales

Monsignor A. N. Gilbey

TAN Books
An Imprint of Saint Benedict Press LLC
Charlotte, North Carolina

Nihil obstat: Michael Quinlan, J.C.D.

Imprimatur: ✠ Thomas, *Ep. Salf.*
Salfordi, 5th October 1982

The Nihil Obstat and Imprimatur are a declaration that a book or pamphlet is considered to be free from doctrinal or moral error. It is not implied that those who have granted the Obstat and Imprimatur agree with the contents, opinions or statements expressed.

Retypeset and published in 2013 by TAN Books, an Imprint of Saint Benedict Press, LLC, Charlotte, North Carolina, with Americanization of word spelling.

Cover design by Caroline Kiser.

Front cover image: *The Transfiguration*, 1594–95 (oil on canvas), Carracci, Lodovico (1555–1619). Pinacoteca Nazionale, Bologna, Italy. Alinari, The Bridgeman Art Library.

Cataloging-in-Publication data on file with the Library of Congress.

ISBN 978-0-89555-316-4

Published in the United States by
TAN Books
An Imprint of Saint Benedict Press, LLC
P.O. Box 410487
Charlotte, NC 28241
www.tanbooks.com

Printed and bound in the United States of America.

To
William Guy
Adrian Mathias
Christopher Monckton
Victor Walne

Contents

PART I: FAITH

PART II: HOPE

PART III: CHARITY

APPENDICES

Note on the Text

THE text has been divided into chapters. Each chapter corresponds approximately to one of the weekly parts of the course, mentioned in the Preface, some of which have appeared in *The Universe*, the Catholic newspaper.

Selected quotations from the documents of the Second Vatican Council, which are grouped together at the end of the Commentary, are indicated by superscript numbers in the text.

The edition of the Catechism used is that of 1971. Quotations from the Holy Bible are in the Douay translation or in the Authorized Version. The latter is indicated by "AV." Quotations from the documents of the Second Vatican Council are taken from the compendium edited by Fr. Austin Flannery O.P. and published by Costello Publishing Company Inc.

The Fen Ditton Penance, mentioned in Chapter 16, is described in Chapter IX of *Cambridge Revisited* by Arthur B. Gray (Cambridge: W. Heffer & Sons, Ltd., 1921).

Author's Preface

THIS book is based upon recordings of a course of Instructions in the Faith, which I have given to enquirers. It is consequently conversational in tone, colloquial in vocabulary and frequently repetitive. I gave the Instructions at weekly intervals and hoped that enquirers would have time to ponder the content of each session before coming to the next. This book should be read ruminatively and made the subject of prayer.

It would never have occurred to me to offer these Instructions to a wider public than those to whom they were given. If any reader finds them of value, his thanks are due not to me but to four devoted friends who overcame my diffidence and undertook the whole responsibility of publishing the original edition, although none had professional expertise in this field. It is to them that the book is dedicated.

The idea of making the course into a book came from Adrian Mathias, William Guy recorded my words, Christopher Monckton, through his family connections, had it first printed by the Times of Malta and Victor Walne bore the entire burden of distributing the result. They further persuaded me to include as an Appendix a talk which I gave to a group of Catholic graduates at Oxford, which may be thought to be not wholly irrelevant.

Domine, ne respicias peccata mea, sed fidem Ecclesiae tuae.

A. N. G.

Truth alone is worthy of our entire devotion.

—Fr. Vincent McNabb, O.P.

CHAPTER 1

The Foundation of Faith in Reason

WHAT I propose to do is to take as the basis of our talks The Catechism of Christian Doctrine approved by the Archbishops and Bishops of England and Wales and published by the Catholic Truth Society. The Catechism is an extraordinarily valuable attempt to bring the whole scope of Catholic theology down to a small compass and almost to the vocabulary of a child. The point in taking the Catechism as the framework is that it does cover the whole ground. One of the things I want to emphasize is that Catholicism is one whole philosophy of life and not a series of disconnected statements of belief. It is to this whole philosophy of life that these Instructions, please God, will lead you.

The Catechism tries to cover the whole ground of what Catholics believe. If you turn back to the contents list of this book you will see the scheme on which the Catechism is composed. As you see, the whole scheme is concerned with Faith, Hope and Charity, the three theological virtues, which have Almighty God as their end and object. In accepting and practicing Faith, Hope and Charity we have fulfilled the whole duty of man. The fourth section of the Catechism, on the Sacraments, is only apparently an exception to the scheme. Logically and theologically the Sacraments come under the section of Hope, where I shall discuss them. I can only think that the Catechism puts them in a separate section in order to deal with them at greater length.

Coming now to the body of the Catechism, I shall make one of my few criticisms of a work of which I am a great admirer. That concerns the placing of the word "Faith" before Chapter 1. You will see that the place where it really belongs is between questions 8 and 9. Question 9, "What is Faith?" is the start of a new chapter and that is the point where the Catechism begins to consider Faith. Placing the word "Faith" at the very beginning of the whole work is really misleading because those first eight questions are an attempt to suggest to the mind of a child the preamble of faith, that is the foundation in natural reason that we need to lay before we can talk about Faith, Hope and Charity at all. These three theological virtues, as we shall consider later, are all gifts of Almighty God. What we need to do first is to exercise our minds to try to reach a rational concept of Almighty God, of our own nature, and of our own relationship to Him, before we start talking about His gifts to us.

We believe that it is possible for the unprejudiced human mind, even before consideration of divine revelation, to come to a certain but obviously very limited knowledge of five points: the existence of Almighty God; His nature; the immortality of the human soul; the freedom of the human will; and our consequent responsibility.

These five points—the existence of God, the nature of God, the immortality of the human soul, the freedom of the human will and our consequent responsibility—are a brief summary of what is properly called natural theology.

We believe that men can come to such knowledge and, in fact, that the overwhelming majority of men have come to it throughout the course of human history, conducting their lives in the belief that there is a Supreme Being, that He is a personal God, that we survive death, that we are free in our actions and that we are responsible for them.

The best classical presentation of these truths, which are not, as you see, especially Christian, let alone exclusively Catholic, is in the *Summa Theologica* of St. Thomas Aquinas. His approach to the existence of Almighty God is often spoken of popularly as his "five proofs." It is significant, however, that he does not use the word "proof" himself. I always try to avoid that word "proof," as it is liable to suggest a sort of knock-down argument. The word Aquinas uses is *viae*—that is, "ways"—which lead us to the knowledge of Almighty God. For our immediate purposes we need dwell only on two of the five "ways," but I do want to spend a little time on those two because they are immensely important. They have so many practical applications to the conduct of our lives and are a very necessary foundation of much that we shall consider later in this course.

The first of the five "ways" of Aquinas, which is almost an obsession with me and which I find extraordinarily fruitful, is what he calls "the argument from contingent being." Very simply it is this: nothing that we know exists of itself. There was a time when everything of which we have knowledge or experience did not exist; and there will come a time when it will cease to exist. Existence, or being, is not, therefore, part of its very nature. Being is something lent to everything we know, given to it, communicated to it. Now, unless there existed that Being Who not only has but is being of His very nature, and is able to communicate being, everything that we know would not be or exist at all. The things we know and see were once possibilities: they are now realized facts. If there were not that one Being Who is being of His very nature, Who is able to translate them from the region of unrealized possibility to the region of realized fact, they would be unrealized possibilities still.

This approach, or "way" of Aquinas seems to me to be the most fruitful for many reasons. First, it helps us to understand that all things must not only be called into existence by Almighty God but must be kept in being by Him from moment to moment. Things do not become necessary in the philosophical sense by being called into existence—they remain as "unnecessary" or "contingent," as before their creation. If Almighty God did not keep things in being from moment to moment, they would drop back to the nothingness from which He drew them.

We see from this that the creative power and the conservative power of Almighty God—the power to cause things to be and the power to keep them in being—are two aspects of the same thing. We may consider the creative power as the first of a whole series of conservative acts or the conservative power as a whole series of creative acts.

This concept leads us to an appreciation of the "immanence" of Almighty God, which is His constant presence in and through the whole universe. The consequence of God's immanence is His omniscience. Because He is in and through all that exists—for otherwise it would not exist at all—He must know all that exists: "Yea, the very hairs of your head are all numbered." (*Luke* 12:7).

We see what a wonderful foundation there is here for a life of prayer, or for what is called "practicing the presence of God." We are never out of the presence of Almighty

God. He is in and through not only our bodies and all material objects but also our thoughts, hopes, fears and desires. Without Him they would not exist. We are therefore always in touch with Him.

Of all the approaches to the existence of Almighty God, the argument from contingent being is the one that ties up most immediately with what we know about Him from Holy Scripture. We are not at this stage using Holy Scripture as a foundation for our belief, but as a confirmation of what our reason leads us to. You may remember that incident, recorded in the Book of Exodus, where Almighty God speaks to Moses from the burning bush and charges him to speak to the children of Israel in His name. Moses asks in whose name shall he say he is speaking. In reply, Almighty God gives, as it were, a definition of Himself: "I am Who am" (*Exodus* 3:14), in other words, "I am very being itself: everything else is contingent."

Now, leaping forward to the New Testament and remembering that we are using it only in confirmation of where our reason leads us, one of our Blessed Lord's clearest claims to divinity is when He tells the Jews, "Abraham rejoiced that he might see my day." (*John* 8:56). They say to Him, "Thou art not yet fifty years old, and hast thou seen Abraham?" And the sublime reply, "Before Abraham was made, I am." Not "was" but "am"—"I am Being itself."

That concept of God as Being itself illuminates the whole concept of eternity. We so often make the mistake of thinking of eternity as an infinite prolongation of time, going back, back, back and forward, forward, forward again. That, of course, is not eternity at all. In eternity there is no succession of events. St. Thomas Aquinas has the perfect expression for it when he describes eternity as *perpetuum nunc*—perpetual now. Almighty God is a perpetual presence in all eternity.

There is an analogy which may help to clarify the relationship of time to eternity. Now remember, analogies are analogies only. If they are useful, use them. If they are not useful to you and fail to illuminate the truth to you, have no hesitation at all in discarding them, and remember that you are not discarding with them the truth they are meant to illuminate.

The analogy or comparison which I personally find useful is to think of eternity as the point at the center of a circle. You know from your geometry that a point has no extension in space: it simply exists. In the same way, eternity has no extension in time: it simply exists. When we say of Almighty God in our limited language that He was, is and always will be, it would be for more correct to say—since in eternity there is no succession of events—that He always is. Now, if you think of time as the circumference of that circle, with every single point on the circumference equally and simultaneously present to the center, you may see what we mean when we say that the whole of time is likewise equally and simultaneously present to Almighty God. But to us the succession of events is real indeed: we are successively encountering what is simultaneous to Almighty God. This is a thought to which we shall come back, but I do want you to get our meaning very clear in your mind when we say that God is Being and that everything else is contingent or dependent upon Him and accordingly unnecessary in itself.

The other argument of St. Thomas I want to spend a moment on is what is called "the argument from design." It is a much more popular one, in a sense, and it has a strong appeal to people living closer to nature, such as sailors or shepherds. Anyone who is closely in touch with the material creation will inescapably see evidence of a design or plan. Creation does not work haphazardly. Days and nights, seasons and years, are not a random succession. Things do not just happen out of order or without design. Design necessarily and inevitably implies a Designer, Someone Who has conceived in His mind, and Who has effected by His will, that which we are observing.

The argument from design, applied to Almighty God, takes us one stage further than the argument from contingent being because it leads us to the concept of a personal God. It is, however, very necessary to understand correctly what we mean by "a personal God." This concept is frequently misunderstood in two quite different ways. People are inclined to think either that when we talk of a personal God we are looking upon Him as though He were an outsize man; or that, though we do indeed believe Him to be God, we refer directly to Jesus Christ.

By a person we mean a being who has a mind and a will. By a personal God we mean that He Who is, He Who has called all things into being and keeps them in being, has a mind to conceive and a will to execute the whole of the visible and invisible creation.

These two approaches, the argument from contingent being and the argument from design, lead us to the thought of Almighty God as Being itself—not as a blind force but as a personal God. In ordinary speech we generally confine the word "person" to human beings, but its real meaning is far wider than that. We can use it theologically to express our belief that Almighty God is a person, the angels are persons, the devils are persons. For they are all beings who have minds and wills.

Let us now consider in what sense we are made in the likeness of God. Our likeness to Him lies in this: that we have minds that can conceive and wills that can execute. We have minds that are, however distantly, reflections of the Wisdom that is Himself and wills that are reflections, however distantly, of the Power that is Himself. It is that which makes us the Godlike creatures that we are—we are made in the image of Almighty God. We are unique in the whole of the visible creation in having these two Godlike characteristics: a mind that can conceive and a will that can carry into effect. Invisible spirits such as the angels and devils have minds and wills, but in the material creation nothing but man has the Godlike power to know and to do.

Man alone of the whole material creation survives death. His body plainly dies and corrupts. His soul, we believe, survives death. The terms "body" and "soul" are entirely acceptable but may be misleading if they cause us to think of body and soul as two separate entities brought together for the space of a human life. It may be more helpful to think of man as a single entity acting on two planes at once—the material and the spiritual.[1]

The material goes the way of all material things, being resolved at death into its material parts. The spiritual, we believe, survives death precisely because it is not material and has no material parts into which it can be resolved.

In this life, of course, the material and the spiritual are constantly interacting. The spiritual is being fed all the time by impressions received and communicated to it by the material senses and is in its turn using those senses to express its thoughts, judgments and reflections. But this activity is not a material one.

The senses, for example, are constantly registering "this

man" and "that man" and "the other man." We can see, hear and touch our fellow men. The mind, reflecting on these impressions, reaches the abstract concept of Man and the yet more abstract concept of Humanity. The mind goes further and passes abstract judgments on abstract concepts, as when it says, "Man is mortal." All this is at the very lowest level of thought of which the human mind is capable. But it is enough to show the completely different nature of the physical and the spiritual activity of man. The senses can only register an enormous but ultimately finite number of phenomena. The mind or soul can reach abstract concepts and pass abstract judgments about them. No material thing can do that; the mind or soul is therefore not a material thing.

The other reason that impels us to believe that the mind or soul is immaterial is that it has the power of reflection, which no material sense can have. The eye cannot see itself, the ear cannot hear itself, but the mind, the function of which is to think, can think about itself thinking about itself ad infinitum. No material thing can do that.

We believe that that immaterial faculty which enables us to think and to will is immortal, for although Almighty God could of course extinguish what He has called into being—and at this stage before we come to the assurance given to us by divine revelation, we cannot exclude this possibility—it would seem improbable that He should give to our souls an essential characteristic of which He later intended to deprive them.

What I have said so far gives a general outline of three of the five points I have already mentioned—the existence of Almighty God, His nature and our own immortality. We have now to consider the freedom of the human will and our consequent responsibility. The responsibility plainly is this: the fulfilling of the end, purpose or object of Him Who called us into being. He Who has made all things alone knows why He made them. The whole of the inanimate creation fulfills the purpose of Almighty God willy-nilly, simply because it has no mind or will. As I have emphasized, Man alone in the whole of the visible creation has a mind and a will; and therefore has it in his power to seek to fulfill the purpose Almighty God had in mind in bringing him into being. Man also has it in his power to try to oppose that purpose.

Now, with those five considerations in mind—the existence of Almighty God, His nature, our immortality, our free will and our consequent responsibility—I should like to run through the first eight questions of the Catechism, which are an attempt to put something of what we have been saying within the reach of a child. Then I shall relate these eight questions to what we have already said.

Q1 **Who made you?—God made me.**

The three monosyllables of the answer have in them everything of design, purpose, status and responsibility. Think how many people there are who lack those concepts and are consequently miserable and frustrated. They are tempted to think of life as a haphazard series of events with no purpose behind them: whereas the concept we have been considering presumes a purpose in the work of a Creator Who is Wisdom, and Power.[2]

For all that we are intelligent beings with minds which reflect His wisdom, our limited minds cannot expect to grasp His purpose in its entirety. It is sufficient for us to discover the purpose of that tiny, though immortal, part of the whole creation which He has entrusted to us: our own soul. Each person, seeking to fulfill the purpose for which Almighty God brought him into being, makes precisely the contribution required of him for the completion of the whole design. Thus for each man there is design, purpose and consequently status.

What is true of one man is true of every human being and makes every man an object of awe, veneration and love. Therefore each of us has immense importance, which derives not from ourselves or from our achievements but from our being willed into existence by Almighty God and kept in existence by Him.

Think again how many people there are in the world today who are absolutely miserable, questioning their own identity—a disease peculiar to our generation. Many are frequently miserable precisely because they take not Almighty God but their neighbor as their yardstick and feel that they are not wanted, that they have no business to exist. We who have the concept of a personal God before us know that, however purposeless or ineffective our lives may seem to ourselves or others, we do have business to exist. We are here because God wills that we should be here. We are not our own justification: Not that we are sufficient to think anything of ourselves, as of ourselves; but our sufficiency is from God. (*2 Corinthians* 3:5).

The next question in the Catechism asks why Almighty God brought us into being. The answer is:

Q2 **God made me to know Him, love Him and serve Him in this world, and to be happy with Him for ever in the next.**

The sequence of knowledge, love and service is significant. The consequence of knowledge of Almighty God will be that we love Him; and that we shall seek to express that love in service. The second part of that answer is—setting aside divine revelation, which is not yet our concern—hardly one which we can know with assurance.

Q3 **God made me to His own image and likeness**

and with a mind and a will that are a reflection of His infinite wisdom and infinite power. We have free will, the proper exercise of which is to further the will of Almighty God. That is what our free will is for: to cooperate with His will, by fulfilling our part in His plan.[3]

The Catechism continues with a consideration of the soul:

Q4 **This likeness to God is chiefly in my soul.**

My body is something that I share with the lower animals: my soul is a reflection of Almighty God.

Q5 **My soul is like to God because it is a spirit and is immortal.**

This is perhaps a misleading answer because the analogy is not accurate. My soul is indeed a spirit, as is Almighty God, but immortality and eternity are not synonymous. Immortality is defined in the next answer:

Q6 **When I say my soul is immortal I mean that my soul can never die.**

A corresponding definition of eternity might run: "When I say that Almighty God is eternal I mean that Almighty God cannot not be."

I must take most care of my soul, for Christ has said, "What doth it profit a man if he gain the whole world and suffer the loss of his own soul?" Q7

Of course, the answer is "Nothing." I should like to expand this a little, not by changing but by emphasizing the meaning: "What doth it profit a man if (though this obviously cannot be done) he gain the whole world for Christ and suffer the loss of his own soul?" And the answer is again "Nothing," for each of us is brought into this world to establish the kingdom of God in his own soul. If we do that, we shall fulfill the whole purpose of our being.

I want to emphasize this, because so much of our modern Christianity gives the impression that what we are here for is to put the world right. To make a true contribution to putting the world right, we must first establish the kingdom of God in our own hearts. This primary duty is ours all the time and any effect we have outside ourselves will be either an overflow, a consequence or an instrument of that. The primary province for each of us is not the Third World but our own hearts.

A friend was once bewailing the wickedness of the world to St. Peter of Alcantara. The saint replied, "The remedy is simple. You and I must first be what we ought to be: then we shall have cured what concerns ourselves. Let each one do the same, and all will be well. The trouble is that we all talk of reforming others without ever reforming ourselves."

The achievement of sanctity is the complete fulfillment of each man's vocation. It will have repercussions outside ourselves, though it may have absolutely none that the world can see. Consider the life of an enclosed contemplative whose effect on the world is literally immeasurable. We may not see the consequences, but the good a contemplative does is beyond our power to measure.

That point needs spelling out again and again, because in it lies the whole idea of vocation—that each single one of us not only is an individual creation of Almighty God but has a vocation which is absolutely unique and peculiar to himself. Each of us has a combination of gifts and handicaps and tasks to perform which is true of no one else at all. Each man's vocation is unique and peculiar to himself and he achieves sanctity by trying to fulfill it. It is something solely between himself and Almighty God.

I wonder if you know that wonderful phrase that occurs in Cardinal Newman's *Apologia pro Vita Sua* where he says he can never remember the time when there were not for him two, and two only, "absolute and luminously self-evident beings, himself and his Creator." And the only criterion of success or failure in human life is whether we have established that relationship rightly. All others flow out of that. "Thou shalt love the Lord thy God with thy whole heart, with thy whole soul, with thy whole mind and with thy whole strength" and, consequently and relatively, "thy neighbor as thyself"; in other words, in the same way that you love yourself—that is, willing his eternal salvation and fulfillment. We love ourselves as that tiny part of the whole creation confided to us. And that takes precedence over anything else.

Once again I shall use analogies or comparisons. As I said earlier, do use them if they are of use. If not, discard them without hesitation.

One analogy—not often seen nowadays—is that of people making a tapestry sitting on a row of stools, working the canvas from behind, each of them trying to carry out perfectly the bit of design that is in the space allotted to him. Only confusion ensues if any of them think that the man five stools down is not getting on very fast and goes to help him, to the neglect of his own work. If he has done his own patch, well and good. For that is what he is there to do. If each man does his piece perfectly, when they all go round to the other side the whole design comes to life. But if any of them thinks he can improve or change the pattern he has been given, or thinks he should neglect it to help someone else, he causes nothing but confusion.

Another example is that of actors on a stage. Each actor, absorbed in his own part, is that part for the time that he is on the stage. That is his contribution to the play. Only confusion is caused if he thinks, "The leading man is not speaking his lines very well: let me try to do it better." No, each actor, playing his part to perfection, not only fulfills his own function but also contributes assurance to the whole cast.

The rest of this course is in a sense devoted to the next answer:

> **To save my soul I must worship God by Faith, Hope and Charity, that is, I must believe in Him, I must hope in Him, and I must love Him with my whole heart.** Q8

PART I

FAITH

CHAPTER 2

Divine Revelation

I HAVE tried to suggest to your mind the foundation that needs to be laid before we can begin to consider whether God has revealed to us more about Himself than our own reason leads us to—that is to say, whether there has been what is called a revelation from Almighty God to mankind. I have tried to suggest to you that by human reason we can know the existence of Almighty God, His nature, our own immortality, our will and our consequent responsibility. Now, the whole of morality lies in trying to discover the will of Almighty God and in trying to fulfill that will: in this lies not only all morality but the whole fulfillment of our own nature and being; we can fulfill ourselves only through Almighty God.

And I laid stress on the need to establish what I may call the "vertical" relationship between Almighty God and ourselves before we even attempt to establish a horizontal relationship with our fellow men. This may be summarized by saying that there is no meaning in the brotherhood of man without the fatherhood of God. Brotherhood means being the sons of the same Father. Each of us derives his limitless importance from the fact that Almighty God has thought well to bring him into being and maintain him in being. The source of the importance of each one of us is the source of the importance of each of our neighbors.

We go now from that foundation to the quite different question whether Almighty God has revealed to us more about Himself than that. At this stage we may see that it is not improbable, because the knowledge we have, certain though we believe it to be, does not carry us as far as we would wish to go, it does not by any means answer all the questions which we wish to ask, many of which in the nature of things will not be answered until we come into the light of eternity.

The Christian religion teaches that Almighty God has opened a whole cycle of knowledge to us which we could not have reached otherwise. We cannot expect the total content of it to be within our power to attain. That would seem to be incompatible with the whole economy with which Almighty God governs the universe. So we should expect divine revelation to contain truths which we could not reach unaided and which will require us to have faith in the Revealer if we are to accept them. It must be compatible with human reason: all truth must be compatible with all other truth. It cannot be contradictory to reason, though it may be beyond the power of reason to attain. We shall accept it by faith in Almighty God, the Revealer, because we believe Him and because we believe that He is Truth itself.[4]

Now, the distinction between the content of something revealed and the credibility of the revealer is something which we are always making in ordinary life. We continually believe things because other people tell us them. In the case of ordinary life many of these things can be checked by us. But I want for a moment to emphasize how constantly, in the ordinary conduct of our life, we are believing things because we are told them. I want to emphasize it, too, because we ought not to make heavy weather about doing in our relationship with Almighty God what we do daily in our dealings with other people.

Take an immediate example: why do I believe everything I do believe about you? It is precisely because you have told me. Why do I believe your name? I could, of course, check it. I could ring up and ask for confirmation, or ask to see your birth certificate. But that is not why I believe it. I believe it because of your credibility.

Take another example: if a distinguished professor were to tell me something about his proper line of study, which is a completely closed book to me, so that I could not check it at all, I would believe what he told me because he was known to be a truthful and reliable person.

I stress these points because in the revelation of Almighty God the actual content of what He is revealing to us is something beyond our power even to check or, in the case of the mysteries, to understand. We are accepting what has been revealed because we believe it to have been revealed by Almighty God and because we know Him to be the very truth. We believe His revelation, therefore, through faith. And this is the point where we start considering the nature of the act of faith.

You will see that the opening question of this section of the Catechism is "What is Faith?" (This is the point at which the heading "Faith" should have been printed, not at the beginning of the whole Catechism.) The answer is one of those superlatively clear definitions in the Catechism which I want to suggest you should try to learn by heart. There are three or four definitions that you should learn by heart—not many, but do try to do it—and this is very definitely one of them. It is a superb definition:

Q9 **Faith is a supernatural gift of God which enables us to believe without doubting whatever God has revealed.**

In the days when, as a child, I learned the Catechism, we learned the whole thing by heart. I only wish that people still had that power of memory, which they seem to have lost. Some people now deride the system of teaching by heart, saying that it is pure parrot-work without any value. That is nonsense. A child who learned the whole Catechism by heart often did not understand the exact or precise meaning of what he was learning at the time. But once he had got a definition clearly in his mind he had something to come back to and ponder again and again for the rest of his life. In the modern method of teaching, the child has nothing to come back to or to ponder.

If you like to mark your Catechism, there are two words I suggest you underline: they are "gift" and "whatever." Let us start with "gift."

The whole value of that word is that it emphasizes an act of the will, the intellect having been sufficiently prepared to allow the will to act freely. It is the will which, moved by Grace, determines the mind to believe. I have already said that there are two ways in which we resemble Almighty God: by having a mind to know and by having a will to realize or carry into effect. All the supernatural virtues, Faith, Hope and Charity, depend on acts of the will; and the Catechism emphasizes this by describing them as gifts of God. For a gift is something essentially involving acts of the will on the part of two persons. What I am obliged to give you, what you are obliged to receive, is not a gift at all. A gift is of its very nature a free thing. I choose to give you a book or a picture of my free will. You are absolutely free to accept or refuse it.[5]

The very nature of a gift involves a free act of the will; and so it is with Faith: it needs to be freely offered by Almighty God. Certainly it needs to be freely accepted by the individual. It cannot be forced.

And there you see the need for more than an act of the intellect.

Our intellects, faced with their proper evidence, are not free. You cannot possibly follow a whole line of reasoning and accept every successive step without accepting the conclusion. The mind must go as far as the conclusion. You cannot accept the validity of the hypotheses of a mathematical proof and of each successive step in the proof and then say, "Oh, no, I will not accept the conclusion." The intellect is not free to do that. It has reached the conclusion already. Now, an act of faith is completely different from that. Since Faith is a gift from Almighty God, it is within our power to accept or to refuse it. That is why Faith is a virtue.

Accepting the conclusions of reason cannot be a virtue because you have no alternative. You may be praised for the diligence or application which have enabled you to use your reason well. But for reaching the conclusions to which reason leads you, you cannot be praised, for there is no choice in the matter.

Our Blessed Lord is constantly praising people for their acts of faith: "I have not found so great faith in Israel." (*Matthew* 8:10). An act of faith, accepting what Almighty God has revealed to you, is due to a free act of the will. Our Blessed Lord is constantly working miracles in support of His Divinity. These are loosely referred to as "proofs" of His

Divinity. They are not rigorous proofs in the mathematical sense; in other words, they do not leave us with no alternative but to accept the fact that He is God. If you had seen Christ raising a man from the dead, you might be moved to say, "He must be God," but it would not compel you. You could take refuge in saying, "There must be some natural explanation of this phenomenon." You would not have been compelled to believe in the divinity of Christ by witnessing phenomena which you could not explain. The phenomena may be overwhelmingly persuasive. But they cannot in the nature of things be compelling. You cannot prove a mystery.

An act of faith must, as I have said, be compatible with reason. It cannot be nonsense. It cannot be contradictory to what your mind tells you. But when the compatibility of the Christian revelation with reason has been pointed out to you—and the object of a course of instructions in the faith is to show the compatibility of revelation with natural truth—and when you have had experience or knowledge of any number of other phenomena which tend to indicate that revelation is true, the will is still free to accept or refuse the credibility of God's revelation to mankind.

The purely expository character of a course of instructions such as this is well illustrated in the tart reply of a tired priest at the end of a hard day to a convert who said, "You surely don't expect me to believe that, do you?" The priest answered, "Madam, I don't expect you to believe anything. You asked me what the Church teaches and I'm telling you." A revealed religion can be taught only didactically.

So you see what an enormous amount there is in that word "gift"—the offer of faith by Almighty God, and its acceptance on our side, is the offer and acceptance of a gift. In both cases it is a free act. This is the first of many,

many examples we shall have of the sublimity of the human will, which allows us to "play opposite to" Almighty God. Everything I am talking about from now on is connected with this interplay between a finite being like you and me, and Him Who is.

The other word to emphasize in the definition is "whatever." The point conveyed by that word is that we are invited to accept by a single act the whole of the Christian revelation.

People often think that becoming a Catholic entails the acceptance of, let us say, twenty-five successive propositions. No, becoming a Catholic entails the acceptance of only one: namely, that the Catholic Church is God's revelation. With that acceptance comes the consequent acceptance of the whole of the Church's teaching in one single act. The act of acceptance is the same for a philosopher as for a peasant. One, because his natural knowledge is greater, may need a wider-ranging course of instruction than the other: but at the end the act of acceptance is the same for both.

I remember an Anglo-Catholic coming to me once and saying, "I already believe in the sacramental system, in the sacrificial nature of the Eucharist, in the Real Presence, in the place of our Blessed Lady in the scheme of things. How much more shall I have to believe to become a Roman Catholic?" I replied, "You have probably come to believe in those things each in turn, seeing their internal harmony and their value to your spiritual life, and in each case you have exercised your private judgment. Now, if by God's grace you become a Catholic," as I am happy to say he did, "you will accept all those truths and a great many more which I need not specify at the moment, not because you have come to accept them by an exercise of your private judgment but because the Church teaches them. You will have accepted them by a single act of faith. So you see the foundation of your belief is quite different."

A contemporary of our Blessed Lord who came to the conclusion by divine faith that Christ was the Son of God would have said,

"I accept everything that Jesus Christ teaches." Were he to say instead, "Yes, everything that I have heard so far I accept, yes, I accept what Jesus has just said; but I cannot commit myself now to accept what He may say tomorrow," that would not be an act of faith at all, precisely because it is not a single act of acceptance of the whole of the revelation on the strength of faith in the Revealer.

To go back to the example I gave you earlier: I believe you when you tell me about yourself because I think you are an honest and trustworthy person. I do not say, "Oh, yes, I accept everything up till now, but I suspend judgment about what you are going to tell me next." No, it is the person himself, the revealer, who carries conviction and on whose assurance the single act of acceptance is made. Subsequently we may see how the different aspects of the Church's teaching enrich each other and illustrate each other; but still the act of acceptance is a single act and not several successive acts.

Because the Church is the means by which the revelation of Almighty God reaches us, the Catechism follows its sublime definition of Faith with some preliminary questions on the Church, a subject which we shall consider in far greater detail when we come to the ninth article of the Creed. Do not be discouraged because we are now going very slowly: this is the basic foundation of everything. This alone is the motive of divine Faith: God's knowledge and truthfulness.

I must believe whatever God has revealed because God is the very truth, and can neither deceive nor be deceived. Q10

I am to know what God has revealed by the testimony, teaching and authority of the Catholic Church. Q11

Jesus Christ gave the Catholic Church divine authority to teach when He said, "Go ye and teach all nations." Q12

(*Matthew* 28:19)

It is because of His supreme knowledge and veracity that we believe God's word. It is the Church's role to witness what God has revealed through Christ, to convey His teaching and, through the Sacraments, to dispense the grace he won for us on Calvary. The nature of the Church is perhaps best understood if we say that she has the abiding identity of a person running through her whole life from the first Pentecost to the Second Coming of Christ. And just as a person grows in knowledge of himself and in the power of expressing himself, so too does she. She does what a person does. She understands herself better and expresses her thought with increasing precision and clarity.

So, too, the Church has the memory of a person. That is what we mean by the sentence, "She is her own best evidence, her own authority." She never teaches because what she is teaching is recorded somewhere. She is teaching it because it is true. She is, in St. Paul's magnificent phrase, "the pillar and ground of truth" (*1 Timothy* 3:15), so she admits to no appeal from her teaching to any higher or other authority, such as people expect when they ask, "Where did she get that from?" What the Church teaches is constantly confirmed by the Scriptures, archeology, human history, experience and the rest, but she is never teaching it because of that confirmation.

A person can tell you much more about himself by increasing his intellectual skills. If I were to take a course in psychology, medicine or economics, shall we say, I could tell you more facts about myself that I can now. The Church, in the same way, is constantly adopting other disciplines than her own to explain the unchanging truth which she has always believed. Let me give you some examples.

We believe that the Apostles knew Jesus Christ to be man and believed after the Resurrection, if not before, that He was very God himself. But not for centuries did the Church use the vocabulary of Greek philosophy, as she did at Chalcedon and Nicaea, to make her belief precise.

Again, the Church has always believed in the Real Presence of Christ in the Holy Eucharist, but the precise statement of her belief had to await the adoption of Aristotle's vocabulary of substance and accidence.

Again, the concepts of biology and evolution may be used nowadays to explain the nature of the Church as Christ's mystical body, yet the Pauline text, "Being many we are one body in Christ" (*Romans* 12:5), shows that St. Paul shares our belief, though not our vocabulary.

Let us pause to summarize the ground we have been covering. I have been trying to put before you a concept of revelation—that is to say, a body of truth opened to us by Almighty God and otherwise inaccessible and beyond the reach of our reason. And I have outlined the concept of the act of faith, whereby we accept that revelation. I have stressed that we accept divine revelation because of our faith in the Revealer rather than because of the compelling nature or content of the revelation itself, which, as I labored to make plain, cannot of its nature be attained by human reason, though it must of necessity be compatible with reason because truth cannot contradict truth.

We went on from that point to the Catholic Church here on earth as the vehicle or bearer of that revelation. She makes the claim that she alone holds God's revelation to mankind, and expounds that unchanging truth with a constantly increasing degree of precision and understanding. The truth itself is by its very nature unchanging and, by the same token, the identity of the Church is unchanging because we see her as continuing Christ in corporate form from the first Pentecost till the Second Coming.

Now, out of the concept of the unchanging identity of the Church comes clearly the idea that she is not expounding anything other than herself. She has not, so to speak, a source that she is expounding; she is frequently confirmed by the sources and the evidences, but she is never expounding something which she has found elsewhere.

You see at once how completely that presentation of Christianity differs from any other presentation, at least in the West, with which we are familiar. All other presentations of Christianity see the Church or "churches" as expounding something other than themselves, be it the Bible or the teaching of the undivided Church or the teaching of the first five Councils. But why do we believe a person? I gave you the example earlier about your telling me your name. I believe you because of your own credibility. Had you at that moment started trying to produce documentary evidence from your pocket I should have become suspicious, because it is only an imposter who produces that sort of evidence in support of the truth of what he is saying. An honest man is believed because of his obvious honesty and the conviction which he carries.

In the same way the claim of the Catholic Church to be God's revelation to mankind is confirmed. To take an obvious example, the Church teaches what she teaches about the divinity of Christ not only because of the Gospels—she was believing and teaching what she teaches now before they were ever written. She does not teach the doctrine of the Holy Eucharist because of the account of the Last Supper or because of the sixth chapter of St. John, though they confirm what she teaches and what she believed and taught before they were written. She is her own best evidence, her own authority, and therefore either she carries conviction in herself and all history, archeology and experience confirm that or we reject her claim altogether. External reasons for her credibility can only be confirmation of it.

One of the best accounts of the Church's concept of revelation is contained in a book by a largely forgotten writer, W. H. Mallock (1849–1923), who leaped to fame whilst an undergraduate with a very amusing satire called *The New Republic*, a satirical novel in the manner of Thomas Love Peacock. It has no plot and consists of a series of conversations by all the great pundits of the period, such as Jowett and Matthew Arnold, renamed but undisguised. Like all satires, it suffers from being dated.

The book that I wish to recommend to you is *Doctrine and Doctrinal Disruption* (London: A. & C. Black, 1900). Like other books by Mallock it is burdened with a dissuasive title. Another thing against it is that it is embedded in a controversy which is no longer topical.

The book begins with an attack on three Protestant presentations of Christianity, those that find authority for

Christian doctrines in the intuition or the interior witness of the individual; in the beliefs of the early Church; and in the consensus of the Church as a whole. These points of view were vigorously held by many people at the time Mallock was writing. But having done that destructive work, which does not really concern us who are seeking a positive presentation, he turns in Chapter IX to "the theory of authority which is rejected by all Protestants but which, when adopted, completes their own theories, reconciles their contradictions and makes of them a logical whole." Mallock devotes the last part of the book to showing that the Roman Catholic exposition of Christianity avoids all the difficulties considered in the first part.

The theory which he expounds with quite extraordinary penetration and gift of exposition is that the Church is her own best evidence. Let me quote a paragraph:

> The result which its possession of this complete, organic character has on the Church of Rome as a teaching body is obvious. Being thus endowed, as we have seen, with a single brain, the Church is endowed also with a continuous historic memory; is constantly able to explain and to restate doctrine, and to attest, as though from personal experience, the facts of its earliest history. Is doubt thrown on the Resurrection and Ascension of Christ? The Church of Rome replies, "I was at the door of the Sepulcher myself. My eyes saw the Lord come forth. My eyes saw the cloud receive Him." Is doubt thrown on Christ's miraculous birth? The Church of Rome replies, "I can attest the fact,

> even if no other witness can, for the angel said
> Hail! in my ear as well as Mary's."

That is what the Church means when she takes her stand on

Scripture and Tradition. Once again we have to remind ourselves—as we have done in the case of Faith, Hope and Charity—that the colloquial use of technical words is far removed from the Church's use of them and may even be opposed to it. When we say, for example, "there is a tradition that Queen Elizabeth slept in that bed," we are repeating a pious belief: which we may ourselves share and are even suggesting that it is one which there is reason to accept. When the Church speaks of Tradition she claims to have just such a knowledge as is claimed by a person with regard to events which he has himself experienced.

If you grasp this theory of revelation you will see how it is that the Church continues her teaching through the centuries not only with increasing clarity but also with increasing understanding of it, just as a person can understand himself better as he gets older and can expound to others with increasing clarity and precision his deepening, but essentially unchanging, thought.[6]

God's revelation is summarized in the Apostles' Creed. We now read the answers to the next three Catechism questions. After that, the next nine chapters will be devoted to the Creed.

Q13 **The chief things which God has revealed are contained in the Apostles' Creed.**

I believe in God, the Father Almighty, Creator of heaven and earth; —and in Jesus Christ, His only Son, our Lord; —Who was conceived by the Holy Spirit, born of the Virgin Mary; —suffered under Pontius Pilate, was crucified, dead and buried; —He descended into Hell; the third day He rose again from the dead; —He ascended into Heaven; —sitteth at the right hand of God the Father Almighty; —from thence He shall come to judge the living and the dead.—I believe in the Holy Ghost; —the Holy Catholic Church; the Communion of Saints; —the forgiveness of sins; —the resurrection of the body; —and life everlasting. Amen. Q14

The Apostles' Creed is divided into twelve parts or articles. Q15

Before we come on to considering the content of divine revelation in detail, I want to go back for a moment just to give you one more reading confirming, or rather clarifying, the major role of the will in the act of faith. The book, from which I am going to give you an extract now, is one which I am sure you will find interesting in itself. It is a novel called *Peradventure*; or, *The Silence of God* by Robert Keable (London: Constable, 1922). It came out just after the First World War, but it is set in the Cambridge of just before the War and centers on the experiences of an undergraduate coming up to Magdalene College from an extremely evangelical home. His father is a parson. The boy has taken up street-corner preaching on coming up to Cambridge and falls in with a priest called Father Vassall, who was in reality Fr. R. H. Benson, a very famous priest in his day. Mgr.

Benson became a Catholic at the age of thirty and spent only ten years or so as a Catholic priest, in the course of which he poured out an immense series of books and sermons, and died early in his forties. But he must have been a man of most extraordinary personality. He had more to do with my being a priest than anyone I never knew. And in *Peradventure* there is a most lifelike picture of him and of the effect he had on the undergraduate from an evangelical home.

One of its great virtues is that it paints every position it describes, from the extreme evangelical one to the Catholic or the agnostic, with extreme sympathy, never putting into the mouth of a character views to which he would not have subscribed in life.

But there, that is a long way round to telling you that the undergraduate falls under Fr. Vassall's influence, begins instruction with him at Cambridge and stays with him in his house in the country after completing his course of instruction. The priest says, in effect, "Here, I have given you everything on the intellectual side that I can. I have given a complete exposition of Catholic doctrine to suit your mind. It is up to you now to accept the gift of faith by an act of your will. I am not going to persuade you. Go on your last morning and pray in the chapel for the gift of faith."

There can be no doubt that it is an autobiographical novel. The whole of the Catholic part of it is accurately described, the presentation of Catholicism in the book could not be better in a work of fiction and the author shows an extraordinarily accurate understanding of what is meant by the gift of faith. Here is the passage:

> "My dear," he said, stammering badly, "you gggo tommmorrow. And we've kept the ttruce."
>
> Paul nodded. Silence.
>
> The priest spoke again. "I don't know," he said. "I can't stick my fingers into your soul. I dddon't want to. Only God's been good to you, you know. And—and He's a jjjealous God."
>
> "Oh, I don't know," burst out the boy. "Father, I don't know! There's so much for and against. And I've prayed and prayed and prayed, and—and God hides Himself."
>
> "He's given you all the lllight you need. He's shown you! He's sent His Son and appointed His Church and ppput it bbbang in your ppath. What else do you want? Do you want a special rrrevelation?"
>
> "Oh, I don't know," wailed Paul. "I don't KNOW!"

And the next morning Paul goes to pray in the chapel as he has been encouraged to do:

> Paul shut his eyes. He was so tired. He turned deliberately away and thought of Edith. He remembered Hursley Woods, and the little brown cap, and the brown leaves, and the blue sky. A thrush, too, that looked at them out of beady eyes. And here he was, in a Popish chapel, Father Vassall's chapel.
>
> He looked up. In the clear morning light, the chapel was all so plain. . . . A little to the right the white tabernacle veil hung in the folds to which Father Vassall had adjusted it this morning. And behind lay the mystery. If only he knew... Paul Kestern grew afraid. The utter

> silence of the chapel grew on him, bore down on him, wave on wave. Why wouldn't God speak? Just a word, a flicker of a curtain... It was all so still. Not even a wind. The silence listened, that was the awful thing; it listened for him to pray. And if he prayed—oh, if he prayed, he would break down like a baby, and surrender, and he would never really have known.

It is a very accurate and very terrible passage. Keable got the whole thing so clear. Preparation over and complete, Paul is urged to pray to be offered and to accept the gift of Faith. And then at that point he requires a physical assurance. "Why wouldn't God speak? . . . Just . . . a flicker of a curtain." And, you see, if either of those things had happened, it would not have proved the truth of our Blessed Lord's revelation just as His own miracles did not prove His divinity. The act of Faith remains a free act depending on the decision of the will to seek and accept God's grace: "Lord, I believe; help thou mine unbelief." (*Mark* 9:24).

And that is why there is virtue in the act of Faith. It cannot be simply the result of reason; the mind cannot help but go where reason leads it: whereas with an act of Faith the will can be withdrawn and the gift of Faith lost. That is why Catholics believe that the loss of Faith may be blameworthy and is in all circumstances the greatest of all misfortunes.

It should be recorded that W. H. Mallock was received into the Church only in extremis and Robert Keable never.

CHAPTER 3

THREE PERSONS IN ONE GOD

WELL now, we go on to embark on a consideration of the content of divine revelation as summarized in the Creed. Significantly enough, the first article of the Creed works retrospectively over the foundation of faith in natural reason, lending the added assurance of faith to truths to which the reason itself has led us:

> **The first article of the Creed is, "I believe in God the Father Almighty, Creator of heaven and earth."** Q16

The next question is "What is God?" and the answer is one of the most superb in the whole Catechism:

> **God is the supreme Spirit, Who alone exists of Himself, and is infinite in all perfections.** Q17

People now deride the teaching of the Catechism by heart, saying, "How could a child understand that?" But the whole point of teaching by heart is to leave a child in sure possession of something absolutely true, on which he can meditate to his dying day without exhausting the content of it. Give him something vague and amorphous and he has nothing to ponder.

Here is a wonderful, theological definition of the greatest accuracy, of which one phrase, "Who alone exists of Himself," sums up in a few words the whole approach to the existence of Almighty God from the argument from contingent being. God is Being of His very nature and all other things have only a shared or participated being, communicated to them by Him Who is. All other things are—in the philosophical sense—"unnecessary."

The next half-dozen questions and answers have a consistent theme running through them. I wonder if you will see something of this. It is certain that I, as a child, did not, and they seemed singularly unconnected, though accurate, observations. But they are not unconnected. They are very closely knit together. We go from the definition of Almighty God as the supreme Spirit Who alone exists of Himself to say:

Q18 **God is called "Almighty" because He can do all things: "With God all things are possible."** (*Mark* 10:27)

Q19 **God is called "Creator of heaven and earth" because He made heaven and earth, and all things out of nothing, by His word.**

Q20 **God had no beginning: He always was, He is, and He always will be.**

Q21 **God is everywhere.**

Q22 **God knows and sees all things, even our most secret thoughts.**

Q23 **God has no body; He is a spirit.**

I wonder if you see what binds those answers together? As a child I remember thinking of the last of them as the most inconsequential of all. The sequence of the thought is really very close. It all goes back to that approach of Aquinas which is an obsession with me, the argument from contingent being, one of the "ways" of Aquinas discussed in Chapter 1. It is an attempt to clarify in the mind of a child the relationship between the Creator and His creation, between Him Who is and all those things to which He has communicated being. First it considers that there is nothing except Him Who is and what He has Himself made. That which he has made cannot possibly limit His power. So we say of Him that He is Almighty.

Everything that we know had a beginning in time. Had He a beginning? No: that is to miss the whole point. He is. We say of Him in our limited language that He always was, He is and He always will be. As we considered in our first talk, it would be far more accurate to say that He always is, for eternity is not an infinite succession of time but a perpetual now.

You see, we do not hold what is called a "mechanistic" view of the universe: that is, a Creator calling things into being and then letting them take their course. No, things do not become necessary in the philosophical sense through having been brought into being. They remain as unnecessary as before. The "conservative power" of Almighty God, as it is called, is required to maintain them in being from moment to moment as much as His creative power was required to call them into being in the first place. Almighty God is lending being to all things all the time. Otherwise they would cease to exist.

The consequence, of course, is that Almighty God is everywhere. He permeates the whole of the universe more intimately than we are permeated by the air we breathe. He is in and through everything that exists.

Consider sunlight flooding a room. To an observer looking into that room from outside, it is the sunlight that brings into being every single object in the room. Without the sunlight, he would not be able to observe the objects in the room at all.

That is a very faint analogy of the action of Almighty God on the whole universe, with the obvious difference that if He were not in and through all that exists, all that exists would not exist My analogy fails there, for the furniture would be in the room even if the sunlight was not.

Another analogy, if you will, is to be found in *The Life of John William Walshe, F.S.A.* by Montgomery Carmichael (London: Burns & Oates, 1901). This book is a biography of a fictional character, but so convincingly done that many people have taken it to be a genuine biography. The story is of a young man running away from his home in Manchester, where he had been put to work in a countinghouse. It is an entirely romantic story. The young man takes boat to Italy, where he encounters the Catholic Church for the first time, becomes a Catholic and marries an enchanting girl. They live happily ever after. The passage I want to quote occurs when he is at sea (the book is written in the character of a son writing about his father):

> My father read the Bible and the Imitation of Christ throughout the voyage. He tried Shakespeare and Rogers but he was in too exalted a state. He tried Sterry but the salt of the sea seemed to take all the savor out of its mysticism. He had never been at sea before. The sea invigorated him and lifted him out of himself. The sea seemed to him so scriptural. It brought him nearer God. It seemed to him like a type of

> god; creatures lived in it moved in it, had their being from it. So men lived and moved in God and had their being from God and yet were distinct from God. Praise was in his heart.

A lovely passage! That is, of course, what St. Paul is telling us when he says of Almighty God that "in Him we live and move and have our being." (*Acts* 17:28 AV)

Now, what is the consequence of the immanence of Almighty God? Plainly, the omniscience of Almighty God. If He is in and through everything that exists—for otherwise it would not exist—then He must know everything. He is not looking into His creation from outside. He is in and through it. When our Blessed Lord tells us, "The very hairs of your head are numbered" (*Matthew* 10:30), He does not mean that Almighty God needs to count them. He has no need to count them; He is in and through them or they would not exist. When He tells us that not a sparrow drops from Heaven but our heavenly Father sees it, He does not mean that Almighty God is leaning over the battlements of Heaven and saying, "There is a sparrow falling." He is in and through the sparrow and the whole surrounding air. His omniscience is the immediate consequence of His immanence. Therefore,

> **God knows and sees all things, even our most secret thoughts.** Q22

I rather regret the word "even," which suggests that to know our secret thoughts is one degree more difficult for Almighty God than knowing material objects, but of course in this respect all created things are in the same category. None of them is necessary.

A clear grasp of the concept of immanence will help greatly to a better understanding of miracles. You will find that critics, especially those who hold the mechanistic view of creation described on page 26, will speak of miracles as though they were a sudden and brusque intervention of Almighty God into the Universe from outside—almost as though a coach on the bank were to try to correct the faulty course of a boat by a thrust from a bargepole. If you were to take that rather fantastic analogy the action of Almighty God in working a miracle is far more akin to the all but imperceptible action of the cox (who is very much within the boat) whereby he brings the boat on to course.

I have already said that the concept of the immanence and omniscience of Almighty God is a great help in the whole life of prayer. This idea, if kept in mind, helps us to develop that attitude of constant prayer which is urged upon us by St. Paul:

"Pray at all times." (*1 Thessalonians* 5:17). St. Francis of Sales expands the idea when he writes in the Introduction to the Devout Life:

> Remember always to make many withdrawals into the solitude of your own heart whilst you are outwardly in the midst of conversation and business: and this mental solitude cannot be hindered by those who are always about you, for they are not about your heart but about your body, so that your heart may remain always alone in the possession of God.

See here a form of prayer which can be practiced at all times and does not require that we should retire to church or to some private place. Try to cultivate that habit of mind so that whenever your mind is free it will effortlessly drop back into recognizing the presence of Almighty God and your closeness to Him.

Now we come to the last of these half-dozen answers:

God has no body; He is a spirit. Q23

The purpose of this answer is to guard us against pantheism, which is a distortion of the concept of immanence. It is the idea that Almighty God is, as it were, sunk in His own creation and is limited or confined by it, as in this life we are by our bodies. This is not so. For Almighty God existed from all eternity before ever He called anything into being. He will exist through all eternity and even if every single thing in the universe were to drop out of being, He is. But, so long as anything exists, He is in and through it without being limited or contained by it.

Now, as you see, in going through those last six Catechism answers we are merely having fresh insights into what we have sought to establish in natural reason and bringing to it the added assurance of faith. From this point, however, we go into the region of pure revelation, something that the human reason could not have reached at all. Even now that it has been opened to us by Almighty God, it needs the gift of faith, offered by Him and received by us, for its acceptance. Not only do we see that we could not have reached it by our unaided reason; we cannot understand or grasp it by our unaided reason. Thus we are coming from the concept of Almighty God as the one necessary Being to a concept that we owe entirely to revelation: that in this one, single, indivisible Spirit, which is God, there are three distinct Persons:

There is only one God. Q24

There are three Persons in God: God the Father, God the Son and God the Holy Spirit. Q25

Q26 **These three Persons are not three Gods: The Father, the Son and the Holy Spirit are all one and the same God.**

Q27 **The mystery of the three Persons in one God is called the mystery of the Blessed Trinity.**

Q28 **By a mystery I mean a truth which is above reason but revealed by God.**

Mysteries are above reason. They cannot be attained by reason. They cannot be grasped by reason. We believe them not because our reason has impelled us to do so—though we must be able to see that they are compatible with reason—but because Almighty God has revealed them to us.

The basic mystery of the whole of the Christian revelation is the doctrine of the Blessed Trinity: that in the one, single and indivisible God there are three distinct Persons, each of Whom is wholly God and neither of Whom is the other two. This is plainly a mystery. We know it only because Jesus Christ has revealed it to us. He reveals it to us implicitly by claiming that He is God; by speaking of the Father as distinct from Himself and also God; and by speaking of the Holy Spirit as distinct from either and also God. And He reveals it to us explicitly when He sends out the Apostles to teach and to baptize in the name not the names, of the Father and of the Son and of the Holy Spirit. There is only one God, but there are three distinct Persons, the Father, the Son and the Holy Spirit.

Now, though we cannot come to a knowledge of the truth about the Blessed Trinity unaided, and though we accept it only on the all-sufficient word of Jesus Christ, which is enough, we can—and this is true of all the mysteries of faith—ponder it and apprehend something of its depth, its richness and its internal coherence. That really is what Catholic theology is all about. It is the pondering of a revealed truth. Here I am going to say something I shall probably repeat many times: namely, that this is a matter in which Catholic theology differs completely from every other intellectual discipline. In every other intellectual and academic discipline, what are we doing but trying to push back the boundaries of knowledge? Whether it be in science or history, we are constantly trying to seek further knowledge. Now, with Christian theology the position is completely different. The actual truth communicated to us is not one that we can discover nor one, therefore, that we can enlarge. A revelation has been given to us, "the faith once delivered to the saints." As we have seen, our appreciation of it is growing and developing. Our appreciation of divine revelation grows deeper and deeper through thinking about it. It is not for nothing that our Blessed Lady is the patron of Catholic theologians. "Mary," if you remember, "kept all these words, pondering them in her heart." (*Luke* 2:19). Catholic theology is exactly that: the constant meditation on an unchanging revelation, a deepening appreciation of it and a deepening understanding of it.

We cannot add to divine revelation, any more than we can add to any other living thing. You cannot add to a tree or to a body. Growth must be organic and must come from within. Catholic theology is just like that. It never changes the identity of the revelation as given to us by Jesus Christ our Lord, but it sees deeper meaning in it and increases our understanding. And so it is with a profound mystery like that of the Blessed Trinity. As a subject of thought it is inexhaustible. Though we find it impossible to grasp and understand, yet it yields fruit to our contemplation.

Here is an illustration to fix this in your mind. There is a story that St. Augustine, one of the greatest minds that the Christian Church has ever had, was taking his evening walk one day on the seacoast of North Africa, bringing that great mind of his to try to seek a rational approach to the mystery of the Blessed Trinity. He came upon a little boy who had dug a hole in the sand and was running backwards and forwards filling it with water from the sea. St. Augustine said to the little boy, "What do you think you are doing?" and the little boy replied, "I am going to put the whole sea into this hole." St. Augustine replied, "You will never do that, my little man." The boy said, "I shall do that as soon as you reach a rational understanding of the mystery of the Trinity," and disappeared. A sharp lesson to St. Augustine, which illustrates the limits of what the human mind can do.

But we can make fruitful use of analogy. One of the best analogies of the Trinity, and one which particularly appeals to me, is that which the medieval Schoolmen developed from the opening—the sublime opening—of St. John's Gospel:

> In the beginning was the Word. And the Word was with God. And the Word was God. The same was in the beginning with God. All things were made by Him, and without Him was nothing made that was made.

Inspired by that, they thought of God the Father as the eternal Mind and used the term "Word" to indicate the thought occupying that Mind.

Our minds cannot be vacant even for a split second of conscious time, but must always be employed with some thought, trivial or otherwise. The perfect Mind of Almighty God must from all eternity be occupied by a Word or thought which is no less eternal than itself. But God alone is eternal. We cannot escape the consequence: "the Word was God." So the mind conceiving (God the Father) and the thought conceived (the Word, or God the Son) are, if we may use that phrase, "coincident in eternity." Neither precedes the other. And between the two, between the mind conceiving and the thought conceived, there must be a complete identity of will and purpose, God the Holy Spirit. That, as we shall see when we come to treat of Charity, is what we understand by Love. Love is essentially a reciprocal and mutual thing. Love, uniting the mind conceiving and the thought conceived, proceeds therefore equally from both. Again, never for an instant of eternity has there not been this complete accord between the mind conceiving and the thought conceived. The love between Father and Son, and Son and Father, is as eternal as they, and is therefore very God.

It is a lovely analogy, and it is my favorite because it is independent of any material symbols. I am never very happy with shamrocks or other symbols of the Blessed Trinity. They may be good enough as symbols but they do not teach us very much. But this is a completely nonmaterial analogy. The mind conceiving (God the Father), the thought conceived (God the Son) and the complete unity of will and purpose between them (God the Holy Spirit) are wholly non-material.

We, with our limitations, cannot help thinking of a certain precedence in time between the Persons of the Blessed Trinity, though of course there can be none. We cannot help but think of Father, Son and Holy Spirit in that order. But the analogy we have been considering helps us to see how They are coequal and coexistent in eternity. Whatever order of precedence we inevitably attribute to Them, the order of precedence is not in Them, the three divine Persons, but in our minds as we consider Them. Between Them there cannot be any other than complete and absolute equality. The Father, the Son and the Holy Spirit are all absolutely equal and coeternal.

Now, before we finish with analogies, the Catechism itself has one, which I as a child failed to appreciate. But the more I have thought about it since my childhood, the more valuable I think it. Going back to the Catechism you will see:

Q29 **There is this likeness to the Blessed Trinity in my soul: that as in one God there are three Persons, so in my one soul there are three powers.**

Q30 **The three powers of my soul are my memory, my understanding and my will.**

And the reason why it is an analogy is this. Almighty God is a pure Spirit. So is your soul a wholly immaterial thing. And yet this one, indivisible, immaterial thing has three completely distinct functions, neither of which is the other two. It is your soul that is your memory, your soul that is your understanding and your soul that is your will. Yet these three functions of one, indivisible, immaterial thing are not parts of it. You cannot have parts of a spirit. It is only material things that can be divided into parts. But a purely spiritual thing can have functions. Those functions of the soul—the memory, the understanding and the will—are an analogy of the three divine Persons of the Blessed Trinity. It is an analogy which perhaps means little to a child, because, as in my case, a child does not appreciate what is meant by a spirit, The soul is something quite other than the five senses or the brain; it is a purely nonmaterial thing, having no extension or parts. And yet it has these three distinct functions, so that your memory is not your understanding, your understanding is not your will and your will is not your memory. In a parallel way we say that the Father is God, the Son is God and the Holy Spirit is God, but the Father is not the Son, the Son is not the Holy Spirit and the Holy Spirit is not the Father.

In medieval art you often see the Blessed Trinity represented by a diagram. At its center there is a circle bearing the word DEUS. At equal distances from the circle there are three other circles, labeled PATER, FILIUS and SPIRITUS SANCTUS, arranged at the vertices of an equilateral triangle and joined to each other by bands bearing the words NON EST and joined to the central circle by bands marked EST.

Besides forming analogies or comparisons to illuminate a mystery, we can also set it out schematically. A very good example with regard to the Blessed Trinity is the Athanasian Creed, which is a wonderful statement of what we believe about the Trinity. We can say, "Here is a truth, communicated to me by the gift of God. I accept it by faith and this is what I understand by it."

The Athanasian Creed is enormously long and is now all too seldom heard. The Church of England omits it, partly because it has comminatory clauses excommunicating people who will not accept it, which are thought to be very uncharitable. The Catholic Church has abolished the office of Prime, where it was frequently recited. But here are the relevant articles of the Creed, from Lord Bute's translation of the old Roman Breviary:

Now the Catholic Faith is this, that we worship One God in Trinity, and Trinity in Unity. Neither confounding the Persons, nor dividing the Substance. For there is one Person of the Father, another of the Son and another of the Holy Ghost.

But the Godhead of the Father, of the Son and of the Holy Ghost is One, the Glory Equal, the Majesty Coeternal. Such as the Father is, such is the Son and such is the Holy Ghost The Father Uncreated, the Son Uncreated and the Holy Ghost Uncreated. The Father Infinite, the Son Infinite and the Holy Ghost Infinite. The Father Eternal, the Son Eternal, and the Holy Ghost Eternal. And yet They are not Three Eternals but One Eternal. As also They are not Three Uncreated, nor Three Infinites, but One Uncreated and One Infinite. So likewise the Father is Almighty, the Son Almighty and the Holy Ghost Almighty. So the Father is God, the Son God and the Holy Ghost God. And yet They are not Three Lords but One Lord. For, like as we are compelled by Christian truth to acknowledge every Person by Himself to be God and Lord, so we are forbidden by the Catholic Religion to say, there be Three Gods or Three Lords. The Father is made of none, neither created, nor begotten. The Son is of the Father alone, not made, nor created, but Begotten. The Holy Ghost is of the Father and the Son, not made, nor created, nor begotten, but Proceeding. So there is One Father, not Three Fathers; One Son, not Three Sons; One Holy Ghost, not Three Holy Ghosts. And in

> this Trinity is nothing afore or after, nothing is greater or less; but the whole Three Persons are Coeternal together, and Coequal. So that in all things, as is aforesaid, the Unity in Trinity and the Trinity in Unity is to be worshiped. He therefore that willeth to be safe, let him thus think of the Trinity.

So far we have talked about the foundation of faith in natural reason; revelation and the nature of the act of faith whereby we accept it; and the Apostles' Creed as a summary of that revelation. We have dealt with the first article of the Creed, "believe in God, the Father Almighty," and the consideration of the first article fell clearly into two different parts. The first part showed that one of the functions of the act of faith is to go back over the foundation of faith in reason and lend to that foundation the added assurance of faith. So the whole of the first part of this chapter has been concerned with considering once again what we meant by Almighty God as summed up in that wonderful definition, God is the Supreme Being Who alone exists of Himself (q17). I pointed out that that phrase, "Who alone exists of Himself," is really a summary of the very first approach we made to the existence of Almighty God by way of the argument from contingent being, emphasizing that God is Being itself, whereas all other things have existence, or being, communicated to them by God. I also pointed out that those next half dozen Catechism answers are all a consideration of the consequence of that approach to our thought regarding the relationship between Creator and creature. Implicit in that concept of Almighty God is His immanence; that is, He must be in and through the whole of Creation for it to exist at all. He not only brings it into being but keeps it in being from moment to moment. From His immanence follows His omniscience; and yet, as that last question of those half dozen points out, Almighty God is not sunk in His own creation or limited by it: *God has no body; He is a spirit* (q23).

The second half of this chapter went on from the consideration of the act of faith, confirming its foundations in reason, to something which is purely in the realm of revelation, wholly beyond the power of reason to attain: that is, the doctrine of the Blessed Trinity. We accept this doctrine, as we accept all the other mysteries of faith, on the word of our Lord and Saviour Jesus Christ. He reveals it to us in an indirect way by Himself claiming to be God and by speaking of the Father as distinct from Himself and also God, and of the Holy Spirit as distinct from either and also God. He reveals it directly by sending out the Apostles to teach and to baptize in the name, not the names, of the Father, the Son and the Holy Spirit. This is a perfect example of a mystery, which is defined in the Catechism as "a truth which is above reason but revealed by God." (q28). From this moment on, we are entirely in the realm of mysteries—truths which our unaided reason could not come to, but which we believe have been communicated to us by our Lord and Saviour Jesus Christ.

CHAPTER 4

Jesus Christ, God Incarnate

The second article of the Creed is, "and in Jesus Christ, His Only Son, our Lord." Q31

The second article of the Creed is concerned with the very central doctrine of the whole of the Christian revelation, the Incarnation. The coming of God into His own creation is, of all the truths which we believe, the central one which gives meaning and coherence to all the others. No single part of the Christian message makes any sense unless we see it centered on that truth, the truth that God in the Person of His Son comes into His own creation and becomes Man.

At this point I want to alter the order of questions in the Catechism. For the Catechism now considers the Incarnation in detail and then asks Question 43, "Why was God the Son made man?" I think it more helpful to start with that Question before we go on to consider the Incarnation in detail. The Catechism answer is:

God the Son was made man to redeem us from sin and hell, and to teach us the way to heaven. Q43

That question poses very briefly what we might call the "why?" of the Incarnation and, as I say, I think it is more helpful to consider that question before the "Who?" Question 43 asks, "Why was God the Son made man?" and answers, "To redeem us from sin and hell and to teach us the way to heaven"—in other words, to undo the consequences of the Fall, which barred Heaven to mankind.

I propose now to consider that doctrine of the Fall of Man and to preface it at once, as one ought to do with every single article of the Creed, by saying, "Of course, we are considering a mystery." I may not remember always before each article to say,

"Remember, this is a mystery." I hope you will remember to do so yourself. Each article of the Creed is something beyond reason and revealed by God. It seems to me that, of all the mysteries in which we believe, none prepares us better by reason, or is better confirmed by experience, than the Fall of Man. This is not to say that the Fall is discoverable in its entirety by reason, but only that reason does prepare us for it and experience confirms what revelation tells us in greater detail.

The doctrine of the Fall is that at the very beginning of human history there occurred some catastrophe in human nature, the consequences of which are with us still.[7]

Reason prepares us for the doctrine of the Fall by posing a dilemma: how can a God Who is the very Good Himself have brought into being a creation that is, as it seems to us, manifestly flawed and imperfect? There is a disparity between a perfect God and a creation that appears to us to be flawed or, in other words, evil.

This dilemma lies at the very root of the problem of evil, which has exercised so many minds, Christian and non-Christian alike. The whole pagan concept of a Golden Age, a time when all things were perfect, recognizes this dilemma. But it may be pointed out that Christianity is the only one of the great religions of the world that puts the guilt of that dislocation fairly and squarely on the shoulders of man. Pagans frequently see God or the gods as outsize human beings, having the flaws and weaknesses of human nature, being quarrelsome, lustful and the like. Christianity, on the other hand, sees God as perfect. The fault lies in the failure of man, through the abuse of his free will, to fulfill the will of the Creator.

God created a world which in its material aspects cannot help but fulfill His will, since it has no will of its own. Man alone in the whole, visible creation has it in his power to seek to do the will of Almighty God or not to do it. It is that idea of the responsibility of man which underlies the concept of the Fall, the concept that there was a rebellion on the part of man at the very beginning of human history. The consequences of it are with us still—not only the visible consequences such as suffering, sickness, death and the like, but also our own internal disorder, which we know by experience.

Generation after generation of mankind has been dissatisfied with the present. It is an extraordinary thing, if you come to think of it, seeing that the present is the only thing any generation has ever known. "The time is out of joint," says Hamlet (Act I, V, 188). That notion is not only found in the Christian tradition, as expressed by Shakespeare and so many others, but is universal. Generation after generation of mankind has idealized the past and talked of the Golden Age or looked to the future and the prospect of better things yet to come. "The good old days" or "the brave new world" are recurrent themes. But never, never, never is satisfaction with the present moment expressed, although it is the only thing of which we have direct knowledge.

Not only is there dissatisfaction with external things; there is also dissatisfaction with oneself. Each of us is constantly conscious of internal discords, stresses and strains, so that, as St. Paul puts it, "We do not the things that we would." (*Galatians* 5:17). There is a war between our higher selves and our lower natures. We have not that complete command of ourselves that we wish to have. We are all constantly humiliated by our limitations both in thought and action.

It is this preparation, both in reason and in experience, which makes us ready to accept what is, after all, a fundamental mystery. The Christian religion comes and reveals to us the truth of what we have instinctively known and felt. It tells us that things are not as Almighty God meant and created them to be. The sin of our first parents has dislocated human nature and the consequences are with us still.

That, in the merest outline, is what we mean by the Fall of Man. At the very beginning of human history, there was a rebellion against the perfect Being on the part of the creature possessed of free will. This is a profoundly mysterious concept; reason would not have led us to it; reason can only show us its compatibility with itself and with experience. It needs the revelation of Almighty God to give us that concept with certainty.

Now, the concept of the Fall of Man is revealed in the opening chapters of Genesis, a narrative composed, of course, much later than the event which it records, and for the benefit of an unsophisticated people who had neither our historical nor our scientific approach. Our approach to the sacred text neither relegates it to pure fiction nor treats it, as do fundamentalists, as if it were a modern scientific or historical record. The fact that there was an abuse of free will on the part of our first parents is effectively conveyed in a literary style proper to the people for whom it was intended. Where allegory takes over from history in the details of man's Fall is a matter for responsible discussion, but at least it would seem that there are pointers in the Bible record. Though plainly our first parents did not use our language or concepts or categories of thought, they must have known the difference between creature and Creator, between the Absolute and the relative, between the contingent and the Necessary. The record, as we have it, suggests that the form the temptation took was that if only man were to challenge his Creator, he would find that he was equal to his Creator: "Eat the forbidden fruit and ye shall be as gods." (*Genesis* 3:5).

We do believe that a rebellion took place and that the consequences of it were the importing into the world of all the things which mar a perfect creation: sickness, suffering and death. No less certainly did it upset the internal balance of our nature, destroying what theologians call man's "integrity." That calamity at the dawn of history is something which man had it in his power to bring about but not to remedy. We believe that it was in man's power to commit an act of infinite malice but not in his power to work a proportionate—that is to say an infinite—reparation. We are helped in this by the principle that the gravity of an offense is measured by the dignity of the person outraged thereby. For example, a slight offense done to someone of lower status acquires a greater gravity if offered to a friend or equal and so on up the scale until, done to a king, it becomes high treason. On the other hand, the adequacy of a reparation is not measured by the dignity of the person we are seeking to placate but by the dignity of the person seeking to make reparation. For example, the submission of King Henry II to being flogged for his share of the responsibility for the murder of St. Thomas à Becket at Canterbury has, in human estimation, a quite different value from a similar punishment inflicted on some poor criminal.

This concept, applied to the Fall, shows that the sin of our first parents was a sin of infinite gravity, since it was committed against Almighty God. On the other hand, their ability to put it right was finite because it was limited by man's finite nature. This may help us to see why the human race from the very beginning has been unable to put right the evil that it did at the outset. The whole course of the dealings between the Creator and His creatures as recorded in the Old Testament points forward to the fact that One would come to repair the damage. If you get that contrast clear between the ability to do wrong and the inability to remedy that wrong, you see the necessity of the Incarnation.

I will now return to the Catechism answers which we left out earlier:

Q32 **Jesus Christ is God the Son, made man for us.**

Q33 **Jesus Christ is truly God.**

Q34 **Jesus Christ is truly God because He has one and the same nature with God the Father.**

Q35 **Jesus Christ was always God, born of the Father from all eternity.**

Q36 **Jesus Christ is the Second Person of the Blessed Trinity.**

And then:

Q37 **Jesus Christ is truly man.**

Jesus Christ is truly man because He has the nature of man, having a body and soul like ours. Q38

Jesus Christ was not always man. He has been man only from the time of His Incarnation. Q39

I mean by the Incarnation that God the Son took to Himself the nature of man: "The Word was made Flesh." (*John* 1:14) Q40

There are two natures in Jesus Christ, the nature of God and the nature of man. Q41

There is only one Person in Jesus Christ, which is the Person of God the Son. Q42

Now, all these definitions are to safeguard the fact that the one Person of Jesus Christ, one single undivided Person, has two natures, each whole, complete and distinct: the nature of God and the nature of man. Every act of our Lord and Saviour Jesus Christ consequently partakes of the divine and the human. He is both, all the time. This is the profoundest and greatest mystery. Only if you accept that mystery—and it is the acceptance of it that makes a man a Christian—do you see the point of the Incarnation. Only then do you see how the Incarnation was essential for the redemption of mankind. The mystery of the Incarnation means that the redemption which our Blessed Lord works for us derives infinite value from the fact that He is God. At the same time it is done by a man having the same nature as ours, done, that is to say, by a member of the fallen human race. It is not God, so to speak, wiping out the record. A redemption is really being effected, the fault really is being remedied, by Someone Who has the power to remedy it because He is God. Yet He is able to do it on behalf of the human race because He is also man. If there were not two natures in the one Person of Jesus Christ, the Incarnation would be ineffective.

There is no mystery equal to the Incarnation for the demands which it makes upon our faith. All other mysteries are best seen as preparatory to it or as consequences of it. This is the central mystery of all and if you accept it you have by implication accepted all the others. There can be none to touch it. Think what it means—it means that the Absolute comes into the relative, the Eternal into time, the Necessary into the contingent, the Creator into His own creation.

Nearly every one of the great Christian heresies has emphasized one of Christ's two natures at the expense of the other, or has weakened or denied the complete union between them. That is why the Church all through the ages has struck great hammer blows condemning an imbalance this way or that or any weakening of the union between Christ's two natures. Because Christianity is a revelation to us of mysteries, there is an inescapable tension in it. Remember always that almost every heresy—perhaps every heresy—is a truth out of context, a truth emphasized at the expense of another truth. Truths have to be kept in balance. Most heresies stem from an imbalance.

To emphasize Christ's divinity at the expense of His humanity was the earliest Christian heresy. To say that Jesus Christ is truly God, really God, He Who made the sun, the moon and the stars, caused all things to exist and keeps them in being, is indeed orthodox. But to go on to say that Christ's humanity is but a mask, a cloak, a phantasm which He adopts in order to appear among men is to destroy the reality of His suffering and death. A phantasm just going through the motions of suffering and dying has no merit at all. Therefore a redemption worked on these terms, so to speak, has no power to redeem.

Then take the other extreme—a heresy that is more prevalent today—the proposition that Jesus Christ is truly man but that He is not truly God. To say, "Jesus Christ is really a man, as you and I are men, having really been born in a moment of time, having truly died on the tree, but His divinity is an approach to the Divine greater than that achieved by any other man," is to deprive His death of the infinite value which derives from His being truly God. A redemption worked on those terms would not have infinite value.

Then again, if you weaken the link between the divine and human natures of Christ and say, "There was not one single Person but a man suffering and dying and a God rising from the dead; oh, yes, He really was a man, Who suffered and died; yes, but it was God Who worked miracles, Who rose again"; if you maintain that there was a conjunction in one person of separate beings, one human and one divine, then the suffering and death are not the suffering and death of God and are therefore not of infinite value. It is only if you believe in these two natures, divine and human, united in one Person that the Redemption is effective, a redemption done by One Who is God Himself and Who, because He is man, truly suffers and so expiates the sins of the human race, of which He is a member.

It always astounds me that people who profess their belief in the Incarnation find such difficulty in believing the consequences. Every other mystery is either preparatory to or consequent upon that central mystery. We have seen how the mystery of the Blessed Trinity prepares us to appreciate who becomes incarnate. The mystery of the Fall prepares us to appreciate why He becomes incarnate. And the mystery which we shall consider in the next chapter, that of our Blessed Lady's place in the scheme of things, is the absolute guarantee of both the divinity and the humanity of Jesus Christ her Son. It is her conception and bearing of Him that links Him to us and to the whole human race. Again all that we believe about the Church stems from our belief that the Church is a continuation of the Incarnation; she is Christ continued in corporate form until the Second Coming. Further, the whole sacramental system whereby He works in and through matter to communicate divine grace to us reflects the fact that the Incarnation—God taking material form to work our redemption—is the Sacrament of Sacraments. All other mysteries flow from the central one of the Incarnation. That is the one on which we are going to concentrate all our thoughts and prayers.

Before we go on to develop this line of thought, we will just for a moment touch on the last three questions, which finish off this section of the Catechism:

Q44 **The holy name JESUS means Saviour.**

Q45 **The name CHRIST means Anointed.**

I rather regret that the practice of referring to our Blessed Lord as the Saviour or the Redeemer has so passed out of common use. For when we refer to Christ as "the Redeemer" or "the Saviour," we are putting our finger exactly on His function, His role, which is to redeem, to save. That is the whole object of the Incarnation—to undo the effect of the Fall and so to redeem mankind.

It is admirable that the next question, "Where is Jesus Christ?"—just such a question as a child might ask—is so courteously given an answer of the greatest theological exactitude:

As God, Jesus Christ is everywhere. As God made man, He is in heaven, and in the Blessed Sacrament of the Altar. Q46

As we have seen, Almighty God is everywhere, permeating all that exists, for otherwise it would not exist. Since Christ is God, He too must permeate all that exists, as does the Father, as does the Holy Spirit. Christ, therefore, is everywhere. As man, Jesus Christ, Who was conceived by our Blessed Lady and born of her, lived His life on earth, died on the Cross and rose from the dead, God made man, united to our nature, is in Heaven, to which He ascended after the Resurrection, and in the Blessed Sacrament, which we shall consider later on.

CHAPTER 5

Our Lord's Birth, Death and Resurrection

NOW, we spent the last chapter considering the Incarnation, which, in a sense, is a subject that we never leave. For the Incarnation is the central mystery of the whole of our faith. Every other mystery is best seen as preparatory to or consequent on the Incarnation or contained in it. There is a real sense in which, in accepting the Incarnation in all its fullness and with all its implications, we are accepting the whole of the Catholic faith. The faith seen from outside may look very complicated, but once you grasp the central truth that Jesus Christ is both God and Man, the many consequences of that mystery fall into position. The Incarnation contains all other mysteries and I have suggested that it is always a matter of surprise to Catholics that people who profess belief in that mystery so often find it difficult to accept the mysteries that derive from it. People tend to accept the Incarnation more easily than other doctrines because we live in a civilization still largely colored by Christian tradition. Were you to try to expound the Catholic Faith to a Brahmin or a Confucian the point at which you would stick would be the Incarnation. Once you had got over that hurdle I do not think he would make much difficulty over the mystical body or the Real Presence.

The next sections of the Catechism consider the mystery of the Incarnation in its different aspects. First, the Incarnation as concerned with the humanity of our Blessed Lord, that is to say, with the fact that He is truly man.

Q47 **The third article of the Creed is, "Who was conceived by the Holy Spirit, born of the Virgin Mary."**

Q48 **The third article means that God the Son took a Body and Soul like ours, in the womb of the Blessed Virgin Mary, by the power of the Holy Spirit.**

Q49 **Jesus Christ had no father on earth: St. Joseph was only His guardian or foster-father.**

Q50 **Our Saviour was born in a stable at Bethlehem.**

Q51 **Our Saviour was born on Christmas Day.**

These answers show why the Catholic Church puts such immense emphasis on the divine maternity of our Blessed Lady. People who do not appreciate the Incarnation in its fullness often find great difficulty in accepting the position we give to Our Blessed Lady, not appreciating that it springs immediately from what we believe about the Incarnation and that it is the great guarantee of orthodoxy with regard to it. The whole inspiration of the Catholic devotion to our Blessed Lady is precisely that God in the Second Person of the Blessed Trinity took His human nature from her. He really is a man, conceived by His Mother, as were you by yours and I by mine. He drew his material existence from her: flesh of her flesh, bone of her bone. He is not, as some heretics have believed, a phantasm. It is not a case of God choosing to present Himself to us in the likeness or guise of a man. He has, as the Catechism says, a body and a soul like ours. We do not believe that His divinity was so to speak, His soul, nor that His humanity was His body. No, a man who had a human body but whose soul was God would not be a man at all. A man is a body and soul: a rational animal. Jesus Christ was just that. He really had a human body. He really had a human soul. He was a man. Consequently He knew, felt and thought as a man knows, feels and thinks. He was not pretending to do those things but really and truly experiencing them. When He asked the woman at the well for a drink (*John* 4:7), He really was thirsty. When He wept at Lazarus' death (*John* 11:35), He was not simulating sorrow or counterfeiting tears. He really felt sorrow; He really wept. He knew things, as we know them, through the senses; He suffered, as we suffer, through mind and body. So many things which might seem incompatible with His divinity are the inevitable consequences of the objective reality of His humanity. He really felt the agony of fear in the garden. When He called out in torment on the Cross,

"My God, my God, why hast Thou forsaken me?" (*Mark* 15:34), He did not believe that He had been abandoned. He was using a psalm to express that feeling of complete abandonment which He was undoubtedly feeling in His human nature. That psalm, 21 (22 AV), beginning though it does with profound abasement and going on to describe in prophetic detail our Lord's sufferings on the Cross (vv. 16–18), moves with perfect trust into the vision of universal redemption won by the Cross (vv. 19–31). Not just verse 1 but the whole psalm passes through His mind.[8]

Only if you believe what we believe about the Incarnation is there any reason for honoring our Blessed Lady as we do. If you follow those heretics who say that our Blessed Lord is a man only, making a closer approach to the Godhead than any man has ever done, then she is the mother of a man, a great man, the greatest of men; but you cannot say of her that she is the mother of God. If you go to the other extreme and say that He is God only and His human nature is a mask, a cloak, a phantasm, then plainly all you can claim for her is that she is the mother of a mask, a cloak, a phantasm, whatever meaning you can attach to that phrase. If, further, you follow those heretics who separate the divine and human natures of Christ and think of the man suffering and dying and the God working miracles and rising from the dead, then our Blessed Lady is at most the mother of the human nature of Christ. But if you say, as we do, that she is the mother of that one, single person, Jesus Christ, Who is both God and man, then you agree with the Council of Ephesus, which defined her as the Mother of God. You see now that all the devotion we pay to our Blessed Lady, far from derogating from the devotion we owe to our Blessed Lord, God Incarnate, is, as I said a moment ago, the very guarantee of the orthodoxy of our Christology. Only if we are orthodox Christians believing in two natures, the human and the divine, each whole, complete and distinct, but both united in one Person, do we believe that our Blessed Lady is the Mother of the one Person of Christ—the Mother of God.

The Catechism now goes on to consider the sufferings of our Blessed Lord.

The fourth article of the Creed is, "suffered Q52
under Pontius Pilate, was crucified, dead and buried."

The chief sufferings of Christ were: first, His Q53
agony and His sweat of blood in the Garden; secondly, His being scourged at the Pillar and crowned with thorns; and thirdly, His carrying His Cross, His crucifixion and His death between two thieves.

The chief sufferings of our Lord are called the Q54
Passion of Jesus Christ.

Our Saviour suffered to atone for our sins and Q55
to purchase for us eternal life.

These answers are merely emphasizing, as we have already said, the reality of our Blessed Lord's sufferings, which can result only from His being man. The appearance or simulation of suffering is not really suffering. Consequently, if our Blessed Lord were not a member of the human race His apparent sufferings would have no value as an expiation and would not have been endured by Him on behalf of the whole human race. The Catechism then says:

Jesus Christ is called our Redeemer because Q56
His Precious Blood is the price by which we were ransomed.

When we were talking earlier about Christ, I regretted how one seldom hears Him referred to now as the Saviour or Redeemer. For to refer to Him thus puts the correct emphasis on what He came to do and did. I think it is most important, whenever you find yourself caught up in one of those profitless discussions about comparative religion as to whether Christians are more or less moral than Moslems or Buddhists or what you will, to remember that the great distinguishing feature of Christianity is not its moral consequences but the fact that of all the great religions of the world Christianity is the only one for which its followers claim that its Founder has done something, as distinct from teaching something. It is not a question of Christianity having a higher moral code than any other, though we believe it has. It is a question of its having affected the relationship between mankind and God. The Incarnation expiated the effects of the Fall and won for Man a higher position than he had before the Fall.

This section of the Catechism ends with some historical observations:

Q57 **Our Saviour died on Good Friday.**

Q58 **Our Saviour died on Mount Calvary.**

Then follow the practical directions about making the Sign of the Cross, with an explanation of its meaning:

Q60 **In making the Sign of the Cross we are reminded of the Blessed Trinity by the words, "In the name of the Father, and of the Son, and of the Holy Spirit."**

As we observed earlier, it is "in the name," not "in the names."

Q61 **In making the Sign of the Cross we are reminded that Christ died for us on the Cross by the very form of the cross which we make upon ourselves.**

In making the Sign of the Cross we make a complete profession of the Christian faith—faith in the Blessed Trinity, the Incarnation and the Redemption. It is a perfect form of prayer, for all its briefness, because it professes the whole of the Christian faith in one phrase and expresses it in thought, word and deed.

After emphasizing the reality of Jesus Christ's humanity, the Catechism goes on to consider His divinity.

The fifth article of the Creed is, "He descended into Hell; the third day He rose again from the dead." Q62

What I want to stress now is the importance attached by our Blessed Lord to His Resurrection from the dead as the demonstration of His divinity. There is a sense in which the crucifixion and death of our Blessed Lord demonstrate His humanity—He could not have suffered and died had He not been man like you and me. Now He Himself takes His Resurrection from the dead as the demonstration of His divinity.

Our Blessed Lord in His own lifetime was constantly claiming to be God. He did not make this claim suddenly, in one single assertion, but suggested that staggering fact by gradually opening the eyes of others to it, so that they came progressively to believe by divine faith that He really was God Himself. The reason why our Blessed Lord does not make His claim to Godhead suddenly is partly, I suppose, because this truth is so overwhelming that His disciples could not have taken it in; and partly because to make that claim unequivocally at the outset of His public life would have resulted in His being immediately apprehended and tried for blasphemy. The capital charge against Him was eventually this: "He claims to be God." All through His public life He was working miracles in support of His claim:

multiplying material things, stilling the tempest, healing the sick, raising the dead.

But all the time He was pointing forward to one miracle more overwhelmingly convincing than any other. All the other miracles have some parallel in the history of the Old Testament and, as we believe, in the subsequent history of the Church. All the time Christ was working those other miracles He was, as I said before, pointing forward to one miracle more powerful than any in demonstrating His Divinity, that of raising Himself from the dead. He foreshadowed His Resurrection when He said,

"Destroy the temple of Jerusalem and in three days I will raise it up." (*John* 2:19–21). His hearers of course, understood Him to refer to the actual building, but He meant the temple of His own body. Again, when He was asked for a sign, He replied, "An evil and adulterous generation seeketh a sign: and a sign shall not be given it, but the sign of Jonas the prophet. For as Jonas was in the whale's belly three days and three nights : so shall the son of man be in the heart of the earth three days and three nights." (*Matthew* 12:39–40).

Then there were Christ's words at His transfiguration. You remember that He took Peter, James and John apart and was transfigured before them. They were being allowed to see that demonstration of His Godhead because they were the very three who would see Him in the agony in the Garden, unmanned and broken down under the fear of what was going to befall Him. As they came down from the mountain He charged them to tell no man of what they had seen "until the Son of Man has risen from the dead." In other words, "You have been given a preview, so to speak. Do not talk of it until then." Later, when the Resurrection did occur, see how the Apostles made it the very cornerstone of their preaching.

Our Blessed Lord was pointing forward to His Resurrection throughout His public life; the Apostles pointed back to it. After the descent of the Holy Spirit in the upper room in Jerusalem, when the Apostles went out to preach the Gospel for the first time, what did they preach? Not primarily those things that you might expect from many modern presentations of the Gospel, such as morality or loving kindness. No, they went out to preach the hard, historical fact that Christ, Who had been crucified, had risen from the dead. It was the whole burden of their mission. This demonstration of Christ's divinity was the message which they carried to the ends of the then known world and in the defense of whose truth they laid down their lives.

What the Apostles did then, the Church has done ever since. The whole life of the Church circles round the Resurrection, so that the sacred day of Christians is not the last day of the week, on which God rested, but is the first day of the week, on which God sprang into new life. Likewise the center of the whole Christian year is not, as modern social observance would lead us to think, Christmas Day, but Easter Sunday. The whole Christian year hinges on it and the moveable feasts are reckoned from it.

I wonder if you see why the Resurrection is such a complete demonstration of Christ's divinity. All the other miracles, as we have seen, have some parallel elsewhere. This has none. It is not claimed for any Saint or Prophet, however great, that he has raised himself from the dead. What power God has given him in life dies with him. Had Christ been man alone His miraculous powers would have ceased at death. But no! He was very God, the one necessary Being, He Who could not not exist. His omnipotence therefore continued eternally when His enemies destroyed His human life. So the Resurrection of our Blessed Lord from the dead is a demonstration of His divinity, as His crucifixion demonstrates His humanity.

The Catechism now turns to Christ's descent into Hell:

Q63 **By the words "He descended into Hell," I mean that, as soon as Christ was dead, His blessed Soul went down into that part of Hell called Limbo.**

Q64 **By Limbo I mean a place of rest, where the souls of the just who died before Christ were detained.**

Q65 **The souls of the just were detained in Limbo because they could not go up to the Kingdom of Heaven till Christ had opened it for them.**

The next question we have already considered:

Q66 **By the words, "the third day He rose again from the dead," I mean that, after Christ had been dead and buried part of three days, He raised His blessed Body to life again on the third day.**

Q67 **Christ rose again from the dead on Easter Sunday.**

That part of the fifth article of the Creed, the descent into Hell, is, I imagine, the part of the Creed least remembered by Christians. It was not always so. In the Middle Ages there was a constant reference to what was called the "Raking of Hell." You see it portrayed in medieval wall paintings; you see it in medieval mystery plays; you see it in one of the south windows of King's College Chapel at Cambridge.

Now, I imagine that the reason why the descent into

Hell is mentioned so seldom by Christians is that its vocabulary is misleading. "Hell" does not here mean Hell in the strict sense, because Hell is the state of eternal separation from Almighty God. The Hell we are talking about here is called Hell by analogy. It is very important to know what it means, because this article of the Creed brings home to us the absolute necessity of the Redemption. We, living nineteen centuries after the Redemption took place, take it for granted and say to ourselves, "If only I do what is right and act according to my lights I shall be saved." Yes. But that is only because of what Jesus Christ has done—His suffering and dying for us. Every attempt on our part to lead a good and holy life is of value only because it is complementary to His dying for us. Our efforts would have been of no avail had He not done so.

What is clearly implied by this article of the Creed is that all the saints and the prophets of the Old Testament simply could not enter Heaven until Christ's sacrifice was complete. They were in Limbo. They had not yet been redeemed. The curse of Adam was still upon them. Their lives of virtue were lived in expectation of the Redemption and needed the Redemption in order to come to fruit. This article of the Creed means that the moment the Redemption took place its consequences were applied to them. Their good works, their lives of virtue, sprang into life; the gates of Heaven opened to them.

We ought to thank God every day of our lives that we are living after the Redemption and that our attempts to lead lives of holiness are effective precisely because the Redemption has taken place.

CHAPTER 6

The Ascension, the Second Coming and the Holy Spirit

IN OUR last two chapters we have been thinking about the Incarnation, which is, as I have so often emphasized, the nub of the Christian revelation, the central truth that Jesus Christ is wholly God and wholly man, two natures united in one single Person, the Person of Jesus Christ. And we have been considering how the Passion and death of our Blessed Lord demonstrates the reality of His humanity—He really is a man with a human body and a human soul, torn apart in death on the Cross—and how the Resurrection of our Blessed Lord is the great demonstration of His divinity. Precisely because the union of the two natures in the Person of God the Son was not interrupted when He died on the Cross, both body and soul continue to be His even when separated from each other in death. And their coming together again is even more directly responsive to His divine power than the recall of Lazarus, the widow's son, or Jairus's daughter to life.

Now we come to consider the Ascension into Heaven. It is so much less in people's minds than it ought to be. Its theological importance lies in its demonstration of that indissoluble union between the two natures of Christ, human and divine.

Q68 **The sixth article of the Creed is, "He ascended into Heaven and is seated at the right hand of God the Father Almighty."**

Q69 **By the words, "He ascended into Heaven," I mean that our Saviour went up Body and Soul into heaven on Ascension Day, forty days after His Resurrection.**

This means that at the Ascension into Heaven, as recorded for us in the Acts of the Apostles, Jesus Christ was taken up out of the sight of the Apostles and entered Heaven after forty days of His risen life, during which He appeared frequently to His followers and taught them. The point to remember is that the Word Who came down, thirty-three years before, and became incarnate in the womb of His mother, returned to Heaven not the disincarnate Godhead that had come down to earth, but God-Man. In a sense you can think of our Blessed Lord's Ascension into Heaven as being the first fruit of His own Redemption—He is taking human nature up with Him, never again to be separated from the Godhead. It is helpful to think of Him as being the Head of that Body of which we are members; and of His going up into Heaven as being a guarantee that we will attain to Heaven. As we shall consider when we come to discuss the Catholic Church, we see ourselves always as being grafted into Him and forming one Person with Him. He Who is our Head has already achieved the end for which we are destined, so that Man is, as we say in picturesque language, seated at the right hand of God the Father Almighty.

As far as I know, no artist has ever brought together on

one canvas or in a triptych those three events which perfectly show forth the humanity of Christ, the divinity of Christ and the indissoluble union between them: namely the Crucifixion (Jesus Christ really and truly dying on the Cross, showing forth His humanity), the Resurrection (Jesus Christ raising Himself from the dead, showing forth His divinity) and between the two the Ascension into Heaven (showing forth the complete and indissoluble union between them). He Who now ascends into Heaven ascends no longer the disincarnate Word that came down at the Incarnation but the Incarnate Word ascending into Heaven and sitting on the throne of God.

The concept of our Blessed Lord's Ascension into Heaven being the guarantee of our own, is well brought out in the Collect for Ascension Day, which, in the old rite, used to run: "Grant, we beseech Thee, Almighty God, that we who believe that Thine only-begotten Son our Redeemer this day ascended into Heaven may ourselves live in mind of heavenly things," as if to say that where our mind is, our body will follow. This is even more clearly brought out in the Preface, when we pray "through Christ our Lord, Who after His Resurrection appeared and showed Himself to all His disciples; and while they beheld Him was lifted up into Heaven, so that He might make us partakers of His Godhead."

The last answer about the Ascension is:

> **By the words "is seated at the right hand of God the Father Almighty" I do not mean that God the Father has hands, for He is a spirit, but I mean that Christ, as God, is equal to the Father and, as man, is in the highest place in Heaven.** Q70

That is, in the place of God.

Q71 **The seventh article of the Creed is, "from thence He shall come to judge the living and the dead."**

Q72 **Christ will come again from Heaven at the last day, to judge all mankind.**

Q73 **Christ will judge our thoughts, words, works and omissions.**

Q74 **Christ will say to the wicked, "Depart from me, ye cursed, into everlasting fire, which was prepared for the devil and his angels."** (*Matthew* 15:41)

Q75 **Christ will say to the just, "Come, ye blessed of My Father, possess ye the kingdom prepared for you."** (*Matthew* 25:34)

Q76 **Everyone will be judged at death, as well as at the last day: "It is appointed unto men once to die, and after this, the judgment."** (*Hebrews* 9:27)

With that we complete the cycle of human history. We started our consideration of this cycle with the Fall of Man; that is, the separation or gulf between Man and his Creator caused by the rebellion of our first parents. Then we considered the remedy of that appalling catastrophe by the Incarnation, which bridged the gulf which that catastrophe had made. The Second Coming of our Lord and Saviour Jesus Christ represents the completion of the cycle.

We believe that at the end of human history He will return, as He has promised us He would, to judge the whole of the human race in the light of His redemption of it. Moreover, the Catechism tells us that over and above the

Last Judgment we shall be judged at the very moment of death, each one of us individually.

It is very important that we should try to clarify in our minds the notions of judgment, punishment and reward, because there is the constant danger that we may think of them in human terms. It is unfortunate that we speak of the law, the judgments and the punishments of Almighty God in just the same terms as we speak of the law, the judgments and the punishments of men. The law, the judgments and the punishments of men often arouse our resentment, particularly, of course, when we experience them. This is understandable because the laws of men are all in varying degrees arbitrary and when we fall foul of them we believe they could so easily have been otherwise. The overwhelming majority of our laws are arbitrary; not, of course, those which are rooted in the moral law, such as the laws against murder or theft, but the ordinary ones that we in the course of our lives are likely to come up against—traffic regulations or tax laws, for example. There is no inherent reason why we should drive on the right or the left of the road or why we should pay £5 or £50 in income tax. These are things arbitrarily determined by men of judgment as fallible as our own. Consequently, if we fall foul of them we feel a resentment at their arbitrary nature. If we are prosecuted for a breach of one of those laws, it seems to us arbitrary whether we are convicted or acquitted. Much depends on the counsel that we have been able to engage, on the judge before whom we appear, on whether the jury likes the look of us or not. When the verdict goes against us we say, "It could easily have gone the other way, if only my counsel had made that point a little clearer, if only I had not muffed something in the evidence," and so on.

And then the punishment is arbitrary: when we have been convicted under a law which is, as we think, arbitrary, by a process which seems to us to be arbitrary, it seems most arbitrary whether we are sent to jail or are fined or are given a suspended sentence. It could be any of those things, so again our resentment is aroused.

When we use that vocabulary to talk about the law, the punishments and the judgments of Almighty God, we are in danger of importing this feeling of resentment, which is a consequence of the arbitrary nature of human laws. But the laws, the judgments and the punishments of Almighty God are not arbitrary. Almighty God could not conceivably have made the Commandments other than they are, because they are the reflection of His perfect and unchanging nature.

The judgments of Almighty God are not arbitrary. We in our human affairs are constantly giving other people the benefit of the doubt. With Almighty God there can be no doubt. Our standing in His sight is absolutely certain. The consequences of willingly breaking His law cannot be other than they are. If we quite deliberately turn our will away from His, He will not override that free will which he has given us, with all the awful possibilities of good or ill which free will implies. A will which can only choose good, or will be overridden if it chooses evil, cannot be said to be free.

The consequences of disregarding God's laws are not arbitrary but are carried in the actions themselves. In this respect they resemble the laws of nature. The consequences of disregarding the laws of nature do not arouse our resentment as do the consequences of disregarding the laws of men. If we step off a cliff, our being dashed to pieces at the bottom is not an arbitrary punishment. So, too, the consequences of disregarding the law of Almighty God are inevitable. Our very action in diverting our wills from His will means that we cannot come to Him in Whom alone our fulfillment lies. Nothing but a return of our will to His, which is what we mean by an act of contrition or sorrow for sin, can bring us back to Him.

That perhaps makes it a little clearer why we are told that we are judged at the very moment of death as well as at that solemn Assize on the last day. At the very moment of death the condition to which we have brought our souls for good or ill is revealed to us. We know at that moment whether the grace of God is in our souls—as we pray it is—or whether in fact we have driven it out by our own actions. There is therefore what is called a "private judgment" at the moment of death. Our fate at that moment is sealed for all eternity. But we also believe on the strength of our Blessed Lord's own words, that there is a last solemn Judgment of the whole human race at the end of human history; not in the sense of an appeal from what has happened at the moment of death but rather a proclamation or confirmation of it.

This is one more example of the recognition by Almighty God both of our own absolutely unique importance and of our inescapably social nature. Our social commitment runs through all our thinking. Each single one of us is uniquely the creation of Almighty God, brought into the world by Him, fashioned by Him, kept in being by Him. And yet, for all that, we cannot live outside society. We come into a family on which we are dependent for our shelter, food and drink, being unable, unlike the lower animals, to fend for ourselves for the first decade or two of our lives. This dependence applies not only to our physical needs but to the development and exercise of our powers of speech and to our intellectual faculties.

You see this recognition of our double nature at the beginning of human history, where, in the Fall, the action of individuals has consequences for the whole human race, and again in the Redemption, where the action of one individual God-Man reverses the consequences of the Fall. In St. Paul's words, "As in Adam all die, so in Christ all are made alive." (*1 Corinthians* 15:22).

We shall consider later the consequences of our individual and social natures in the mission of the Holy Spirit. The Holy Spirit has a dual function: a personal one and a social one. He dwells in the soul of each of us by His grace: He dwells in the whole Catholic Church as her abiding and life-giving spirit.

It is in that light that we ought to see the two judgments, the immediate one at our death, at that moment where the state to which we have brought ourselves is revealed to us, and then the Last Judgment at the end of human history.

With that we round off the consideration of the Incarnation. We started, you remember, by considering the mystery of the Blessed Trinity, where we learned Who became incarnate; the mystery of the Fall, which tells us why He came incarnate; and ending with the consideration of that central mystery, the Incarnation itself. The Word becomes Man, works our redemption on behalf of the human race, of which he is a member, and endows that redemption with an infinite value because He is God. We shall come back many times to the Incarnation: it will be seen to run through our concept of the Church, the Sacraments and the Real Presence. I cannot too often emphasize its absolutely central importance, as well as the fact that the demands it makes on faith are greater than those made by any other mystery. It can be said that the man who has accepted the Incarnation has by implication accepted the whole Catholic faith.

The Catechism now turns to the Holy Spirit.

The eighth article of the Creed is, "I believe in the Holy Spirit." Q77

The Holy Spirit is the Third Person of the Blessed Trinity. Q78

The Holy Spirit proceeds from the Father and the Son. Q79

The Holy Spirit is equal to the Father and to the Son, for He is the same Lord and God as they are. Q80

The Holy Spirit came down on the Apostles on Whit Sunday, in the form of "parted tongues, as it were, of fire." Q81

The Holy Spirit came down on the Apostles to confirm their faith, to sanctify them and to enable them to found the Church. Q82

We come now to the consideration of the Third Person of the Blessed Trinity. We must bring our minds back to that fundamental mystery of the Trinity. We must remind ourselves that it is a mystery. We could not have come to it by unaided human reason. It is a mystery revealed to us by our Blessed Lord Himself indirectly when He claims to be God, when He speaks of the Father as distinct from Himself and also as God and when He speaks of the Holy Spirit as distinct from Himself and His Father and also as God. He teaches it directly by sending the apostles out to teach and to baptize in the name of the Father and of the Son and of the Holy Spirit: that is, in the name, not the names, of the one, indivisible God, in Whom none the less there are three distinct Persons, each of Whom is God Himself, neither of Whom is the other two.

The first thing to stress is the complete equality among the three persons of the Trinity. We must remind ourselves again that when we put them one Person after another, as we do, there is no sequence of the Trinity. Our minds are prone to consider the Persons of the Trinity in temporal succession, although they are, of course, coeternal. We considered that point when we first talked about the Trinity, quoting the opening of St. John's Gospel:

"In the beginning was the Word and the Word was with God and the Word was God." The Eternal Mind from all eternity is contemplating the Eternal Word, no less eternal than Itself. From all eternity there is complete Harmony between the Eternal Mind and the Eternal Word. Mind, Word and Harmony are all equally eternal and therefore all equally God. There is no succession. We must never think of the Eternal Mind successively contemplating the Eternal Word and next establishing an Eternal Harmony of will between them. The Father, the Son and the Holy Spirit are at one and at once in eternity; not for a split second of time was there first the Mind, then the Thought occupying it, then the Identity of will and purpose between them. They are completely coeternal. It would be impossible to have degrees of inequality in Almighty God: all three Persons are equally God.

I mentioned a moment earlier how we are inescapably individual and unique and yet no less inescapably social. I find it profitable to think of that as a sort of reflection of the Trinity. We say that man is made in the image of Almighty God primarily because he has a mind and a will, reflecting the Wisdom and the Power which is God Himself. Further, there is a resemblance to the Blessed Trinity in our own nature, which is unable to realize itself or grow to its full stature without contact with others. Man needs to go outside himself to be fully realized. We are not self-sufficient. We need to love and to be loved. St. John tells us, "God is love." (*1 John* 4:8). There at the very center of the Godhead, of the one necessary Being, is Love from all eternity, the Father loving the Son, the Son loving the Father, that Love being personified in the Holy Spirit Love is a mutual, reciprocal thing, something going out from one and returned by the other, something between two persons. So at the very center of the Godhead, the very center of Being itself (which is what God is), there is Love. This is what we mean when we say that the Holy Spirit proceeds both from the Father and from the Son.

A great controversy divided the Western from the Eastern Church when that fact, which the Church has always believed, was expressed in the Filioque clause of the Creed.

Love is essentially a two-way traffic. The Holy Spirit does not only proceed from the Father towards the Son and remain there, but also comes back from the Son to the Father. So for all eternity this motion of outgoing and returning is at the very heart of Being.

With regard to the Blessed Trinity we believe that, in the words of theologians, all the *operationes ad extra*, that is, the works of the Trinity outside Itself, are common to all the Persons of the Trinity. The *operationes ad intra* are personal to each. Though all the Persons of the Trinity are at one in the work of creation and conservation, we do tend by a process that theologians call "attribution" to particularize Creation to the Father, Redemption to the Son and Sanctification to the Holy Spirit.

We must always correct a tendency to think that any of the work outside the Trinity can be exclusive to any one Person by reminding ourselves that, though we are inclined to think of the Father as the Creator bringing all things into being, yet the Son and the Holy Spirit create as one with Him. The opening of St. John's Gospel states this point clearly: "In the beginning was the Word and the Word was with God and"—consequently—"the Word was God. All things were made by Him and without Him was made nothing that was made."

Then again, though it is the Word alone, the Second Person of the Blessed Trinity, Who becomes incarnate, yet Father, Son and Holy Ghost in common caused the Word to become flesh. The Incarnation, like all other effects of omnipotence, comes from the nature of God, in which the Persons are one.

Finally, because of the descent of the Holy Spirit at the first Pentecost, we tend to attribute the work of the sanctification of the Church and all her members to the Holy Spirit. Yet the whole Trinity indwells in the whole Church and those who are in a state of grace.

Within the Trinity, all is common where no personal relationship (Father to Son, Son to Father, Holy Spirit to Father and Son) intervenes.

With these cautions in mind, we return to our consideration of the Holy Spirit. The Holy Spirit, we believe, descended upon the Apostles at the first Pentecost, as recorded in the Acts of the Apostles (2:3). He descended upon them, as the Catechism says, to enable them to found the Church. He came to them to be the indwelling spirit of that social organization here on earth, the Catholic Church.

He stands in that relation to it which our souls do to our own bodies.

Always remember when you are tempted to be impatient or critical of that human body here on earth, the visible Church, that she depends for her authority and sanctity not on those through whom she comes to us but on the indwelling of the Spirit. The Catholic Church on earth derives her whole value only from the fact that the Holy Spirit dwells in her. Just as your body and mine are worthless once the spirit goes out of them, so in the same way the whole vast and intricate organization of the Catholic Church on earth would be of no value if the Spirit were withdrawn.

The Holy Spirit came on the Apostles first, in a corporate and social mission to enable them to found the Church. Further, He dwells in the heart of each individual who is in a state of grace. This is what St. Paul means when he tells us, "Ye are living temples of the Holy Spirit." (*1 Corinthians* 6:19).

Once again we have an illustration of our twofold character. Each single one of us is a unique individual, yet all of us are inescapably social. The Holy Spirit indwells in us both individually and corporately.[9]

If you want to see with what power the Holy Spirit comes, you have only to look at the effect of His coming on the Apostles. The Apostles after the Crucifixion and even after the Resurrection were a band of bewildered men not daring to go out and preach the Gospel. They were utterly demoralized by the death of our Blessed Lord: at the time of His Passion and Trial one betrayed Him, one denied Him repeatedly and only one was found to stand at the foot of the Cross when He was dying. That was the material on which the Holy Spirit had to work. That was the material which He completely transformed. The moment the Holy Spirit descended upon the Apostles, they went out to preach the Gospel for the first time. They went out into a hostile world to carry the good tidings of the Resurrection to the ends of the earth. They laid down their lives in witness of the Resurrection. That is the effect the Holy Spirit had on them.

What He did to them He can do to us. The extent to which He does depends entirely on our cooperation. Everyone in a state of grace carries about within him the Third Person of the Trinity, God Himself, Who can make each of us a saint.

CHAPTER 7

The Church

WE HAVE now finished considering the Holy Spirit, the Third Person of the Blessed Trinity, Who is mentioned in the eighth article of the Creed. With the ninth article the Creed goes on to:

> **the Holy Catholic Church; the Communion of Saints.** Q83

The order is significant and deliberately so. The Catholic Church has her origin and life directly from the Blessed Trinity. In the Nicene Creed this truth is more explicitly stated. There we declare our faith in the Holy Spirit, the "giver of life." But to whom does the Holy Spirit give life? To "the One, Holy, Catholic and Apostolic Church." So the Catholic Church is a mystery of faith bound up with our faith in the Blessed Trinity. She is a visible society of people, a human organization with a human history, but, like our physical body, she has a single, higher principle of life, a "soul," unifying and animating her members.

When the Holy Spirit came, on the first Pentecost, it was with the twofold effect we have already noticed: the personal indwelling of individuals (shown by the parted tongues of fire) and the corporate effect of uniting them in a single body of which the same Holy Spirit is the soul. And since He comes as the gift of the Word Incarnate from Whose fullness we have all received, we become one with Christ in the Holy Spirit. We form one mystical body with Him, He the head, we His members. Mystical here does not mean "unreal": it means a reality beyond the natural creation which only faith can apprehend.

This consideration of the Catholic Church shares the centrality of the Incarnation. We stressed that the Incarnation is the central doctrine of all that we believe. The Catholic Church is the Incarnation continued in Christ's mystical body until He comes again. All the mysteries of the Creed in which we profess our belief are rightly seen only in relation to that central mystery that God the Son comes into this world in the person of Jesus Christ.

It is a matter of regret to me that the Catechism treatment of the Catholic Church is not, as I think, quite as clear as it might be. In particular, the order of the questions is unfortunate and I propose to reverse it.

The Catechism starts off, as always when approaching a new subject, with a definition:

Q84 **The Catholic Church is the union of all the faithful under one Head.**

Let me at once point out that that definition, though accurate, is surely inadequate. I would like you to substitute in your Catechism for that word "union" the much stronger and more accurate word "incorporation," so that we should read the definition as follows:

Q84b **The Catholic Church is the incorporation of all the faithful under one Head.**

Of course, the stronger term necessarily includes the weaker.

Whenever I criticize the Catechism, it is never because it is wrong but because it is inadequate or gives a misleading emphasis. My criticism of Answer 84 is not that it is wrong but that it is inadequate, because a union may be a purely accidental thing that can be dissolved.

The Head of the Catholic Church is Jesus Christ our Lord. Q85

In Questions 86 to 93 the Catechism goes on from that consideration of the Catholic Church as the incorporation of all the faithful under one Head to consider the Church on earth and the position of the Papacy within it. I prefer to take Questions 94 to 99 immediately after Question 85 and only then to go back to consider the visible Church on earth, because I want to begin by considering the basic concept of the Catholic Church—the complete identity between the Church and Jesus Christ Himself—before turning to the visible manifestations of that identity here on earth.[10]

Our Blessed Lord clearly identifies His followers with Himself in that wonderful discourse after the Last Supper recorded for us in Chapters 14–17 of St. John's Gospel. The New Testament, as we now know it, divides that discourse into four chapters, but it deals with one theme. It is His last testament to His disciples. The particular part I want you to read and think and pray about is the first ten verses of Chapter 15. This particular passage, as is so often the case in our Blessed Lord's discourses, appears to have been suggested to Him by something immediately at hand. through the vineyards from the supper table to the Garden of Gethsemane, where He is about to spend the night in prayer. He says:

> I am the true vine; and my Father is the husbandman. Every branch in me that beareth not fruit, he will take away; and every one that beareth fruit he will purge it, that it may bring forth more fruit. Now you are clean by reason of the word which I have spoken to you. Abide in me; and I in you. As the branch cannot bear fruit of itself unless it abide in the vine; so neither can you unless you abide in me. I am the vine, you the branches; he that abideth in me, and I in him, the same beareth much fruit: for without me you can do nothing. If any one abide not in me he shall be cast forth as a branch, and shall wither: and they shall gather him up and cast him into the fire, and he burneth. If you abide in me, and my words abide in you, you shall ask whatever you will, and it shall be done unto you. In this is my Father glorified; that you bring forth very much fruit, and become my disciples. As the Father hath loved me, I also have loved you. Abide in my love. If you keep my commandments, you shall abide in my love; as I also have kept my Father's commandments, and do abide in his love. (*John* 15:1–10).

There is no distinction between a vine and its branches. There is no such thing as a vine that has no branches, and branches which do not inhere in a parent stock are no vine. Vine and branches are one thing seen in two different aspects, and that is how our Blessed Lord wants us to see our relationship to Him. We become one living, growing, organic reality with Him. And it is not a dead unity. It is not a bringing together of a number of things. That is why I consider the word "union" to be inadequate. A union could be a bundle of sticks: brought together and tied together they form a union indeed, but cut the string and they all fall apart. They are not a living thing at all.

Now, the connection between the vine and the branches is a completely different one. They share a life. Their whole value depends on their sharing that life. They can do nothing without it. There you have our Blessed Lord's picture of the relationship between Himself and His followers—His picture or model of the Church.

The same idea runs through all St. Paul's teaching under the simile of the body and its members. You will not be surprised by his identifying Christ and His followers if you remember the circumstances of his conversion. As he rode down to Damascus, he was asked by our Blessed Lord in a vision, "Saul, Saul, why persecutest thou me?" (*Acts* 9:4). You will notice that He said not "My followers" but "Me," because Christ and His followers are one. At that time our Blessed Lord had been dead, risen and ascended into heaven for some three years. St. Paul presents the identity between Christ and His followers under the simile of the body and its members. (*1 Corinthians* 12:12). Just as we have seen earlier that the value of the branches of a vine depends on their inherence in the parent stock, so the value of limbs depends on their incorporation in a body. (*Ephesians* 5:30). Branches and limbs alike have no value in themselves. Their value comes from their sharing of a common sap or lifeblood. When we consider the Church we are considering not an accidental coming together of things, but an organic unity.

Let us turn to Question 94 of the Catechism, the point to which we have come by altering the order:

Q94 **The Church of Christ has four marks by which we may know her: she is One; she is Holy; she is Catholic, she is Apostolic.**[11]

Now, what I want you to see about those four marks of the Church is that they are all of this essential, organic nature; they are not contrived by men but are of the very nature of the Church herself. Let us go through the Catechism definitions of these different marks of the Church. I warn you that I am rather critical of the definitions, once again not because they are wrong but because they are inadequate and often seem not to distinguish between causes and effects. The cause of all these four marks of the Church is her oneness with Jesus Christ. That is the reason why she is One, why she is Holy, why she is Catholic, why she is Apostolic. If you want to understand at all what a Catholic means by the Church, remember one simple phrase which we have used before: the Church is Christ living on in His followers. All these marks are marks or characteristics of a person who could not divest himself of his characteristics even if he wished to do so.

The Catechism says:

Q95 **The Church is One because all her members agree in one faith, have all the same Sacrifice and Sacraments and are all united under one Head.**

Q96 **The Church is Holy because she teaches a holy doctrine, offers to all the means of holiness and is distinguished by the eminent holiness of so many thousands of her children.**

Q97 **The word Catholic means universal.**

The Church is Catholic or universal because she subsists in all ages, teaches all nations, and is the one Ark of Salvation for all. Q98

The Church is Apostolic because she holds the doctrines and traditions of the Apostles, and because, through the unbroken succession of her Pastors, she derives her Orders and her Mission from them. Q99

You will see what I mean by saying that many of the Catechism answers confuse causes with effects:

The Church is One because all her members agree in one faith, have all the same Sacrifice and Sacraments, and are all united under one Head. Q95

But the real reason why the Church is One is because Christ is One; He is one Person, indivisible as persons are. You cannot divide a person: you can mutilate, amputate, wound, but division of a person is impossible. So the Church is One with an absolute and essential unity. The reason for her being One is the last clause: her members "are all united," or, as I prefer to say, incorporated, "under one Head." The consequence is that all the members agree in one faith and all have the same Sacrifice and Sacraments. These are not the cause of the unity. The unity is absolute because the Church's members are all incorporated into one body and a body cannot be divided. The unity of the Church is in no sense a man-made unity. That, once again, is why the word "union" is so inadequate. If you get a whole lot of people round a table to agree, that is a man-made unity, and they may, as you well know, disagree before they have left the room. The unity which they have made they can unmake.

Now the unity of the Church has quite another character. It comes from her continuing Christ in corporate form. When men are grafted or incorporated into her, they share that unity. When—which God forbid—they break away from that unity, they leave it unimpaired because they have not made it. So when people drop away from the Church, in their hundreds or thousands or millions, as they did at the Reformation, they do not divide the Church, for that is not possible. They will have passed out of that unity, leaving it unimpaired. Always remember that the unity of the Church derives from her continuing Christ Himself, not from the fact of a number of men agreeing to her doctrines.

In just the same way, the holiness of the Church is essential, not accidental. Here again you see in the Catechism answer that failure to distinguish between causes and effects:

Q96 **The Church is Holy because she teaches a holy doctrine, offers to all the means of holiness and is distinguished by the eminent holiness of so many thousands of her children.**

I would rather say the Church is holy because she derives her life from Christ, Who is the fountain of all holiness. And just as members of the Church have not created their unity but derive their unity or their agreement from their membership of a Church which cannot lose it, so members of the Church do not contribute her essential holiness to the Church but are drawing their holiness from her. She is the source of holiness as she is the source of unity, because her Head is Christ Himself. She dispenses the means of holiness through the Sacraments which He instituted. If, as the Catechism asserts, many thousands of her children are holy—would there were more—they are so because they are using the means she offers. It follows that in one sense the Church is neither more nor less holy according to whether her children are holy or not: her essential holiness is as absolute as her unity is. She cannot lose her holiness any more than she can lose her unity.

Now we come to the universality of the Church. Observe again the failure of the Catechism to distinguish between causes and effects:

> **The Church is Catholic or universal because she subsists in all ages, teaches all nations and is the one ark of Salvation for all.** Q98

But it is the last phrase that is the reason for the Catholicity or universality of the Church: she is the one Ark of Salvation for all. She is the one divinely revealed and convenanted means of men being saved, and her present extension in space or time is accidental. She is Catholic in God's intention and design. He designs her to be the one Ark of Salvation for all. The consequence is that she is very widely spread—would that she were more so—but even if she were more widely spread that fact could not essentially increase her Catholicity. Her Catholicity does not derive from her present geographical extension.

At this point it is necessary to consider what we mean by "the one Ark of Salvation for all," because, as you know, this exclusive claim of the Catholic Church is one of the greatest stumbling blocks to non-Catholics. The Catholic Church's claim is exclusive—never minimize that. It is as exclusive as Christ's own claims to be the one Redeemer. The Apostle says, "There is no other name under Heaven whereby we may be saved." (*Acts* 4:12). No one is saved because of what any other religious teacher or prophet has done. Every single man who is saved, from the beginning of time to the end of time, is saved only because of the Redemption that Christ wrought. And the attempt of any man to live according to his own lights is complementary to that redemption. It would be quite ineffective unless Christ's redemption had been wrought. And so your good Confucian, your good Buddhist, or whatever he may be, is never saved because of what his religious leaders have done. They were powerless to effect anything. Only Christ the God-Man can undo the effects of the Fall. Men are saved when they live according to such lights as they have because Christ's redemptive sacrifice gives supernatural value to their lives.

If you bear in mind that phrase which I quoted, "There is no other name under Heaven whereby we may be saved." (*Acts* 4:12), you will appreciate the real meaning of the Latin *tag extra Ecclesia nul la salus*—"Outside the Church there is no salvation." The Church is Christ's divinely-appointed means of saving mankind. It is the one Ark of Salvation for all. But just as many people are saved, as we hope, because of what Christ has done, even though they are themselves unconscious of what it is that is saving them, so every single person who is saved is saved because of his conscious or unconscious membership of the Catholic Church. He may not have the least notion what it is that is carrying him to his eternal reward. It is the Catholic Church. Many non-Catholics appear to think of salvation as a sort of Dunkirk, an enormous saving operation which may be achieved by a wide variety of craft, the choice of which may be left to the individual. Here is the whole human race in a very tight corner, as the British Army was after the collapse of France, when it was trying to get across to England and using every means to do so—Channel steamers, fishing smacks, racing yachts, any craft to hand. The great object is to get across—never mind the means. The Catholic believes, however, that there is only one means of getting across, which is carrying many passengers who think they are traveling independently. It is as though a man were walking the quarterdeck or swimming in the liner's swimming-bath or rowing in one of the fixed lifeboats, thinking that it was his own efforts that were carrying him. He is in fact being carried across by the one divinely-appointed liner. There is only one way of reaching salvation.

The whole concept of the exclusive claim of the Catholic Church to be the vehicle of salvation—and it is exclusive—makes sense only if you see that claim as the continuation of the exclusive claim of Christ. Indeed, if you want to test the accuracy of any statement about the Catholic Church, see if you can substitute the word "Christ" for "Church." If you can do so and the statement makes sense, then you can be assured of its orthodoxy. If you cannot or it does not make sense, then there is something wrong in the statement. Everything that Christ claims for Himself can be claimed for the Church which is His continuation.[12, 13]

Now we come to the last of the four "marks" of the Church:

> **The Church is Apostolic because she holds the doctrines and traditions of the Apostles, and because, through the unbroken succession of her Pastors, she derives her Orders and her Mission from them.** Q99

This is perhaps the most difficult of all the four marks of the Church to expound. The difficulty is aggravated by the fact that the word "Apostolic" may so easily suggest an appeal to the early Church. That is precisely contrary to what we mean by the term, which is this: that, as I have said, the Catholic Church is one with Christ. She has a continuing identity, right through her history—the same identity that an individual has. In describing herself as Apostolic she is not appealing to the Church of the Apostles but claiming to be that Church.

There are so many things about the Catholic Church which are explicable only if you think of her identity in Christ. She is One with the unity of a person, Holy with the holiness of a person, and so she remains the same, right through from the morning of the first Pentecost until the Second Coming, as you remain the same person from the moment of your birth to the moment of your death and as I do likewise. We are each one person throughout our lives in a way that no one else can simulate, no one can take from us or destroy. Once again, in discussing this mark of the Church we are talking about something that is not man-made or man-achieved. We are talking of essential characteristics of which the Church could not deprive herself even if she wished to do so. Just as she is incapable of losing her unity, her holiness and her catholicity, so she cannot lose her unchanging identity. That body which was born at the first Pentecost, the Church Apostolic, continues as the Catholic Church on earth at the present day and will so continue until Christ comes again, in a way that no other body can change or simulate or claim for itself. And just as a person grows and expands and develops so does the Church, not only physically but, as we shall see, in her understanding of herself, throughout her history.

Now, with every other presentation of Christianity you can put your finger on a point and say, "Yes; this grew out of these circumstances, these social and historical or theological accidents." But no one can say that of the Catholic Church. She began at the first Pentecost.

Someone who has not grasped the concept of the Church as a person finds it difficult to understand her changing superficial aspects. Like a person, the Church is not static at all. Not only is she growing in the obvious, external matters of expansion, organization and the rest, but she is growing too in an understanding of herself. Just as you now understand yourself better than you did at any earlier period of your life, so does she. If you or I were to embark on a new intellectual discipline such as psychology, our understanding of ourselves would increase while our identities would remain unchanged. So, too, the Church has adopted new vocabularies throughout her history to explain what she has always believed. She pressed Greek philosophy into her service to provide the precise vocabulary she required to express what she had always believed about the Incarnation. She did the same when she used the terms of Aristotle's philosophy to describe the Real Presence of Christ in the Holy Eucharist and again when she used the concept of evolution in the nineteenth century to describe the development of doctrines which she had believed in embryo from the first moment of her being.

The Church develops her powers of expression just as a person knows himself better and with much greater precision as he grows older and learns more. I, for example, could not have given this identical instruction word for word fifty years ago. But do I believe something different? By God's grace, no.

All the time, the Church is understanding herself better and explaining herself better. That is what she is doing when she defines doctrines: she is not innovating or initiating them but making precise the "faith once delivered to the Saints." (*Jude* 3). Catholics do not believe that our Blessed Lady was made immaculate in 1854 or that the Pope became infallible in 1870. The deposit of faith closed with the death of the last Apostle. The Church's deepening understanding of it has continued ever since.

Another parallel with a person is this: just as you do not need to establish the consistency of your identity—you are consistent without needing to give thought to it—so, too, the Church has no need to give thought to establishing the consistency of her own identity. You see how different her approach to her past is from that of all those Christian bodies who look back to the past for authority in the present. But not so the Church. Whatever authority she has had at any period of her life, she has now. That is why the word "Apostolic" is liable to give the wrong impression. When the Church says she is Apostolic, she is not appealing to the Apostles or to the Church of the earlier centuries, as do so many other presentations of Christianity. She claims to be that Church.

But she has that natural interest in her past that every person has in his. If you, for example, were to come upon a diary you had kept at school or, when turning out drawers, found letters you had written several years ago, I am sure you would find them very interesting. Natural vanity makes us read such things. But do they have any power to dictate to you what you are going to do tomorrow? Must you use those letters as models for the ones you are going to write this evening? Of course not. You have a consistency with your past. You are the same person. Probably you yourself, who did those things and have the same characteristics, would see there in embryo a foreshadowing of what you are spontaneously doing. Yet you are not consciously modeling yourself on your former self. You have an identity with your former self which requires no effort on your part.

So none of the four marks of the Church is man-made. The Church does not need to take thought to be One, to be Holy, to be Catholic, to be Apostolic—that is, to be identical with the Church of the Apostles. She is all those things. None of them are achieved by effort or will or scholarship. She has that God-given identity because she continues Christ Himself until He comes again.

CHAPTER 8

The Visible Church

WE HAVE been considering the ninth article of the Creed, the Holy Catholic Church. We have changed the order of the questions and strengthened the definition in the Catechism: instead of defining the Catholic Church as the union of all the faithful under one Head, I suggested that we should substitute the word "incorporation" for "union." I pointed out how a union may be a purely accidental thing which can be lost even more easily than it can be achieved, whereas an incorporation is an organic thing involving the sharing of a common life. We saw how our Blessed Lord's own analogy of the vine and the branches emphasized that concept of the Church, as also did St. Paul's of the members of one body united under Christ, Who is our Head. In both cases the analogies are with living things, not dead things.

With that in mind, seeing the Catholic Church always as the continuation of the Incarnation, seeing her as a Person, that Person being Christ, we went on to consider the marks of the Church: that she is One, Holy, Catholic and Apostolic. I pointed out to you how the Catechism often fails, as it seems to me, to distinguish causes and effects. The cause of all those four "marks" of the Church is that she continues Christ Himself—One with His unity, Holy with His holiness, Catholic with the universality of His redemption and Apostolic in the sense of being one abiding person from the moment of the descent of the Holy Spirit on the Apostles to the Second Coming of Christ. All those marks, as we saw, are essential, not accidental; they are marks that are the very character of the Person we have been considering.

Now I want to go back and fill the gap which we purposely made by changing the order of the Catechism questions which we considered in the last chapter. For the Catechism, having defined the Catholic Church, goes on immediately to consider the visible Church here on earth. What I want you to consider now is this: that this mystical body, whereby we are incorporated into Christ and form one body with Him, is itself incarnate or embodied in a visible institution here on earth. The Catholic Church is not an invisible body any more than the Incarnation was an invisible presence. At the Incarnation the Word, the Second Person of the Blessed Trinity, was conceived in the womb of our Blessed Lady, was born by her and came into the world as a visible, material man like you and me, having height, weight, displacement and the rest. He was not a spirit pure and simple: He was really and truly a man. And we believe that that Incarnation of Christ continues in the Church, so that she is not an invisible and disincarnate entity. We believe, therefore, in what is called the visible unity of the Church.

Now, though it is very seldom emphasized, that really is the dividing line between ourselves and all other Christians, certainly in the West. You may deny or disagree with that statement; but come to consider it yourself and ask what other body of professing Christians claims to be the Church, as the Catholic Church does. As you know, they all say, in the Apostles' Creed,

"I believe in the Catholic Church," but if you press them you will always find that they are professing belief in an invisible entity. When they say they believe in the Catholic Church they may mean that they believe in the unity of all those in a state of grace, the oneness of all true believers or a hundred and one other things, but never do they identify the Catholic Church with a single, visible, organized body here on earth. Dr. William Temple, Archbishop of Canterbury, used to say, "I believe in the Holy Catholic Church, and sincerely regret that it does not at present exist."

The error underlying this remark is, despite all superficial differences, precisely the same as that of the Reformers in the sixteenth century when they appealed to the primitive church. Both are effectively saying that in the here and now Christ's promises have failed. But the here and now is the only time I have, in which, with God's grace, to work out my salvation. In that task the ideal Church whether of the past or of the future is powerless to help me.

The doctrine of the visible unity of the Church is specifically the Catholic doctrine which divides the Catholic Church from every other presentation of Christianity. What we believe about the Church, what we are going to consider now, is this concept of the visible Church. We have been considering the Church in her mystical aspect as continuing Christ Himself. Now we come on to see that the Church is incarnate and embodied, no less than He.

So we pass from the Catechism definitions concerning the Catholic Church, which we strengthened to read, "The Catholic Church is the incorporation of all the faithful under one Head," and, "The Head of the Catholic Church is Jesus

Christ our Lord," to consider the visible Church on earth and, in particular, the concept and the role of the Papacy within that visible body. We shall start our consideration of that, again, with a slight verbal emendation, this time in the answer to Question 86, which, in the Catechism, reads as follows:

Q86 **Has the Church a visible Head on earth?**
The Church has a visible Head on earth, the Bishop of Rome, who is the Vicar of Christ.

It should, in my view, read thus:

Q86b **Has the visible Church a Head on earth?**
The visible Church has a Head on earth, the Bishop of Rome, who is the Vicar of Christ.

The visible Church—the concept we are about to consider—has a Head on earth, who is the Pope. Because the Church is visible, her Head on earth is visible.

Before we go on to consider the role of the Pope within the Church, let us digress for a moment to look further at this concept of the visible Church. Why is it so immensely important and central to the whole Catholic theology of the Church? It is because we always see the Church primarily as the means whereby the revealed truth of Almighty God is communicated to us. That again, if you come to consider it, seems to be something peculiar to the Catholic Church. We believe that her primary role is to be, in St. Paul's words, "the pillar and the ground of truth" (*1 Timothy* 3:15), the means whereby divine revelation reaches us; and that her secondary and consequent role is to be the teacher of Christian morality. This is not to say that Christian morality is less important. Always remember that the purpose of the Catholic Church is to communicate revealed truth to us. That is why the Catholic Church puts such immense emphasis on visible unity. Truth is one, inevitably and inescapably one. No truth can contradict any other truth. Since the whole object of the Church is to be "the pillar and the ground of truth," to be the channel whereby truth reaches us, it is of her very essence that she, the visible, organized Church here on earth, should be one. She is bearing witness to one, indivisible truth and must consequently be one herself. You cannot have a divided, contradictory witness to one truth.

In the last chapter, when we were talking about the mystical concept of the Church as Christ continued, and considering that her marks are Christ's marks, I quoted to you the opening of Chapter 15 of St. John's Gospel, which is the discourse of our Blessed Lord after the Last Supper. I would like you to read through those four chapters again, beginning with Chapter 14. They are an arbitrary division of Christ's discourse about His relationship to the Church, from which we quoted the simile about the vine and the branches.

Now we turn to five verses beginning with St. John 17:17. These are the verses in which our Blessed Lord states the role of the Church as the mouthpiece of truth and the consequent need for unity. Remember always that He sees His own role as that of witness to the truth. He has other roles—Redeemer, moral teacher, prophet—but at the most solemn moment of His life, when He is asked to define His mission, our Blessed Lord gives this as the answer: "For this was I born, and for this came I into the world; that I should give testimony to the truth." (*John* 18:37). Truth takes precedence over everything. If you can ask without disrespect or blasphemy what Christ is for, it is to give testimony to the truth. He has been sent as the Truth itself. That Truth, speaking to His Apostles, says, "As the Father hath sent me, I also send you." (*John* 20:21). That is the primary mission of the Church. Everything else—the dispensing of the Sacraments, making men holy, the spreading of the Gospel, every other work the Church does—flows out from and is subsequent to her primary role as "the pillar and ground of truth."

With that in mind, we come to those five wonderful verses from Chapter 17. Our Blessed Lord, as you may remember, is praying to the Father for His disciples:

> 17 Sanctify them in truth. Thy word is truth.
> 18 As Thou hast sent me into the world, I also
> have sent them into the world. 19 And for them
> do I sanctify myself, that they also may be sanc-
> tified in truth. 20 And not for them only do I
> pray, but for them also who through their word
> shall believe in me. 21 That they may all be
> one as Thou, Father, in me and I in Thee; that
> they also may be one in us: that the world may
> believe that Thou hast sent me.

Starting with that immense emphasis in verse 17 on truth, saying in verses 18 and 19 that the whole function of the Apostles is to communicate the truth, our Blessed Lord prays in verses 20 and 21 for us who through the Apostles' word believe in Him that "they may all be one, as Thou, Father, in me and I in Thee; that they also may be one in us: that the world may believe that Thou hast sent me." In other words, our Blessed Lord prays that not only the Apostles but all His followers may be united with a unity as close as that which binds the Father to the Son and the Son to the Father, than which we can imagine no closer unity. The consequence of that unity subsisting between His followers is that "they also may be one in us," that is, that our membership of the Church catches us up into the divine life of the Godhead. St. John says elsewhere, "But as many as received Him, he gave them power to be made the sons of God." (*John* 1:12). The unity which binds us together is the very thing that catches us up into the divine life and the end of verse 21 contains the punch-line:

"That the world may believe that Thou hast sent me"—that the consequence of our being knit together in the truth, in a unity as close as that which binds the Father and the Son, will be that we are caught up into the divine life, and that our being so caught up, being so knit together into one thing, may be the evidence to the world of the divinity of Christ and of His mission.

What follows from that? Plainly, the fact that the truth that binds us together must be a visible one. If the world is going to see in our unity the best evidence of Christ's mission, it must be a unity that the world can see. There are other unities—and ideally all these unities are coincident. Ideally the unity of all true believers, the unity of those in a state of grace, the unity of the ultimately saved should all coincide; but these are unities the world cannot see. They are not visible. The only unity the world can see is that of a visible, unified body here on earth.

Visible unity, of course, is the one thing that the world does see in the Catholic Church. The world knows that this extraordinary body, spread very unevenly but throughout the greater part of the known world, is absolutely at one as to what a man should believe and do to be saved. People outside the Catholic Church have every sort of misconception of Catholic doctrine. They very seldom get a single fact right. But this one fact they do understand. And this, our

Blessed Lord says, should be enough to prompt them to ask, "Is Christ's mission divine?"

That is what we mean by the visible unity of the Church. And this visible unity is not and cannot be claimed by any other body. Now you see the immense value we set on unity: for it is the guarantee and the evidence of the truth which Christ came to communicate to us. Verse 21, "that they also may be one in us," is constantly quoted now by people who are shocked by the division of Christians but who overlook the fact that the unity that Christ promised actually exists. Some forms of ecumenism seem to imply a denial of what is to us the absolutely basic proposition that this unity does already exist and that everybody needs to be gathered into it. Christianity if you like, Christendom certainly, has been broken up and divided. The Catholic Church is not and cannot be divided. As we considered earlier, people can drop away from the Church in their hundreds or thousands or millions, but her unity is not broken by that fact. Her unity, which Christ promised would be the evidence of the divinity of His Mission, continues still.

So you can appreciate the immense importance which we attach to the visible unity of the Catholic Church. You can see how it is in a sense the touchstone of orthodoxy, the guarantee that we are part and parcel of that Church which Christ came to establish here on earth.

Now, it is only if you have understood the concept of the Church's visible unity that you can appreciate the importance we attach to infallibility, or, as I prefer to call it, inerrancy. The word "infallibility" has so many overtones now.

If we have decided that we must belong to the Church because we have recognized her claim to be Christ's revelation to mankind and to be the pillar and ground of truth, then it follows that she must be incapable of leading us into error. In other words, she must be infallible or inerrant. The choice of word is not important as long as we understood that if there is a visible body here on earth, the Church, to which we have decided that we must belong once we have come to see her in the light in which she sees herself, then she cannot impose the acceptance of error on us as a condition of membership.

Now I think we are in a position to look at those Catechism questions which are largely about infallibility. Never try to consider in your own mind, still less try to expound to other people, the concept of infallibility without first clarifying in your mind the concept of visible unity. Infallibility out of the context of visible unity is not only the most arrogant of claims, which it is always thought to be, but is really nonsense. If there are several different expositions of Christianity, all more or less authentic, it is the height of arrogance for one to claim, "I am the only one which is right." What the Catholic Church is claiming is that there can only be one authentic exponent of Divine revelation and that all the others are right only in so far as they approximate to her.

Now we come to those answers starting from the amended form of Question 86:

> **The visible Church has a Head on earth—the Bishop of Rome who is the Vicar of Christ.** Q86
>
> **The Bishop of Rome is the Head of the Church because he is the successor of St. Peter, whom Christ appointed to be the Head of the Church.** Q87

Q88 I know that Christ appointed St. Peter to be the Head of the Church because Christ said to Him: "Thou art Peter, and upon this rock I will build my Church, and the gates of hell shall not prevail against it. And to thee I will give the keys of the kingdom of heaven."

Q89 The Bishop of Rome is called the Pope, which word signifies Father.

Q90 The Pope is the spiritual father of all Christians.

Q91 The Pope is the Shepherd and Teacher of all Christians, because Christ made St. Peter the Shepherd of the whole flock when He said: "Feed my lambs, feed my sheep." He also prayed that his "faith" might never fail, and commanded him to "confirm" his brethren.

Q92 The Pope is infallible.

Q93 When I say that the Pope is infallible, I mean that the Pope cannot err when, as Shepherd and Teacher of all Christians, he defines a doctrine concerning faith or morals, to be held by the whole Church.

We now go to Question 100—the Catechism order at this point is really very curious:

Q100 The Church cannot err in what she teaches as to faith or morals, for she is our infallible guide in both.

I know that the Church cannot err in what she teaches because Christ promised that the gates of hell shall never prevail against His Church, that the Holy Spirit shall teach her all things, and that He Himself will be with her all days, even to the consummation of the world. Q101

I would have preferred to alter the Catechism order again and put question 100 before the others, because we believe that the Church is infallible and that her various organs of infallibility—Pope, Councils, Bishops and people—derive their infallibility from her. The Church is infallible in the sense which I have mentioned earlier—she cannot lay down as a condition of membership the acceptance of what is untrue.

That concept is a negative one, as are both the Catechism definitions: "The Church can not err in what she teaches," and, "When I say that the Pope is infallible I mean that the Pope can not err. . . ."[14]

I think it will be useful to see infallibility as a negative promise given to us that since we are bound, if we see the Church in the light in which she sees herself, to belong to her, we must be able to say, "I cannot be asked to accept what is untrue as a price of my membership."

If you want a yardstick to know when you are covered by this negative guarantee, you should ask yourself, "When does the Church lay down doctrines which I must believe as a condition of membership?" For when she does, they must be true.

The most formal method of defining doctrines is in a Council of the Church, when the whole body of Bishops comes together and lays down what is the Catholic Faith and condemns what is not. Whenever the Church lays something down at a Council, as she did at Nicaea, Chalcedon, Trent or the First Vatican Council, that must be truc because the Church exacts assent to that truth.

On what other occasions does the Church lay down doctrines which we must believe as a condition of membership? In a less formal way the whole body of Bishops throughout the world are constantly laying down conditions of membership. When at the end of a course of instruction someone asks me to receive him into the Church, I have to apply to the Bishop of the diocese for leave to receive him. If he says that I cannot receive this man into the Church unless he accepts this or that doctrine, I can always go to another Bishop. But if they all lay down the same condition, plainly there does reside in the whole body of Bishops *collegialiter sumpti*—"taken as a College"—that negative guarantee against error whose protection I claim. If all the Bishops lay down the same condition, it cannot be untrue.[15]

The Catholic Church is nothing if not a teaching Church. She is teaching all the time—a diocesan Bishop writing his pastoral letters, parish priests preaching, lecturers teaching philosophy and theology in seminaries, nuns teaching in schools, enquirers being instructed. This great daily outpouring of teaching in the Catholic Church cannot possibly, wherever her duty of giving faithful witness to divine revelation is essentially involved, be erroneous. Any one teacher can surely say something wrong, for no one teacher can define doctrines. The whole body of them effectively do, and the whole body of them can never go awry.

Is there one single person who has the power of defining doctrines as conditions of membership of the Church? Yes, the Pope, as Head of the visible Church, has the power of defining a doctrine and imposing its acceptance as a condition of membership. That is not to say that infallibility does not reside in the whole body of the Church because, as we have seen, it plainly does. But the Pope is the only single person who is individually protected against teaching error.[16]

People talk about infallibility as though it could be claimed only when something is defined. On the contrary, it is in operation twenty-four hours a day, sixty minutes of every hour. It is, so to speak, a brake on all the time. The Holy Spirit, if one can say this without disrespect, is working overtime to see that fallible men do not make a travesty of the truth, do not misinterpret the truth, do not impose conditions of membership that are untrue. That is what infallibility means. It is the other side of the coin to visible unity, and that is why infallibility is impossible to understand until you have got that first point that there is, here on earth, a visible, organized body which the world can see. That body is the Catholic Church, the expounder of God's revelation to mankind.

Such a body cannot possibly make acceptance of error a condition of membership.

Now, you will see from question 91 that the Pope has two offices: Shepherd and Teacher of all Christians. He has, uniquely as an individual, his teaching office, in which he is protected by infallibility. But over and above all that he has, precisely because the Church is a visible body, the power of ruling. He is the ultimate authority in the Church. Therefore he is the supreme ruler of the Church in such matters as setting up or dividing dioceses, establishing religious orders and the rest. The ultimate responsibility before Almighty God is his. And in the Pope's power of ruling, precisely because it makes no demands upon faith at all, we have no guarantee of infallibility, as we have in matters of faith.

Because the Church is a visible, organized body here on earth, and because we are members of the Church, we have that duty towards her of obedience, respect and loyalty that we have to all bodies to which we belong, though because she is the most important of all, to a higher degree than to any other.

As soon as you belong to any organization, be it a club, a regiment, a college, a country, it imposes conditions of membership, it rules with authority and it enforces its authority with sanctions.

Every visible society has power to define membership, to legislate, to enforce legislation with sanctions, to expel. That is true of all the societies I have mentioned. Societies legislate, some about important things, some about trivial matters. Societies enforce their legislation by sanctions of varying degrees of gravity. All those societies have the power to expel. You may think the legislation mistaken, the policy faulty. So long as you do not think it sinful you are bound to obey it if you wish to continue your membership, but even if you do think it is sinful and oppose it, as in conscience you must, you have to take the consequences in sanctions.

Because the Church is a visible society in the sense that very few non-Catholics either recognize in her or claim for their own presentation of Christianity, she, too, legislates and enforces her laws by sanctions. And when you hear people expressing great resentment at her doing that, what they are really resenting is her claim to be a visible society. They do not believe that the Church is an embodied entity. They think always that Christianity, religion, what you will, ought to be something purely spiritual, non-institutional, disembodied and certainty not employing sanctions, let alone expulsion. When you came to consider it, the point of cleavage is the one that I suggested at the very beginning: the visible, organized body here on earth, having all the characteristics we have considered. As a Catholic one obeys laws within the Church, whether one agrees with them or not, so long as one does not believe them to be sinful.

Take the liturgical changes through which we have been passing. Many people may have found them distasteful, others desirable, but there is no question that you must obey them. You cannot go along your own way in withstanding the authority of the Church. Or take something of greater importance: the practice of the Church in imposing celibacy on the secular clergy. It is not a question of faith but of law; the law could be changed. It is not part of the divine law. It is part of ecclesiastical legislation. Pray God it will not be changed, but it is the sort of thing that could be changed. If it were changed, some people would think, mistakenly, that the Church had altered some fundamental part of her teaching and had therefore ceased to be herself. But the Church would remain the same Church whether her priests were allowed to marry or not. Her ecclesiastical practices may change, but her essential doctrines—and her own nature—do not and cannot change.

CHAPTER 9

The Communion of Saints

IN THE last two chapters we have been working through the section of the Catechism on the ninth article of the Creed, "The Holy Catholic Church, the Communion of Saints." We began in Chapter 7, where the Catechism defined the Catholic Church as "the union of all the faithful under one Head" (q84), and went on to tell us that "the Head of the Catholic Church is Jesus Christ our Lord" (q85). We considered that the Church should be seen as a person, that Person being Christ, and we saw that the essential marks of the Church—that she is One, Holy, Catholic and Apostolic—are the inescapable consequences of her being the Incarnation continued. They are not ideals that she needs to aim at but characteristics which she is incapable of losing.

We spent a long time dwelling on the Church's unity, which is not an accidental thing. Only when I had tried to present that concept to you clearly did we go back in the last chapter to consider the six or eight questions of the Catechism dealing with the position of the Pope within the visible Church, which we had deferred. Only if you have first understood the concept of the Catholic Church as being primarily the expounder of revelation—and only consequently a teacher of morals—will you understand the immense emphasis that Catholics put upon the visible unity of the Church.

Well, now, I want to go on to the much bigger concept of the Catholic Church in her entirety, not just that part of the Church which is visible here on earth. The last eight questions on the Catholic Church in the Catechism are concerned with the Church in Heaven, on earth and in Purgatory. It is a mistake to think of the Catholic Church as being only that part which is here on earth, which is numerically a very small fraction of the whole, the tiny tip of a vast iceberg. That is why the ninth article of the Creed groups the Holy Catholic Church and the Communion of Saints together.

Q102 **By the Communion of Saints I mean that all the members of the Church, in Heaven, on earth and in Purgatory, are in communion with each other, as being one body in Jesus Christ.**

Q103 **The faithful on earth are in communion with each other by professing the same faith, obeying the same authority and assisting each other with their prayers and good works.**

Q104 **We are in communion with the Saints in Heaven by honoring them as the glorified members of the Church, and also by our praying to them, and by their praying for us.**

Q105 **We are in communion with the souls in Purgatory by helping them with our prayers and good works: "It is a holy and wholesome thought to pray for the dead, that they may be loosed from their sins."**

Purgatory is a place where souls suffer for a time after death on account of their sins. Q106

Those souls go to Purgatory that depart this life in venial sin; or that have not fully paid the debt of temporal punishment due to those sins of which the guilt has been forgiven. Q107

Temporal punishment is punishment which will have an end, either in this world or in the world to come. Q108

I prove that there is a Purgatory from the constant teaching of the Church; and from the doctrine of Holy Scripture, which declares that God will render to every man according to his works; that nothing defiled shall enter Heaven; and that some will be saved, "yet so as by fire." (*1 Corinthians* 3:15) Q109

Questions 102–109 are concerned with the much larger concept of the Church which we have in mind when we define her as the incorporation of all the faithful under one Head, Who is Jesus Christ our Lord (qq84–85). We are now considering all those souls who have been grafted into Christ and caught up into His mystical body, not just that tiny part of the whole which we see here on earth. Underlying that concept are concepts going back to the very beginning of what we have been considering—in particular, the uniqueness of every individual. Here we need to emphasize yet again that in the whole visible universe the important thing is ultimately each individual soul. When all other things have passed away what will matter for all eternity is what use that soul has made of the space between birth and death. Each single one of us, having infinite capacity, can realize that capacity only in Almighty God, Who brought us into being. The one concern that each of us should have is to try to know and fulfill the will of Almighty God in this life and consequently to come to the eternal enjoyment of Him in the next.

The Communion of Saints means that there is a real communion between those who are in via, on their pilgrimage through this world, those who after death are in a preparatory state for Heaven and those who are already enjoying the beatific vision.

As with the marks of the Church, where I suggested that the Catechism did not sufficiently distinguish between cause and effect, so here there is something of the same inadequacy. We saw that the marks of the Church are at the deepest level the consequence of her being Christ continued and are not produced by the actions of her members. So here the communion of all the faithful is the consequence of the Church's oneness with Christ, in Whom we are all incorporated. The basis of our communion with the Saints in Heaven is that we pray to them and they pray for us. We are able to do this precisely because of our incorporation into Christ, which bridges time and eternity and is not broken by death. That grafting into the body of Christ continues and indeed only achieves its fulfillment in the next world.

Now, this concept of a life of grace and of our communion with each other not being broken by death is one that is often obscured by the popular view of death. People frequently talk of death making a complete break in the relationships which we enjoy in this life. Consequently one of the doctrines that have worn most thin in the popular mind is that of oneness with the dead.

The Protestantism of the sixteenth-century reformers,

which might be called classical Protestantism, since so many non-Catholic Christians have now departed from it, rejects the invocation of the Saints and further rejects the doctrine of Purgatory. This has done a great deal to popularize the notion of a breach with the dead. All sorts of people who would not have subscribed to the concept of a complete break seemed to do so in unconsidered speech and thought.

Let me give you a personal illustration. Our parson at home was our nearest neighbor and a great friend. I remember well how shocked my dear mother was—she was a Spanish Catholic with a profound practical belief in Purgatory—when after his wife's death the old gentleman said, "It is such a snuffing out, you know." I am sure that if you had challenged him on whether he really thought it was a snuffing out he would have qualified it, being a believing Christian. But that was his instinctive reaction to death.

A more considered expression of the same outlook occurs in the Diary of Lord Shaftesbury, the great nineteenth-century Evangelical. On the day of his wife's death he wrote, "Tonight will be a terrible event. For the first time since we married, I must omit in my prayers the name of my precious Minnie."

You get a popular expression of the finality of death in the cult of mourning in the nineteenth century. The First World War, if it did no other good, did, I think, change people's outlook on death. In that terrible holocaust, in which so many people lost those they loved, cut off in their youth, they became less willing to accept death as a complete break. This refusal took various curious forms, like the burial of the Unknown Soldier in Westminster Abbey. The first Unknown Warrior was buried under the Arc de Triomphe and when the cult was imported here I remember thinking, and not being alone in thinking, that this was a great reversal of the popular outlook, that and the planting of crosses, poppies round the Abbey and the like. Another example was the great revival of Spiritualism which took place at that time. All these were attempts to fill that longing in the human soul for an assurance that we are still in communion with the dead.[17]

Catholic doctrine puts a very strong emphasis on the fact that our link with the dead is not broken. The dead do not lose their identity as persons and consequently they are still concerned for us and still effectively united to us in love as we to them.

From the concept of our unbroken link with the dead there follows the Church's practice of invoking the Saints and private approaches to our own nearest and dearest who, we have reason to think, have died in the grace of Almighty God and are now in His presence, to pray for us. Of course, the supreme authority of the Church alone can decide when one of her departed members is worthy of public veneration.

The concept of our praying to the Saints and of their praying for us is completely consistent with an idea basic to Catholic thought—that Almighty God is always reaching us through human agency. We speak of Him rightly as our Creator while acknowledging that He achieves our creation through our being begotten by our parents. He communicates His grace to us by the Sacraments at the hands of a priest. He communicates His truth, both natural and revealed, to us through teachers. In this life our progress towards Him is advanced or retarded by our association with others. We owe much to those who pray for us. This support does not cease but is intensified and clarified by their being in the presence of God. It is to us a most unacceptable concept that a mother should pray for her son in life but should neither pray for him nor to him in the next world when he is taken from her by death.

Invocation of the Saints runs very strongly through popular Catholic devotion and practice. We invoke different saints for different things and regard saints as being patrons of particular countries, occupations or callings. It is important to see that this practice, often dismissed as superstitious, is in fact not just a sentimental devotion. It is really rooted in a whole concept or philosophy of life. It goes right back to the concepts with which we started—the uniqueness and individuality of every human being and our continuing as the persons we are for all eternity. The measure or yardstick for any person is how close he has come to Almighty God in his passage through this life and how nearly he has corresponded to the grace of Almighty God and has grown in sanctity and knowledge of Him.[18]

Going back now to the Catechism questions, the idea of the Communion of Saints is worked out on three levels. The faithful on earth are in communion with each other because of our incorporation in Christ. The consequence is that we profess the same faith. It is not ultimately that profession of the same faith which makes us one; our common profession of faith is the consequence of our being one. Obeying the same authority and assisting each other with our prayers and good works are again the consequences. The whole of the Church on earth is dependent for her momentum on the attempt of each individual to grow in sanctity and holiness and to advance the sanctification of the whole world by first of all advancing his own sanctification and then communicating what he has achieved within himself to others. Praying for each other is common, I suppose, to Christians of all traditions, but you will find us putting emphasis on it all the time, asking people to pray for us or for our friends in need. When you finish your confession to a priest and he gives you his blessing he often says, "Say a prayer for me." This idea of our responsibility for each other and our need to advance each other's sanctification runs very strongly through the practice of the Christian life.

Q104 **We are in communion with the Saints in heaven by honoring them as the glorified members of the Church, and also by praying to them, and by their praying for us.**

Again, at the deepest level, we are in communion with them not because we honor them as the glorified members of the Church, but because they are members of the mystical body and we honor them as having attained the end for which we are all made. We also ask them to pray for us. Once again, it is impossible to imagine that the ties formed by human love or relationships are broken. As I said, if a mother prays for her own child in this world and asks that he will advance in the knowledge of Almighty God and in the attempt to fulfill His will, she must do so with redoubled intensity when she comes to enjoy the vision of Almighty God Himself, not only with redoubled intensity but with complete knowledge of what that child needs to fulfill the purpose of his existence. We in this life often pray mistakenly for each other or for ourselves by asking for things that would not be good for us or for the people for whom we are praying. Please God these prayers are fulfilled in a more profitable way. When people come to the beatific vision, at least their prayers will be rightly directed to things that are really to our good.

Thirdly, we pray for the souls in Purgatory: we are in

communion with them because the link with the mystical body is not broken but, as with those in Heaven, intensified or clarified by death. In old age one thinks very frequently of the harm one has done and the mistaken impression that one has given to other people, or the lack of love one has shown. It is a great comfort always to remember that when our friends come to the beatific vision they see us as we are and our intentions as they were. No longer can there be any misapprehensions or misunderstandings between ourselves and those whom we love as there can be so easily in this world. We are in communion with the souls in Purgatory, once again, because this link with them is not broken but strengthened by death, as we help them or seek to help them by our prayers and good works. And that leads us on to the consideration of the doctrine of Purgatory, once again a doctrine rejected by classical Protestantism.

We believe that there is a distinction between the guilt of a sin and the consequence of it which we need to expiate. That distinction lies at the root of the doctrine of Purgatory. It is a distinction we make constantly in ordinary life, as when something that we have done brings physical harm to another. That person may perfectly well forgive us completely—if he is a good Christian he will—but none the less, and quite compatibly with complete forgiveness, he may demand compensation for the harm he has suffered. The forgiveness of the offense is quite distinct from and independent of any idea of putting right the evil that has been done.

Almighty God, we believe, when we repent of our sins, forgives us completely, utterly and entirely: "Though your sins be as scarlet, they shall be whiter than snow." (*Isaiah* 1:18). Our sins are washed away completely by Christ's redemption; so completely that there is no longer any difficulty, strain or awkwardness between Almighty God and ourselves such as so often there is when we receive human forgiveness. No, we are absolutely in harmony with Him. He loves us as much as before, but there is still the need to try to expiate what we have done wrong.

And that is the point—or a very large part of the point—of practicing voluntary mortification in this life, of going against our own will, of doing disagreeable things, fasting, abstinence and the like, on which all too little emphasis is laid in the present day. All those things are an attempt to put right the consequences of our evil rather than the evil itself, because we have repented of the evil and have been forgiven. And we know well enough in our own lives how constant following of an evil course may harm us in soul and body and may have consequences which need to be corrected by self-discipline.

That process in the course of most of our woefully unmortified lives may very probably be incomplete at the moment of death. We shall not have made anything like adequate compensation for what we have done. Before coming to the presence of God we shall not only need, we shall positively desire, to be prepared and made worthy to come into His presence, to have all those things put right that we have done wrong. We shall not want—we cannot want—to appear before Almighty God with the disfigurement that we have wrought in ourselves, but we shall want the consequences of our sins to be purged away. That, we believe, is the function of Purgatory.

There may be those who have prepared themselves by a holy life for an immediate enjoyment of the beatific vision, and this is the teaching of the Church about martyrs. Our Blessed Lady, who was completely sinless, was assumed directly into Heaven; but probably for the overwhelming majority of the human race passage through Purgatory is a necessary preparation.

I always think of Shaw's play *Pygmalion* as an example of Purgatory. You cannot imagine Eliza Doolittle wanting to be thrust into the final scene at a grand ball before she was ready to play her part in it properly.

And so with ourselves: we cannot possibly want to come to the enjoyment of Almighty God until we have been purged of the consequences of our sins. We cannot imagine how that purgation will be effected. One plausible consideration is that when we come before Almighty God at the private judgment we shall realize how much we long for Him and how unfit we are to enjoy Him. Our very separation from Him may be the purgative suffering which fits us for Him.

Let us go back to the concept of the Communion of Saints. Our link with those who have been separated from us by death is not broken and, just as we are able to help and benefit each other in this life, so must we seek to accelerate that process whereby those whom we have known and loved in this life are prepared for the eternal enjoyment of Almighty God. And that is what we mean by praying for the souls in Purgatory. Because their salvation is assured, since they are certainly coming to Almighty God, we also invoke their prayers and pray to them. Once again, this great nexus of praying for each other is carried on into the next world.

The Catechism ends this section with an attempt to prove the doctrine of Purgatory by scriptural quotations. This is typical of the Catechism, which was originally inspired by a desire to refute Protestant errors and consequently made free use of scriptural quotations. Though I believe the quotations do refer to the existence of Purgatory,

I do so because the Church tells me their meaning. I think you might have difficulty in convincing a Protestant objector of the existence of Purgatory from these quotations alone. I would prefer to take my stand on "the constant teaching of the Church." I believe the Church's interpretation of the Bible because I believe the Church to be the one divinely appointed bearer of revelation to mankind.

CHAPTER 10

The Forgiveness of Sins

WE HAVE completed our consideration of the section of the Catechism on the Church. Now we start on the tenth article of the Creed,

the forgiveness of sins. Q110

By "the forgiveness of sins" I mean that Christ has left the power of forgiving sins to the Pastors of His Church. Q111

Sins are forgiven principally by the Sacraments of Baptism and Penance. Q112

As you appreciate, Baptism and Penance will be dealt with later, in Chapters 14 and 16, in the section on the Sacraments. What we are here concerned with is not the means by which sins are forgiven but the concept of sin itself. The Catechism definition of sin is as follows:

Sin is an offense against God by any thought, word, deed or omission against the law of God. Q113

I want to stress that in the final analysis, all sin is primarily internal and is a matter of omission. Always remember that sin is a negative thing. The Christian religion is about fulfillment. It is all about our fulfilling that purpose for which

Almighty God has brought us into this world by opening our minds to His mind, bringing our wills to His will. By so doing, we come to our complete fulfillment for all eternity in the enjoyment of Almighty God.

Now, sin is a failure on our part to bring our mind to the mind of Almighty God, to bring our will to the will of Almighty God. It is the frustration of ourselves and of our own fulfillment. Before the other manifestations of sin which the Catechism describes as "thought, word, deed or omission" (q113) comes the failure of our own will. It is well, therefore, to think of sin chiefly as an omission which may, but need not, be manifested in word or deed. Sin can exist in the mind and will alone and it is there that the sin occurs.

It is very important to remember that distinction, because we are living in a world where evil, if it is thought of at all, is thought of as being some external word or deed which is, in the current jargon, "antisocial," something doing harm to other people. The Christian concept of sin, however, is of something affecting our relationship to Almighty God, and whether that sin is externalized is secondary. The sin occurs within us at that moment when we withdraw our mind and our will from the mind and will of Almighty God. Whether we go on to commit an external act in consequence of that withdrawal is comparatively insignificant because the relationship between ourselves and Almighty God has already been broken by that internal act of our mind and will.

Our Blessed Lord makes that point very clearly indeed when He tells us that, "He who looks at a woman to lust after her has already committed adultery with her in his heart." (*Matthew* 5:28). So far as Almighty God is concerned, the sin was committed at that moment when we withdrew our mind and will from that of Almighty God and consented to a lustful desire. Whether we go on to perform a lustful act is comparatively insignificant, except for the poor woman concerned. So far as Almighty God is concerned our relationship with Him was broken at that moment when we consented to lust.

St. John makes exactly the same point when he tells us that he who hates his brother is a murderer. (*1 John* 3:15). You will notice that he says, "is a murderer " and not "is in danger of becoming a murderer": he is a murderer at that moment when he has so hated his brother as to be willing to take his life. The sin is committed then. Once again, whether he goes on to take his brother's life is a matter of comparative insignificance, except perhaps for the poor brother and his family.

Remember for your comfort that the reverse is true: those acts of virtue which you have really willed, and not just idly wished, to perform are as though you had performed them. The good occurs at that moment when you have given your mind and will to Almighty God for the fulfillment of His purpose.

For example, someone who feels called to devote his life, shall we say, to working in a leper colony for love of Almighty God and sets out to do so but is shipwrecked on the way, stands in the sight of Almighty God as though he had carried his intention into effect. The fact that he has not been able to realize it does not make invalid the complete harmony of his mind and will with the mind and will of Almighty God.

The Catechism now moves on to consider the different kinds of sin:

> **There are two kinds of sin: original sin and actual sin.** Q114

The next four answers in the Catechism pertain to original sin. Original sin is a consequence of the Fall of Man, which we have already considered as the necessary preamble to discussing the Incarnation. Unless we consider what the situation was which Jesus Christ our Lord became incarnate to remedy, we can scarcely appreciate the purpose of the Redemption. "The Good News of the Redemption" which we are urged to proclaim, has very little meaning unless we first believe "the Bad News of the Fall."

Q115 **Original sin is that guilt and stain of sin which we inherit from Adam, who was the origin and head of all mankind.**

Q116 **The sin committed by Adam was the sin of disobedience when he ate the forbidden fruit.**

Q117 **All mankind have contracted the guilt and stain of original sin, except the Blessed Virgin, who, through the merits of her Divine Son, was conceived without the least guilt or stain of original sin.**

Q118 **This privilege of the Blessed Virgin is called the Immaculate Conception.**

Since the Fall, everyone who is born comes into this world estranged from the love and friendship of Almighty God as the result of the sin of our first parents. That sin was a willful act whereby man put himself out of the love and friendship of Almighty God, with all the consequences in the wounding of human nature and the disorientation of ourselves from which we are all suffering.

The consequence of that act of disobedience, that act of rebellion against Almighty God, which we call the Fall of

Man, is something which we all suffer. It inflicts a wound on our nature, so that our lower powers are with difficulty controlled by our higher powers and are in constant rebellion against them. We come into this world out of a state of grace; the state of grace being that sharing of the divine life, that friendship with Almighty God, which the sin of our first parents has lost for us. But for the redemption which Christ wrought for us, it would have remained for ever out of our reach.

We believe that original sin and our consequent separation from God are the common fate of all mankind. The single exception is our Blessed Lady. We believe that she was never for one single moment of her life from her conception out of the love and friendship of Almighty God. It would be inconceivable to anyone who has the least concept of the horror of sin that she, who was to give humanity to our Saviour by consenting to His being conceived and born by her, should be for a moment under the power of Satan and out of the love and friendship of Almighty God.

The concept of our all being born in this unfortunate state is so widely rejected that, as has been observed, people at the present day do not so much deny the Immaculate Conception as consider it to be universal.

The dogma of the Immaculate Conception of our Blessed Lady was defined only in 1854. This does not mean that it was not believed until then. We have seen how doctrines implicit from the beginning have come to be defined with greater precision and clarity throughout the Church's history.

All that we have said recently has been concerned with original sin, not with what is ordinarily understood by sin—that is, our own misdeeds. It is a consequence of this dreadful weight of original sin that we are drawn towards sin rather than towards virtue. We start life with that bias.

The next group of Catechism questions, 119 to 121, is concerned with actual sin—every sin which we ourselves commit. The Catechism divides that concept of sin into mortal sin and venial sin and defines mortal sin as "a serious offense against God."

Q122 **It is called mortal sin because it is so serious that it kills the soul and deserves hell.**

Q123 **Mortal sin kills the soul by depriving it of sanctifying grace which is the supernatural life of the soul.**

Q124 **It is the greatest of all evils to fall into mortal sin.**

Q125 **They who died in mortal sin will go to hell for all eternity.**

Q126 **Venial sin is an offense which does not kill the soul, yet displeases God, and often leads to mortal sin.**

And then one of the less happy definitions in the Catechism:

Q127 **It is called venial sin because it is more easily pardoned than mortal sin.**

I shall have more to say about that in a moment. But to start off with that great distinction between mortal sin and venial sin: it is one of which classical Protestantism is very impatient. Many think it a bit of hairsplitting and casuistry: if all sin is sin, why suggest that some sins are less heinous than others? If you press such people, you will find that they frequently do not really believe in Hell. The moment you believe in Hell, the moment you believe that it is possible for you and me by deliberate misuse of our minds and wills to separate ourselves eternally from Almighty God, it becomes of immense practical importance to know what are the conditions that produce that appalling result of eternal separation from Him. If you do not believe in Hell, plainly it is unimportant whether there can be a distinction between venial and mortal sin. If all sin is sin but no sin separates you eternally from Almighty God, it is not a matter of very much concern to make such a distinction.

We do believe that it is possible to separate ourselves eternally from God. But you must not think that because Catholics make a distinction between mortal sin and venial sin they think lightly of venial sin and consider that it can be committed with impunity. The parallel between physical and spiritual health is exact and illuminating. Just as the man who has no care for his physical health may find, when a serious illness attacks him, that he has so undermined his constitution by his neglect that he has no powers of resistance, so the man who constantly and carelessly commits venial sins will find when the temptation to commit mortal sin assails him that he has so weakened his will that he falls.

"No; not the least venial sin that was ever committed" wrote Cardinal Manning, "can be absolved but through the Precious Blood which was shed upon the Cross. Little sins! God have mercy on those who talk this language." The whole question of our salvation and sanctification is, using the word properly, an awful one. It is within our power so to misuse our Godlike qualities of mind and will as to remain completely unfulfilled for ever. It is not kind to allow a man who is standing on the edge of a precipice to think that he has no need to walk circumspectly.

I always wish the Catechism were more specific about

mortal sin and that it spelled out the three conditions which theologians hold are necessary for a mortal sin. So important are they that I would suggest your making a note of them in the margin of your Catechism: grave matter, full deliberation and full consent. First of all, the thing done or not done must be a matter of consequence. Secondly it must be done with full knowledge. Thirdly it must be done with full consent.

Plainly a mortal sin must be a matter of consequence. You cannot commit a mortal sin about a trifle. A hasty word, a lie of no consequence to ourselves or to others, a momentary impatience, cannot conceivably be mortal sins.

When we were talking about Almighty God in Chapter 1, I stressed that the really Godlike thing about us is our mind and our will. We shall come back to that several times. And I told you, when we were first establishing that concept of our being Godlike precisely because we have the power to know and to will, that these concepts would recur again and again in the Catechism. They come out very clearly now.

The heinousness of mortal sin comes from the fact that we use those gifts which are most Godlike against Almighty God, in rebellion against Him Who gave them to us. That mind which was made to come to a knowledge of Him and to think about Him is used in order to offend Him; that will which has been given to us so that we may promote His will and extend His kingdom on earth is used against His intention; so in the ways in which we are most Godlike we deliberately offend Almighty God.

For a sin to be of the gravity of mortal sin it is necessary that we should know clearly what we are doing. You cannot commit a mortal sin in a moment of inattention. As I was saying earlier, we are living in a world where people so often think of evil, in so far as they think of it at all, in terms of the consequences to our neighbor. But to kill a man accidentally, to set fire to a house accidentally, however appalling the consequences, cannot be mortal sins at all. They may be sins of carelessness, but a mortal sin needs definite knowledge of what we are doing.

No less surely a sin cannot be mortal unless it is done with a free exercise of the will. It cannot be done under extreme duress or pressure from outside. Though we may have ultimate control of our wills, there are moments when, weak as we are, our wills are overborne by pressure from without. We believe, of course, that, whatever pressures are exerted, proportionate grace will be given to resist them. But there may come a point where the will is not acting freely. Where that is so, you cannot commit a mortal sin.

Again, to take something of which we are very conscious now. If you are brainwashed, as we all are by the media, it is possible that your whole mind and will can become so blurred that you are incapable of normal, human behavior and that your responsibilities are immensely diminished. Heaven knows how many people are taught by those means that things which are evil are not really evil at all. Plainly the whole barrage of sex in the media, for example, must lead innumerable people to think that every exercise of our sexual powers is of itself innocent—a God-given gift (if they use that vocabulary) which it is far better to exercise than to try to discipline or restrain. It is perfectly possible for our mind and will to be so weakened that, even though the thing we do or do not do is of grave consequence to others and to ourselves, the act is not accompanied by those two further conditions that are necessary for mortal sin—full deliberation and full consent.

Well, let us come back and dwell on the awful

responsibility that is ours. It is possible for us to divert our minds and our wills from Almighty God's mind and will with appalling consequences for all eternity. Now, any deviation from the will of Almighty God that does not fulfill those three conditions—grave matter, full deliberation and full consent—is called a venial sin. The word "venial" comes from the Latin word *venia*, a pardon, but I think the Catechism is a little misleading when it says of venial sin that it is more easily pardoned than mortal sin. All sin is pardoned, and can only be pardoned, upon one condition—repentance.

That applies to mortal and to venial sin alike. No sin is more or less difficult to pardon. The condition for pardon is always the same: a complete withdrawal of our will from the matter in which we have offended Almighty God and the bringing back of our will to His. It is called repentance or sorrow for sin and, when we come to consider the Sacraments—that of Penance in particular—we shall need to dwell again on the fact that sorrow for sin is other than a feeling.

Feeling plays no part—or only an accidental and subsidiary part—in the practice of the Christian religion. Sorrow for sin is an act of the will and is quite compatible with a lack of any feeling at all. It is a bringing back of our will to the will of Almighty God, a realization that we have acted contrary to the will and purpose of our Creator and a determination never to do so again. It is compatible with a complete lack of feeling, though obviously it is an immense help if, besides being sorry for sin, we can also feel sorry for sin; and you will find in the Missal a prayer for the gift of tears, a petition that we may have what the spiritual writers call "compunction"—that is, that we may feel sorry. But we cannot control our feelings: if God gives us that gift, so much the better, let us ask for it. But if He does not give it to us, we must none the less be sorry for our sins. Not being given the gift of feeling sorry does not exempt us from the need of being sorry.

CHAPTER 11

The Resurrection of the Body and Life Everlasting

WE NOW turn to the last two articles of the Creed, the eleventh and the twelfth:

The eleventh article of the Creed is, "the resurrection of the body." Q128

By "the resurrection of the body," I mean that we shall all rise again with the same bodies at the Day of Judgment. Q129

The Catechism, as you see, deals with or dismisses one of the most profound mysteries in just one question and a definition. It is as well at this stage to remind ourselves once again that every article of the Creed is a mystery, "a truth above reason but revealed by God" (q28). It is very important that we should remind ourselves constantly of that because, as you know, there is a curiously selective approach to the Christian religion on the part of unbelievers whereby some of the articles of the Creed are dismissed more contemptuously than others. To the believer all are equally true and all are equally mysteries—truths that we could not reach by our own unaided reason. All of them are truths revealed to us by

Almighty God and acceptable only by faith in Jesus Christ, the Revealer.

The eleventh article of the Creed, "the resurrection of the body," is particularly difficult for unbelievers. We believe that those visible, tangible, physical bodies which are ours now and which quite plainly die and decay, returning to the earth whence they came, will at the general resurrection at the Second Coming of Christ be called into being again. That is a truth that human reason could not discern unaided and finds difficult, I should say impossible, to believe without the gift of faith. You may remember how St. Paul, preaching to the Areopagites, found a receptive audience until he came to mention the resurrection from the dead, at which they laughed and said, "We shall hear you about that another time." (*Acts* 17:32).

Nonetheless the resurrection of the body is an essential part of the Christian religion. It is one of those mysteries for which reason has at least done something to prepare us. We have already considered the nature of man. Man is neither a spirit caught and imprisoned in an animal body nor an animal raised to a higher level than the level of the beasts. He is a single entity, a rational animal, body and soul, a single human being acting on the material and the spiritual plane all the time. Consider, then, what we have in common with the lower animals—physical existence, the same physical needs as theirs, and the power to propagate. Yet we reach whole flights of abstract knowledge, abstract judgment and experience which are, so far as we can see, completely denied to the lower animals. We have observed that, though it is perfectly acceptable to use the traditional vocabulary of body and soul, there is a danger in using it of our thinking that here are two separate things brought together for the space of a human life and then torn apart by death. We need to appreciate that man is not two separate entities but one single entity and that his disruption at death is a consequence of the Fall of our first parents. Man was destined by Almighty God to be moving always on the material and the spiritual plane at once. The violent separation of body and soul at death is not part of Almighty God's plan and design: it is the consequence of sin. Christ's triumph over sin will not be complete, His work will not be done, unless that consequence of the Fall is remedied. So we shall, in a manner wholly beyond our understanding, once again be clothed in our bodies. We should not be complete and Christ's triumph would not be complete unless that were going to happen.

The materialist mocks the whole idea of rising again and asks how the limited amount of matter in the world, which is being used again and again, can furnish bodies for millions of people. At our death our bodies will break up into their component parts, to be absorbed again into the totality of matter and reabsorbed into the bodies of other people. The materialist obviously sees in that an objection to the doctrine of rising again.

We do not know how our bodily resurrection is to come about; but we do know that even in this life our own bodies are being constantly reconstituted and, though they do not have a particle-by-particle identity, they are in common speech considered to be the same, identical bodies throughout our lives. Our consideration of the nature of man helps us to accept the profound mystery of the resurrection of the body.

The only risen body of which we have any knowledge is that of our Blessed Lord Himself. As we have seen when considering the Incarnation, it is basic to the Christian faith that Christ did rise again, with the same body in which he suffered and died: we do believe in the physical Resurrection of that same body that was formed in our Blessed Lady's womb and borne by her, that suffered, was crucified and died on the Cross. When St. Mary Magdalen and the holy women on Easter morning went to the tomb, it was the body which had been laid to rest three days before which had risen from the dead. It was that body which ascended into Heaven.

That is a pledge of the resurrection of our own bodies. It is all part of that same triumph over sin and death without which the redemption of our Blessed Lord would be at least partially ineffective. Death is the consequence of sin and sin is not routed if our bodies do not rise again.

We now come to the twelfth article of the Creed, which is closely bound up with the eleventh.

Q130 **The twelfth article of the Creed is, "life everlasting."**

Q131 **"Life everlasting" means that the good shall live for ever in the glory and happiness of heaven.**

Q132 **The glory and happiness of heaven is to see, love and enjoy God for ever.**

Q133 **The Scripture says of the happiness of heaven: "That eye hath not seen nor ear heard, neither hath it entered into the heart of man, what things God hath prepared for them that love Him."**

The wicked also shall live and be punished for ever in the fire of hell. Q134

These questions bring us to the consummation of human history. Remember, as I said earlier, how very different is the measure by which Christians judge time from that of the vague progression of time without a starting-point or finishing-point. A Christian sees the whole of history against the staggering background of three events: The Fall of Man, the Redemption and the Second Coming of Christ. The time-scale of the Christian is at once infinitely greater and infinitely more personal and particular. The thing that really matters is what takes place between each individual human birth and each equally individual human death. Everything happens in that comparatively tiny time-scale against the vast time-scale of the Fall, the Redemption and the Second Coming. The whole of human history is working towards the Second Coming, when we believe the Last Judgment will take place—the separation of the whole human race between the saved and the damned, between those who, however partially or imperfectly, have fulfilled God's plan or design for them and those who have knowingly, willingly and unrepentantly refused to cooperate in Almighty God's plan. Let me remind you once again that the whole process of sanctification and salvation is a mutual process between Almighty God and the individual human soul. We are neither pawns to be moved about by Almighty God nor creatures able to raise ourselves up by our own shoestrings. The whole process of our sanctification and salvation is something requiring the interplay of two wills, the divine and the human. We shall go into that more fully when we come to the concept of Grace.

At the Second Coming, the division of the whole human race into the saved and the damned will depend entirely on the extent to which we have sought to cooperate with Almighty God and the extent to which we have deliberately, by an act of our mind and will, rejected that cooperation. The consequence of our cooperation is, we believe, that we shall come to the eternal enjoyment of Almighty God. "Life everlasting" means that the good shall live for ever in the glory and happiness of heaven (q131). That is a concept of which we can form no accurate mental picture. Once again it is important to see both how experience supports this approach—in that nothing short of Almighty God satisfies the yearnings of the human soul for perfection—and yet how completely inadequate the human mind is to imagine Heaven. I am always grateful to the Catechism for giving at this point the quotation, "That eye hath not seen, nor ear heard, neither hath it entered into the heart of man, what things God hath prepared for them that love Him." (*1 Corinthians* 2:9).

It seems to me one of the most useless speculations for us to try to imagine what Heaven or Hell are like. We have no means of knowing. Naturally the human mind, being what it is, makes symbols or pictures of both. You will find plenty in the Old and New Testaments: symbols of Heaven, such as palms, harps and the rest, and symbols of Hell, such as a prison and a torture-house. But the point to come back to again and again is the realization that, while symbols are of little value and probably even deceptive, nothing can exceed the joy of Heaven or the misery of Hell. Let us rest on that fact. Heaven will be the complete fulfillment of ourselves at every level, the absorption of ourselves into Almighty God, the sharing of His mind and will, the consummation of all good. Hell will be the complete frustration of ourselves and the complete impossibility of ever remedying that frustration.

Rest in that thought, which is primarily a matter of revelation but is none the less one which the human reason can appreciate and understand. In St. Augustine's words, "He Who made you without your will cannot save you without your will." If, then, we die with our wills averted from His, nothing can bring us to Him. On the other hand, if we try all the time to bring our wills to His, we inevitably come to Him. Rest in that thought, come back to it again and again and try to steer clear of all temptations to picture Heaven or Hell.

We have come to the end of the section of the Catechism on Faith and it may be profitable to run through the whole ground from the very beginning before going on to the section on Hope.

Very briefly, you remember we started off by trying to lay the foundation of faith in natural reason, which we summarized briefly in five points—the existence of Almighty God, His nature, our own immortality, our free will and our consequent responsibility. Those five points are suggested rather than expounded in the first eight questions of the Catechism.

It is only on that foundation that we go on next to the consideration of revelation and the act of faith whereby we accept that revelation. We go on to consider that the whole Christian religion is a revelation, a cycle of knowledge unattainable to the human mind until opened to us by our Lord and Saviour Jesus Christ. That cycle of knowledge is summarized in the Apostles' Creed and we have gone through the Creed article by article. You know now in retrospect what perhaps was not so clear at the time: that the whole of the Creed centers round the greatest mystery of all, the Incarnation. Every other article of the Creed is best seen in relation to that central one. In accepting the Incarnation you accept all the others, at least by implication.

In the order in which we consider them in the Catechism we start with the Trinity and the Fall of Man. Our consideration of both of those is most profitably seen as preparatory to our consideration of the Incarnation. The Trinity answers the question Who it is that becomes incarnate—the Second Person of the Blessed Trinity—and the Fall answers the question why He becomes incarnate—to undo the effects of the Fall. The central mystery of all is that the Second Person of the Blessed Trinity takes human nature and in that human nature undoes the effects of the Fall by working a salvation to which He gives infinite value because He is very God Himself. None the less He does it by and on behalf of the human race because He is very man, as you and I are men. So human nature, which of itself would be unavailing to undo the consequences of the Fall, is empowered to do so by its union with the divine nature.

All the other mysteries of the Christian faith are consequences of that central mystery of the Incarnation, starting with the place of our Blessed Lady in the scheme of things, because it is Christ's being conceived and borne by her that guarantees His humanity. Our Lord really draws His human existence from her, is really conceived by her, is really borne by her, is really a member of the human race. He is not a phantasm, mask or cloak for God.

Then the Church is seen as the continuation of the Incarnation. Just as God becomes man not in some vague and amorphous manifestation of humanity but in a very real, identifiable, physical body born at a precise moment of time, so His redemption of us, His teaching and His Sacraments are administered to us through a body no less identifiable, no less clear-cut than Himself—the Church. That is why our concept of the Church is so very central to our presentation of Christianity. It is seen always as Jesus Christ continued in corporate form. Our devotion to the Church, which strikes non-Catholics so often as disproportionate or fanatical, is seen by us as devotion to the Person of Jesus Christ Himself.

PART II

HOPE

CHAPTER 12

Grace and Prayer

THE whole Catechism is concerned with the three theological virtues, which are Faith, Hope and Charity. We have finished the section on Faith and now we are beginning the second of the three great sections, the one on Hope.

The opening question on Hope is a curiously dated one. The Catechism says:

> **Faith alone will not save us without good works. We must also have hope and charity.** Q135

Our Catechism was really aimed as a reply to the Protestant heresy. I believe that the first catechism was composed by Luther to expound his theology of faith, so that every German father of a family could have a simple statement of his theology. Not until later did the Church think of adopting that catechetical form, when St. Peter Canisius, the great sixteenth-century Jesuit, raised by divine Providence to counter the Protestant movement in central Europe, composed the catechism from which nearly all Catholic catechisms are derived. That accounts for many features of our Catechism, one of which is the habit of adducing texts from Holy Scripture.

Question 135 is directed at the classical Protestant error

that man is saved by faith alone, which is, like nearly every heresy, a truth out of perspective.

As you may have noticed already, the whole of the Christian religion is full of tensions. An example, as we have already seen, is the doctrine of the Trinity—three in one. One God, yes, but Three Persons. The Incarnation is another example—God indeed, very God of very God, begotten not made, yes, but at the same time man, as you and I are men. These tensions run throughout the Christian revelation, for what has been revealed to us by Almighty God is truth beyond human understanding.

Both faith and works are essential to the leading of a Christian life—both the acceptance of the faith revealed to us by Jesus Christ our Lord and the consequent need to put that faith into practice by good works. Neither faith alone nor works alone is sufficient for the complete practice of the Christian life. Both are essential.

First we must accept what we have been considering so far—the truths revealed to us by our Blessed Lord. They are beyond the reach of our reason but we accept them because He has revealed them. The mere doing of good works for purely natural reasons has its consequence or its reward, if any, here on earth. The philanthropist who does good deeds either because of some natural urge on his part or because he wishes to gain the praise of men may have his reward here and now.

Secondly, faith without works is dead. The mere believing of the truths of faith without any effect on our lives is valueless for eternal salvation. Thus both faith and works are necessary. First we must believe Christ's redemption of mankind. The acceptance of His redemption raises us to the supernatural life and we must accordingly show in practice the consequences of that belief, thus deepening and strengthening that supernatural life.

Nowadays the popular non-Catholic belief concerning faith and works has gone full circle. It would appear to be, "It does not matter what a man believes, so long as he does what's right"—in other words, man is saved by works alone. Luther reacted against what he thought was the excessive emphasis put upon good works. Much of the practice of the Christian religion in his time seemed to him to be concerned with external observances only and to have very little foundation in a real, living faith in the merits of Jesus Christ our Lord. Seeking to correct that in-balance, he went to the opposite extreme and put the whole emphasis on faith, as though the acceptance of the redeeming sacrifice of Christ by a single act of the will was all that was necessary for salvation. He consequently derided the value of works and dismissed the Epistle of St. James, in which they are commended, as "the Epistle of straw."

Luther's thought, being less incisive than that of Calvin, a scholastically trained, logically minded Frenchman, did not carry this concept to its logical conclusion: if man is saved by faith alone, if works are valueless and if, further, faith is, as we believe, a gift of Almighty God, then the Calvinistic doctrine of predestination naturally follows. If Almighty God gives that gift which is going to save or damn, man is, from the first moment of his being, predestined to salvation or to damnation. And our correspondence to God's grace and revelation is irrelevant.

If we can reduce a far-ranging and profound theological controversy to its simplest terms, this emphasis on faith without works is the root inspiration first of the Lutheran and then of the Calvinistic revolt against the teaching of the

Catholic Church. At the other end of the scale the Pelagian heresy, a much earlier one than those which I have been discussing, taught that man can be saved by his own efforts. It is amusing to note that, while Luther was a German and Calvin a Frenchman, Pelagius was a Briton: he was a theological Samuel Smiles. Self-Help may be good worldly wisdom: when it comes to the things of God it can only be a half-truth.

Well, the truth of the matter, according to Catholic teaching, holds the balance between these two extremes. The whole of our salvation or sanctification is something to be worked out by the interplay of two independent free wills, that of Almighty God and our own, God offering the means of salvation, we cooperating. Almighty God neither saves nor damns us regardless of our own acts of will. Nor, as we shall see under Question 138, have our acts of will the power to save us without the initial activity of Almighty God. As we saw at the very beginning, we believe that, as a consequence of the Fall, man comes into this world separated from the love and friendship of Almighty God and is powerless to remedy his condition. But Almighty God offers us the possibility of doing so. The whole business of our sanctification and salvation must be seen always as a mutual or reciprocal activity between Almighty God and ourselves.

We see a parallel in the great yearly repeated miracle of nature. It is not the farmer who makes the seed burst from the ground and come to ripening—no, of course not. Those things come about by action wholly beyond the farmer's control. But it is his skill in preparing the ground, in ploughing, sowing, clearing stones, weeding, watering if need be, and so on, that allows this miracle of growth to be fruitfully repeated year after year. He is not himself bringing about the miracle, but he is furnishing the conditions in which it can happen most fruitfully.

This is a very exact parallel to the life of grace, used by our Blessed Lord Himself in the parable of the sower. Almighty God gives us the initial grace and our corresponding with His grace does just the things the farmer does—clearing the ground of weeds and uprooting in our lives those things which are offensive to Almighty God—and allows the miracle of grace to bear fruit. And it is this gift of grace that gives us Hope, the virtue that we are to consider now.

The Catechism section on Hope, after the opening given by Question 135, starts, as do all the sections of the Catechism, with a definition. As most of them are, it is a splendid one:

> **Hope is a supernatural gift of God, by which we firmly trust that God will give us eternal life and all the means necessary to obtain it, if we do what He requires of us.** Q136

The definition is a close parallel to the definition of Faith, which we have already considered in Chapter 2. The definitions of all the three theological virtues start in just the same terms: Faith, Hope and Charity, each is described as a supernatural gift of God. I want to stress again that word "gift." As with Faith, so with Hope and, as we shall see in Chapter 18, with Charity, each requires this mutual and reciprocal activity—Almighty God offering, we accepting. In the case of Hope, which we are now considering, He is offering the assurance that He will fulfill the whole purpose for which He has brought us into being, if we cooperate with Him in the life of grace. And the key word of that definition is the word "trust."

The names of all the theological virtues have passed into colloquial speech. In doing so, they have lost much of their precision and meaning. Theological Faith does not mean a vague belief; no, it is an assurance of the truth of revelation. In the same way, Hope in the Catechism does not mean what it means in colloquial speech, where it has come to have a very weakened meaning. When we say, "I hope you are well," or, "I hope it is going to be a fine day," we mean little more than a wish—"I should like to think you are in good health," or, "I should like tomorrow to be a fine day."

Theological hope is much more akin to the colloquial meaning of the word "trust." That is why I would like you to underline that word "trust" in your Catechism. It is a sure and certain hope by which we trust: not a vague hope or a wish but the absolute assurance that the purpose for which Almighty God has brought us into being is going to be fulfilled if we cooperate with Him.

Remember that all the theological virtues, Faith, Hope and Charity, need to be exercised. I said of the gift of Faith and will later repeat of the act of Charity that we, living in a civilization so far remote from nature, are inclined to think of a gift as the passing of some nonliving object from one person to another. If I give you a book or you give me a picture, we are passing something that needs no cooperation. The book, I suppose, ought to be read, the picture ought to be looked at appreciatively; but there they are, dead things in themselves. But we get a far livelier concept of what we mean by the gifts of Almighty God if we think in terms of giving living things. If you give a child a pony or a puppy, the child will get out of it as much as he or she puts into it. The book can be put on the shelf, the picture on the wall, and not looked at again. The transaction has taken place when the gift has been passed from one to another. But you cannot lock the pony in the stable or the puppy in the kennel and never give it another thought. Give it some hay, give it a bone, give it some care and attention and you will get a reward proportionate to your cooperation. The girl who has been given a pony thinks about it twenty-four hours a day; yes, but the amount she gives it she gets back many times over.

So, too, with these three gifts of Almighty God. Faith is not the work of a moment. It needs to be deepened and strengthened by thinking about it, reading about it, loving, studying and living it. We know that faith becomes a dead thing if we think no more about it. A terrible dislocation is liable to take place if we do not increase our knowledge of our faith proportionately to our knowledge of other things. When the disparity between them develops, we shall be tempted either to treat the truths of faith as though they had no relevance to natural knowledge or to jettison them.

So, too, with Hope or trust; unless it is exercised by a life of prayer and talking to and listening to Almighty God—which is what prayer is—it will likewise wither and die. Hope—trust—if not properly exercised and deepened, can be lost in two ways, by excess or by defect. By excess we mean that attitude which suggests that, since Almighty God wants us to come to Him, He will fulfill that purpose without our needing to bestir ourselves. That is the sin of presumption. At the other end of the scale is the man who says, "Here am I, poor weak creature, riddled through by selfishness and sin of every kind. I cannot do anything about it." That is the sin of despair.

Always remember that the essence of the Christian life is never, never, never to stop trying. However little progress you seem to have made, however poorly you think of yourself, never stop trying. The moment you stop, Almighty God cannot help you because, as I say, this process is entirely a mutual or reciprocal one. As long as you are trying, there is hope.

The Catechism now asks, "Why must we hope in God?" In that question and in its answer I should prefer the word "trust" to "hope":

Q137 **We must hope in God because He is infinitely good, infinitely powerful and faithful to His promises.**

Plainly, as we saw at the beginning, God must have a purpose in bringing all things into being. The whole of the inanimate creation fulfills His will or purpose without merit or demerit. Man alone in the visible universe has, as we have seen, the sublime power of being able to cooperate voluntarily with the will of Almighty God and has consequently an awful responsibility if he seeks to oppose it. But since Almighty God wants His whole plan to reach fulfillment, He will support our own efforts to fulfill our role within it.

The next answer in the Catechism goes back to something that we have been considering recently, at least by implication:

Q138 **We can do no good work of ourselves towards our salvation; we need the help of God's grace.**

As we considered earlier, what we do on a natural plane may meet its reward on a natural plane. What we are considering now is God's plan or intention to lift man up from the natural to the supernatural plane, the life of grace:

Grace is a supernatural gift of God, freely bestowed upon us for our sanctification and salvation. Q139

That definition of grace, though perfectly accurate, is, it seems to me, extremely inadequate. It is always a problem to know how to convey the idea of grace, seeing that of all the concepts we consider this is the most remote from our ordinary experience. Jesus Christ came to undo the effects of the Fall and, more than that, to lift us up to the divine life. The Word became man. Almighty God Himself, the Second Person of the Blessed Trinity, came down to our own level, came down to creature-hood. He came to share our life in order to communicate His life to us. St. John tells us in that wonderful opening of his Gospel:

> The Word was with God, and the Word was God

and goes on to give the whole object of Incarnation. At the end of that passage he says,

> He came to His own, and His own received Him not, but to those who received Him, to them He gave the power to be made the sons of God. (*John* 1:12).

He came to communicate to us the divine life. And that is what we mean by grace. It is the divine life which Almighty God communicates to us.

We can conceive goodness on the natural plane. But what it means to have the life of Almighty God communicated to us is something so remote from our experience that we cannot imagine it. We had, so to speak, a glimpse of it when we were considering the Ascension. Jesus Christ returns to Heaven no longer the disincarnate Word that had come down thirty-three years before. Now, being Incarnate, He carries up humanity into Heaven and is seated as man at the right hand of the Father.

The life of grace exists here and now, though it is not visible to us and we are not conscious of it. At death precisely that measure of grace which we have in this world is translated into an equal or corresponding measure of glory:

> And in Thy light we shall see light.
>
> (*Ps.* 35:10; *Ps.* 36:9 AV).

We take it very much for granted that we can love and be loved by God. Of course, every artist and every creator must love the things that he has created—they are part of himself. But they are not at the same level as himself. There cannot be a real, equal relationship between an author and his book or between a painter and his painting. Patently these are inanimate things which cannot return the love which the creator gives them. But through grace we are empowered to enjoy a quasi-parity with Almighty God, so that we can both love and be loved by Him. He, looking upon us, sees in us the divine sonship which His Son has communicated to us. This communication of grace puts us on such terms with Almighty God that it is possible to talk of a mutual love between ourselves and Him.

Our elevation to the divine life is the greatest of all the gifts that Almighty God has given us. All the other gifts—Faith, Hope and Charity—prepare for or flow from this one. Every other gift He gives us, the natural gift of life, the supernatural gifts of Faith, Hope and Charity, converge in the supreme gift of all, the communication to us of the divine life which enables us to love and be loved by Almighty God, not just going through the motions or pretense or simulation of love but loving with very love itself. Love requires some sort of parity between the lover and the beloved, for otherwise it would not exist. Grace is the pearl of great price for which a man will give up all that he possesses. No sacrifice can be too great since by it we are in love and friendship with Almighty God.

The Catechism, always the most practical of books, now goes on to ask, "How do we obtain God's grace?" The answer is very practical and plain:

> **We must obtain God's grace chiefly by prayer and the holy Sacraments.** Q140

Our plan now is to devote the rest of this chapter to a consideration of prayer and then to go directly to the Sacraments, reversing the Catechism order, which treats the Sacraments after Charity. We should always remember the theological tag *Deus non alligatur Sacramentis*—"God is not tied to the Sacraments." He can and, we believe, does work outside them, but they are the covenanted means by which he communicates His grace to us.

We begin with the definition of prayer, which seems to me to be the best of the great definitions in the Catechism. Not only is it wonderfully clear and simple, like the others; it also has a greater economy than any. ("Heart" here is a synonym for "will.")

> **Prayer is the raising up of the mind and heart to God.** Q141

Once again, as so often, we go back to the beginning of things. I hope that you have begun to appreciate already how accurate it is to say that the whole of the Christian revelation is about one truth, which we have to take in piecemeal because of our limitations. One of the very first things we did was to consider Almighty God and ourselves and to appreciate that we most closely resemble Him in the possession of a mind that can know and a will that can do. Now, to pray is to use the two most Godlike things we have—mind and will—and to direct them Godward. To pray is to raise our mind to the mind of Almighty God and to bring our will to cleave to His will.[19]

This concept implies definite acts. Prayer is not just vaguely thinking about Almighty God and hoping that we are obeying His will, but definitely exercising our mind, trying to bring it to His, considering what He wants us to do and what we have failed to do and resolving to do His will as perfectly as we can for the future.

Q142 **We raise up our heart and our mind to God by thinking of God.**

Remember that always. That is the first movement—just thinking of Almighty God. That is why it is so immensely important to have accurate concepts of revealed truth so that our minds may have something on which to work: the wisdom, power, justice and mercy of Almighty God. The thought of Almighty God is something we ought to be trying to keep in mind throughout the day. The concept of the permeation of the whole creation by Almighty God which we considered at the outset is a powerful help to what is called the practice of the presence of God, which is the best of all foundations for prayer.

Q142 **Consequently we pray by adoring, praising and thanking Him,**

The whole first direction of prayer is entirely Godward—the realization of His allness and our nothingness, simple adoration and praise of Him for what He is. You may be familiar with that most wonderful prayer that we say so frequently, the *Gloria in excelsis* where we praise God for His great glory. There is no thought of self here at all. The first movement of prayer is to adore, praise and thank Almighty God before we give any thought to ourselves. Only then can we properly pray for ourselves:

> **. . . by begging of Him all blessings for soul and body.** Q142

Even prayer for ourselves is God-centered and concerns ourselves only, in consequence of that God-centeredness. Our earlier consideration of the nature of Almighty God will have enabled us to see Him in absolutely everything and all creation as spreading out from Him. The consequence will be that we want the whole of creation to fulfill His purpose, particularly that tiny bit of it entrusted to ourselves—those gifts of mind and body that will enable us to establish the will of Almighty God in our hearts, to establish His kingdom there. So all prayer, even a prayer of petition, is really God-centered: we pray that His will may be done.

We may here observe that just as the words Faith, Hope and Charity have lost their original meaning—so that Faith is considered to be belief in something for no particular reason, Hope an unfounded wish and Charity the performing of the corporal works of mercy—so, in the same way, prayer has come to mean nothing but petition, and self-centered petition at that. Petition is a subsidiary aspect of prayer. Even when we petition, we pray that God's will may be done. Prayer is not just asking for things that take our passing fancy.

The whole of this activity, of course, is in that part of ourselves which is invisible—that is to say, it is in the mind and in the will. Because prayer resides entirely in the mind and the will, plainly the answer to the next Catechism question is:

Q143 **Those who at their prayers think neither of God nor of what they say do not pray well; but they offend God if their distractions are willful.**

Like everything else that matters in our relationship to Almighty God, prayer is an internal thing. We have considered that already, with reference to sin. Sin is an aversion of our mind and will from Almighty God. The sin takes place at the moment when we avert our mind and will from His. And whether we go on to act upon that aversion of our will from Almighty God or not is wholly secondary. If we think unjust or lustful or selfish thoughts, the chances are that we shall do unjust, lustful or selfish acts. These acts are the consequences of sins which we have already committed.

The same applies to prayer; being men we are naturally inclined to externalize our prayer by putting it into words and actions, choosing fixed times, places and ceremonies for its performance. This externalization is the vehicle or expression of prayer, not prayer itself.

Always distinguish sharply in your mind between prayer and prayers. Prayer is the raising up of the mind and will to Almighty God. It is possible to pray, to reach the heights of prayer, without any external actions at all. Prayers, on the other hand, are a form of words into which we cast the raising up of the mind to Almighty God. They are the outward expression of the reality, not its essence.

You will see how it is possible and highly desirable to

pray at all times, as we are urged to do. Prayer ought to be something running through the whole of our lives and not just something confined to the moments of saying our prayers. None the less, these moments are extremely valuable because what we do not do by rule and by habit we are likely not to do at all. So fixed times of prayer, external acts of prayer and public worship are all immensely important, but valueless unless they express an internal reality.

Think of a line of telegraph poles going as far as you can see over the horizon. The posts occur at absolutely regular intervals. The important parts of the picture are the wires going from post to post. The wires are the important thing because they carry the message, but they would not be able to do so if they were not carried from post to post across the landscape. That is a very prosaic parallel but a quite accurate one. We are very unlikely to be living a life of prayer and turning our minds constantly to Almighty God unless we have those moments when at regular intervals we try to make a little space in our lives to think of nothing else but Him. If we do that then there is at least some chance that throughout the day we will bring our minds back to the realization of the presence of God, to the immediacy of our communication with Him and to the need of His help and guidance. We will then be able to carry out the very important task of prayer throughout our life, from one fixed time of prayer to another.

We have seen that Hope is a supernatural virtue like Faith and, as we shall see, Charity. All are gifts of Almighty God, requiring, as we have stressed each time, free offering and free acceptance, so that their acceptance is in the last analysis an act of the will. The three theological virtues are the acceptance of gifts which Almighty God is offering us.

The gift of Faith is the truth of revelation. The gift of Hope is the assurance that Almighty God will do His part in our salvation and sanctification if we do ours. When we come to consider Charity we shall see that that, too, is a gift, the free offering and free acceptance of love.

We have seen that the names of the three theological virtues have lost in common speech their precise theological meaning, being sometimes quite distorted. This is particularly true in the case of Hope. It has been so weakened that colloquially it means very little more than "wish," whereas theologically it is very much more akin to "trust," the absolute confidence that Almighty God will do His part. It is perfectly put in the Anglican Burial Service, which speaks of "in sure and certain hope of the resurrection." That is theological Hope—sure and certain hope, not just a vague wish that it might be so.

Hope in God is founded in the belief that He desires His creation to fulfill the purpose which He had in mind in bringing it into being. The grounds for that confidence in each of us are the indwelling of grace: We can do no good work of ourselves towards our salvation; we need the help of God's grace (q138). Grace is the gift of all gifts, as the very name implies; if Faith and Hope and Charity are gifts, even more so, if possible, is Grace. The very name indicates something freely given. At the outset we dwelt on our Blessed Lord's parable of the sower going out to sow his seed, showing that all these gifts that have been given to us require not just passive acceptance from us but active cooperation. So Faith, Hope and Charity are gifts of which the fruits, as in the case of grace, go on increasing in so far as we are receptive of them and exercise them.

That free gift of grace from Almighty God so far raises us

up to the divine plane that a mutual, reciprocal relationship between Almighty God and ourselves becomes possible. The possession of grace, which raises us up to the divine level, should be seen as the whole object for which the Incarnation took place: "He came into His own, and His own received Him not: but to those who received Him He gave the power to be made the sons of God." (*John* 1:11–12). That is what grace is. The possession of grace is the one thing of supreme importance in the whole of our lives, because just that measure of grace which is ours at the moment of death will be translated into the same measure of glory, which fits us to see Almighty God and to be with Him. Glory is not an arbitrarily added reward for a good life. It is the consequence of being in a state of grace transmuted by eternity.

The Catechism, being, as I have said, immensely practical, now asks how we can obtain grace. The answer is: "chiefly by prayer and the holy Sacraments." So we have been talking about prayer, which is most beautifully defined in the Catechism as "the raising up of the mind and heart to God." We have seen that "heart" is here a synonym for "will" and the possession of a mind and a will is the way in which we most closely resemble or reflect Almighty God and in which we are particularly made in His image. In prayer we raise our mind and will to Him. In prayer we think of Him, seek to sink our mind in His mind and seek to make our will cleave to His will.

We have considered that, since we are men, working always on two planes at once, the spiritual and the physical, the chances are that we shall tend to throw prayer into an outward form of words or actions or place. But the essence of prayer, through all its ritual expression, is the raising up of mind and will. The external action has value only in so far as it expresses the inward reality which is there. Just as love, the highest form of human activity, is something essentially in the mind and the will, though we normally show it by words and actions, so too the value of all the emotions of our mind and will lies within ourselves. And if the externals are not supported by or backed by reality they become sheer hypocrisy. So, too, forms of prayer without real prayer are, as the Catechism says, not only valueless but "offensive to Almighty God" (q143).

And I have tried to emphasize that, though the essential value in prayer is the internal act of the mind and the will, without an external action, prayer is very unlikely to take place at all. Here again there is a parallel with love. A love which is never expressed is likely to wither and it is improbable that it will call forth any response. The external action of prayer should be regular, and gains rather than loses through being the consequence of habit. That is why it is so important to be regular in our morning and evening prayers. Without these props the general turning of our mind towards prayer, our attempts to make prayer real throughout our lives, are never likely to be successful.

The Catechism now gives an encouraging illusion that we are going through it very fast, because the section on prayer begins with an analysis of the Lord's Prayer, which has a beautiful simplicity about it that does not need much exposition, though we can meditate on it for ever.

Q144 **The best of all prayers is the "Our Father," or the Lord's Prayer.**

And how should it not be the best?—seeing that

Q145 **Jesus Christ Himself made the Lord's Prayer.**

In the form in which Catholics say the Lord's Prayer, it is almost identical word for word with the form known to other Christians:

> **Our Father, Who art in heaven, hallowed be Thy name; Thy kingdom come; Thy will be done on earth as it is in heaven; give us this day our daily bread; and forgive us our trespasses, as we forgive those who trespass against us; and lead us not into temptation, but deliver us from evil. Amen.** Q146

And then the Catechism gives the paraphrase to which I have referred:

> **In the Lord's Prayer God is called Our Father.** Q147

> **God is called Our Father because He is the Father of all Christians, whom He has made His children by Holy Baptism.** Q148

> **God is also the Father of all mankind because He made them all, and loves and preserves them all.** Q149

As I said in Chapter 2, there is absolutely no meaning in the brotherhood of man without the fatherhood of Almighty God. Brotherhood depends entirely on having a common father. It is an empty phrase otherwise.

> **We say "our" Father and not "my" Father because, being all brethren, we are to pray not for ourselves only but also for all others.** Q150

> **When we say "Hallowed be Thy name" we pray that God may be known, loved and served by all His creatures.** Q151

Q152 **When we say "Thy kingdom come" we pray that God may come and reign in the hearts of all by His grace in this world and bring us all hereafter to His heavenly kingdom.**

Q153 **When we say "Thy will be done on earth as it is in heaven" we pray that God may enable us by His grace to do His will in all things as the blessed do in heaven.**

Q154 **When we say "Give us this day our daily bread" we pray that God will give us this day all that is necessary for soul and body.**

Q155 **When we say "Forgive us our trespasses as we forgive those who trespass against us" we pray that God will forgive us our sins as we forgive others the injuries they do to us.**

Q156 **When we say "Lead us not into temptation" we pray that God may give us grace not to yield to temptation.**

Q157 **When we say "Deliver us from evil" we pray that God may free us from all evil both of soul and body.**

Let us go back for a moment just to see how perfectly the Lord's Prayer emphasizes the point that the first object of prayer is to praise Almighty God. We must free our minds of the concept of prayer as just asking. The first half of the "Our Father" is direct praise of Almighty God: "Our Father Who art in heaven, Hallowed be Thy name, Thy kingdom come, Thy will be done on earth as it is in heaven." Praise is always the first movement of prayer. Only then follows the prayer of petition—and even that is keyed to the first part. When we are asking, we are asking for the perfect performance of God's will and, more particularly, that His will may be done in that tiny part of creation which we alone can control—our own souls. We begin the petitionary part of the Lord's Prayer by asking for our material needs, not because they are the most important but because—as the theological tag puts it—"supernature is built on nature." The life of grace is founded on the natural life, so we ask for enough of the material things of life to free us from being distracted from the real purpose of our existence by the lack of them. We go on to ask for forgiveness of our sins and we ask to be spared temptation and to be delivered from evil.

I must emphasize again that the first movement of prayer is praise and the second is petition, which is always keyed to the will of Almighty God. People often lightly refer to prayers not having been answered, overlooking the fact that all prayer needs to be shaped to the divine will of Almighty God. We cannot expect Him to give us things that are going to be inimical to our sanctification and salvation nor, in our heart of hearts, can we want such things once we know that they are opposed to the complete fulfillment of the purpose for which He made us. All prayer must be conditioned to the concept of perfect fulfillment of the will of Almighty God and therefore the perfect fulfillment of ourselves.

The Catechism then goes on to a concept with which you are already familiar from our consideration of the Communion of Saints. We have emphasized that we are all part of one another because we are ingrafted into the mystical body which is Christ Himself. So, rightly and properly,

Q158 **We should ask the Angels and Saints to pray for us because they are our friends and brethren and because their prayers have great power with God.**

In Chapter 9 I mentioned that the popular non-Catholic tradition was that death meant a break in human relationships. Thus followers of that tradition no longer pray for the dead or pray to the angels and saints but pray directly to Almighty God, overlooking the fact that Almighty God is constantly working with us through other people. He is constantly using other people as channels of His grace and love to us, from the moment of our conception and birth to our receiving the Sacraments at the hands of other men and to our receiving love from other creatures and giving love to them. All this love, properly understood, is the overflow of the love of Almighty God for each one of us. When another person shows one love and affection, ultimately Almighty God is using that person as a channel.

Since we survive death as the individual human beings that we are, and are not caught up into some anonymous mass of humanity, those who knew us and loved us in this life and for whom we ourselves felt affection have a personal concern for us. So it is that the Catholic Church has always followed the practice of invoking saints for particular purposes as patrons of countries, institutions and colleges. This is right and proper, because those with whom we form close bonds in this life will be concerned in the next to advance our sanctification and salvation and will be better able to promote it.

We can show that the Angels and the Saints Q159
know what passes on earth from the words
of Christ: "There shall be joy before the Angels
of God upon one sinner doing penance."

CHAPTER 13

Our Blessed Lady

AMONG all the angels and the saints our Blessed Lady occupies a unique place. She does so in every way—doctrinally, historically and in our devotional life. Our Lady's consent at the Annunciation to become the mother of God, which we celebrate on Lady Day, is the turning point of all human history. It is impossible to exaggerate how absolutely central our Blessed Lady is to the whole scheme of things. That is why we invoke her aid above that of all other creatures.[19]

The Catechism says:

> **The chief prayer to the Blessed Virgin which the Church uses is the Hail Mary.** Q160
>
> **Hail, Mary, full of grace, the Lord is with thee; blessed art thou among women and blessed is the fruit of thy womb, Jesus. Holy Mary, Mother of God, pray for us sinners now and at the hour of our death.** Q161
>
> **The Angel Gabriel and St. Elizabeth, inspired by the Holy Spirit, gave us the first part of the Hail Mary.** Q162

Q163 The Church of God, guided by the Holy Spirit, gave us the second part of the Hail Mary.

The whole of the first part of the Hail Mary comes straight from Holy Scripture. "Hail, full of grace, the Lord is with thee" (*Luke* 1:28) are the words used by the Angel Gabriel when he came to tell her she was to be the Mother of God. And "Blessed art thou among women and blessed is the fruit of thy womb" (*Luke* 1:42) is the greeting given to our Blessed Lady by St. Elizabeth when our Lady went across the mountains to tell her she was with child. The Church of God has taken these two texts and strung them together, interpolating the holy names of Mary and of Jesus, and has then appended the invocation: "Holy Mary, Mother of God, pray for us sinners now and at the hour of our death."

I hope very much that you will make the Hail Mary an integral part of your prayers. It is a most wonderful prayer and, like all devotion to our Lady, it is all about the Incarnation. The only reason why we honor our Blessed Lady as we do is that by God's unique design she conceived and bore our Blessed Lord, Who drew His bodily existence from her.

The second half of the Hail Mary emphasizes an important point: that there are two moments of time of unique importance to each of us—this very present moment of time, over which alone we have control, and the hour of death, that moment of time when we pass into eternity, a moment which will seal our fate for ever.

We spend too much of our time escaping from the present moment, distracted from it by regrets for the past and by fears and worries about the future, neither of which we can now affect. There is a very good passage in *The Screwtape Letters*, by C. S. Lewis, about this very point. As you may know, these Letters are supposedly written by an old devil teaching a young devil how to tempt humanity. Here is an extract from Letter XV:

> Do we want to encourage our victim's anxieties, or to keep him worried? Tortured fear and stupid confidence are both desirable states of mind. Our choice between them raises important questions.
>
> The humans live in time but our Enemy [Almighty God] destines them to eternity. He therefore, I believe, wants them to attend chiefly to two things: to eternity itself, and to that point of time which they call the Present. For the Present is the point at which time touches eternity. Of the present moment, and of it only, humans have an experience analogous to the experience which our Enemy has of reality as a whole; in it alone freedom and actuality are offered them. He would therefore have them continually concerned either with eternity (which means being concerned with Him) or with the Present—either meditating on their eternal union with, or separation from, Himself, or else obeying the present voice of conscience, bearing the present cross, receiving the present grace, giving thanks for the present pleasure.
>
> Our business is to get them away from the eternal, and from the Present. With this in view, we sometimes tempt a human (say a widow or a scholar) to live in the Past. But this is of limited

> value for they have some real knowledge of the past and it has a determinate nature and to that extent resembles eternity. It is far better to make them live in the Future. Biological necessity makes all their passions point in that direction already, so that thought about the Future inflames hope and fear. Also, it is unknown to them, so that in making them think about it we make them think of unrealities. In a word, the Future is, of all things, the thing least like eternity. It is the most completely temporal part of time—for the Past is frozen and no longer flows, and the Present is all lit up with eternal rays. Hence the encouragement we have given to all those schemes of thought such as Creative Evolution, Scientific Humanism, or Communism, which fix men's attention on the Future, on the very core of temporality. Hence nearly all vices are rooted in the future. Gratitude looks to the past and love to the present; fear, avarice, lust and ambition look ahead. Do not think lust an exception. When the present pleasure arrives, the sin (which alone interests us) is already over. The pleasure is just the part of the process which we regret and would exclude if we could do so without losing the sin; it is the part contributed by the Enemy, and therefore experienced in the Present. The sin, which is our contribution, looked forward.

The point about the second half of the Hail Mary, on which I want to put emphasis, is that in it we ask our Blessed Lady to pray for us at the two moments of time which are eternally important, that particular moment here and now—which is under our control and in which we can do the will of God and advance His kingdom here on earth—and that moment when we pass from time to eternity, a moment which will seal our fate for ever.

The Catechism now turns to our Blessed Lady's role in the Incarnation, which, as I have said, is crucial:

> **We should frequently say the Hail Mary to put us in mind of the Incarnation of the Son of God; and to honor our Blessed Lady the Mother of God.** Q164

As I have stressed, the whole veneration of our Blessed Lady turns on the Incarnation. The Hail Mary reminds us of that, for the words are those used by the Angel Gabriel to tell her she has been chosen to be the Mother of God. So we say the Hail Mary frequently to put us in mind of the Incarnation, which is the central mystery of the whole of our religion.

> **We have another reason for often saying the Hail Mary—— to ask our Blessed Lady to pray for us sinners at all times, but especially at the hour of our death.** Q165

> **The Catholic Church shows great devotion to the Blessed Virgin because she is the Immaculate Mother of God.** Q166

The next answer gives the reason for considering our Blessed Lady to be the Mother of God:

> **The Blessed Virgin is Mother of God because Jesus Christ, her Son, Who was born of her as man, is not only man but is also truly God.** Q167

Just to remind you of something we talked a great deal about much earlier when we spoke about the Incarnation: there have been heresies this way and that. Some have emphasized the divinity of Jesus Christ at the expense of His humanity, saying that He was God only and that His humanity was merely a cloak or mask in which He appeared among men. Others have said that Jesus Christ was only a man and that His divinity was simply a nearer approach to being God than any other man has ever made. But since being God is an Absolute, there can be no question of degrees of being God. The devotion which we pay to our Blessed Lady is the very guarantee of orthodoxy about the Incarnation. Like every other mother, she is not just the mother of a human nature. She is the mother of the Person born in that nature: and He is no other than the Word who "was with God" and "was God" from the beginning. So we rightly call Our Blessed Lady the Mother of God. The Person Whom she conceived and bore was in fact both wholly, or, in the words of Chalcedon, perfectly God and wholly or perfectly Man. He derived His humanity from her, not His divinity, but she was the mother of that single Person and when we venerate her as the Mother of God we are professing with absolute orthodoxy our belief in the profound mystery of Jesus Christ being both perfectly God and perfectly man and uniting two natures in one single Person.

Q168 **The Blessed Virgin is our Mother also because, being the brethren of Jesus, we are the children of Mary.**

This answer shows the connection between our Blessed Lady and Christ's body, the Church. She is the mother not only of His physical body but also of His mystical body.

Catholics interpret the words of our Blessed Lord on the Cross to St. John as spoken to all of us when He says, "Son, behold thy mother."

We now come to the Assumption of our Blessed Lady into Heaven:

> **By the Assumption of the Blessed Virgin we mean that, by the power of God, Mary, at the completion of her life, was taken body and soul into everlasting glory to reign as Queen of Heaven and earth.** Q168a
>
> **The Assumption of the Blessed Virgin is an article of Faith because it has been solemnly defined by the infallible authority of the Church.** Q168b

As you know, we believe that doctrines are not defined out of the blue by being suddenly thought up by the authorities and imposed on the faithful. A definition is a declaration by the Church of what is the belief of Catholics, a belief implicit in the faith once delivered to the Saints, which has become more explicit in the course of time. The doctrine of the Assumption of our Blessed Lady into Heaven was proclaimed by Pope Pius XII as recently as 1950. Belief in the Assumption has developed with increasing appreciation of the sinlessness of Mary and her exemption from the consequences of sin. It was firmly enshrined in the liturgy for many centuries before its definition—*Lex orandi lex credendi.*

It may be worth pointing out that all the Saints and great figures of the New Testament have places which are claimed to be their burial places and which have been centers of devotion. No such claim has been made for our Blessed Lord, Who rose from the dead and ascended into Heaven by His own power, nor for our Blessed Lady, whom we believe to have been assumed into Heaven body and soul by the power of Almighty God.

This and all the doctrines of our Blessed Lady are the reflection and the consequence of her sinlessness. We believe that she was completely sinless—in Wordsworth's lovely phrase, "our tainted nature's solitary boast." She is the single exception to the Fall of Man. For she alone of the whole human race was conceived and born in the love and friendship of Almighty God. She was never out of His grace and consequently she never suffered the dissolution and corruption which are the results of sin.

As I have said, the devotion of Catholics to our Blessed Lady stems from her central role in the Incarnation and her consequent status as the guarantee of orthodoxy in our belief about the divine and human natures united in the single Person of Jesus Christ. We express our devotion in a number of ways—shrines of our Blessed Lady such as Walsingham in Norfolk or Lourdes in southern France, statues of her in every Catholic Church, processions in her honor, prayers such as the Hail Mary, which we have discussed, and the Little Office of the Blessed Virgin Mary. The most popular devotion of all is the Rosary. I say it every day and I very strongly recommend you to do the same. It is a beautiful prayer, in which we meditate on the life of our Blessed Lord and ask our Blessed Lady, His mother and ours, to intercede for us.[20]

You will find at the end of the Catechism that beautiful prayer of supplication, the "Hail, Holy Queen" which is said at the end of the Rosary and which used to be said or sung at the end of Low Mass:

Hail, Holy Queen, Mother of mercy, hail, our life, our sweetness and our hope. To thee do we cry, poor, banished children of Eve; to thee do we send up our sighs, mourning and weeping in this vale of tears. Turn, then, O most gracious Advocate, thine eyes of mercy towards us; and after this our exile, show unto us the blessed fruit of thy womb, Jesus. O clement, O loving, O sweet Virgin Mary.

CHAPTER 14

The Sacraments: Baptism and Confirmation

THE Catechism says, We obtain God's grace chiefly by prayer—which we have considered—and the holy Sacraments (q140). But, as we have said before, in its arrangement of chapters the Catechism puts the Sacraments in a separate section towards the end of the whole work. Having considered prayer, it goes on to consider the virtue of Charity. I think that for our purpose it is better to take things in their logical order and to go straight on from prayer to the Sacraments, beginning at Question 249.

We obtain grace chiefly by prayer and the holy Sacraments. Prayer is, as we have seen, the raising up of the mind and heart to God. It is an activity, as it were, from our end; it is our aspiring towards Almighty God. Now, the Sacraments originate from God's end. Each is instituted by Him. They are His contribution to our salvation as prayer is ours. Consequently the Sacraments are indescribably more important and more effective than prayer.[21]

The section of the Catechism on the Sacraments, like other sections, starts with a definition. Like nearly all of them, it is extremely good:

Q249 **A Sacrament is an outward sign of inward grace ordained by Jesus Christ, by which grace is given to our souls.**

A Sacrament is an outward sign of inward grace: that is to say, a Sacrament has to be something material, impinging on our senses, and also a channel of inward, spiritual grace. It is, therefore, of necessity ordained by Jesus Christ, for only He Who is God can make a material thing the channel of His grace.

And there, you see, are reflected two profound truths which we have already pondered: the nature of man and the Incarnation. The nature of man, as we considered at the outset is twofold, and is expressed in the traditional vocabulary as his having a body and a soul. These are perfectly accurate terms, but they carry the danger of our thinking of body and soul as two separate entities brought together for the space of a human life. It is, perhaps, more illuminating to see man as one, single, indivisible being operating on two planes at once. That is to say, man is essentially a spiritual being having, through the possession of a soul indwelling his material body, power to know and to do. Body and soul are so interrelated that they are constantly interacting on each other. Our minds can only be reached through the senses and only through the senses can we express what is going on in our minds.

Now the Sacraments are a recognition of that fact. They are outward, visible, material forms conveying an inward, invisible grace. The other truth which the Sacraments reflect is the Incarnation. Jesus Christ is one single Person possessing two natures, that of God and that of man. His every act is consequently divine and human. The Incarnation is Almighty God Himself, in the Second Person of the Blessed Trinity, taking our nature and, in that nature, working a redemption of which that nature is of itself incapable.

Thus, just as a Sacrament is the use by Almighty God of a material form for an immaterial, spiritual purpose, so the Incarnation, because in it Almighty God effects a purpose through our human nature which is beyond the power of human nature to achieve, can be considered as the Sacrament of all Sacraments.

All the Sacraments have that same characteristic. Here are material things—water, laying-on of hands, or bread and wine—empowered by Almighty God to effect a spiritual purpose which of themselves they could not do. So every phrase in the Catechism definition of a Sacrament is essential. The outward sign, which impinges on our senses, of the inward grace, which Almighty God wants to communicate to us, is ordained by Jesus Christ, because no one but God Himself could have the power to use material things in such a way that by them grace is given to our souls.

The Catechism continues its consideration of the Sacraments as follows:

> **The Sacraments always give grace to those who receive them worthily.** Q250

The Sacraments are the great outpouring of the love of Almighty God on us. They are so much more effective than our own puny efforts to aspire upwards to Almighty God. Our efforts are necessary and valuable and our cooperation in the Sacraments is essential, but the Sacraments derive their efficacy not from us but from Almighty God. Our efforts to aspire towards Almighty God, such as our prayer, are constantly vitiated by our imperfections, our distractions and our mixed motives. But the Sacraments work infallibly with the power of Almighty God. It is only our faulty cooperation that prevents the reception of any one Sacrament from turning us into saints. A limit is imposed only by the narrowness of our power to receive what Almighty God is offering to us. A complete failure to cooperate, of course, can make the Sacraments wholly ineffective, but there is no ineffectiveness on the part of Almighty God.

That is why the Sacraments are so essential to the practice of a Christian life. They are the means above all others of growing in the knowledge and love of Almighty God, of growing in holiness. And they are effective for the reason that the Catechism gives us:

Q251 **The Sacraments have the power of giving grace from the merits of Christ's Precious Blood which they apply to our souls**

and, consequently,

Q252 **we ought to have a great desire to receive the Sacraments, because they are the chief means of our salvation.**

In the next three questions the Catechism reverses what you might think is the natural order. It tells you that a mark or "character" is given to the soul by three of the Sacraments before it tells you which the Sacraments are. So let us go straight on to Question 255:

Q255 **There are seven Sacraments: Baptism, Confirmation, Holy Eucharist, Penance, Extreme Unction, Holy Order and Matrimony.**

The order in which they are put there may seem a little bewildering. Plainly it is not the order in which they are received. You are unlikely to receive Holy Order and Matrimony after Extreme Unction. The reason for this order is that Holy Order and Matrimony are the Sacraments of special states of life and are not intended to be received by everyone. They are comparatively seldom both received by the same person. So they are put at the end of the list. The first five are the Sacraments which, in the intention of Almighty God, are of universal application. It is Almighty God's intention and design that everyone should be Baptized, should be Confirmed, should receive our Blessed Lord in Holy Communion, should have his sins absolved in Penance and should have Extreme Unction—or, as it is now often called, the Sacrament of the Anointing of the Sick—when he is seriously ill or in danger of death.

A character is given to the soul by the Sacraments of Baptism, Confirmation and Holy Order. Q253

A character is a mark or seal on the soul which cannot be effaced and therefore the Sacrament conferring it cannot be repeated. Q254

These three Sacraments—Baptism, Confirmation and Holy Order—make a complete change in the soul which can never be undone and confer a mark or seal, which is the Catechism's way of saying that they last for ever, to the greater glory of the recipient in Heaven, or to his greater confusion and shame in Hell. Baptism takes a man who until then has not been a Christian and grafts him into that mystical body of Christ which is the Church. Confirmation is the indwelling of the Holy Spirit in order to confirm and strengthen the process which Baptism has started. Holy Order is a Sacrament whereby men are empowered to offer the Eucharistic Sacrifice. These three Sacraments can never be undone and no one can ever be deprived of their consequences. Therefore they cannot be repeated.

We will now consider the Sacraments in turn, starting with Baptism:

Q256 **Baptism is a Sacrament which cleanses us from original sin, makes us Christians, children of God and members of the Church.**

Baptism is the first of the Sacraments. It is the first to be received and it is the necessary gateway to the others. It is the initial process whereby a man is grafted on to that vine which is Christ, incorporated into that mystical body of which He is the head, by which divine sonship is communicated to him and by which, consequently, the supernatural effects of the Fall are wiped out. All the Sacraments symbolize what they actually perform and the symbol of Baptism is, of course, the pouring of water, the washing away of original sin. The consequence of the removal of whatever debars us from being in the love and friendship of Almighty God is that we are in the instant of Baptism caught up into the life of God through Jesus Christ our Lord. Through His redemptive sacrifice the divine life is communicated to us. In that moment we begin to live the life of God and the virtues of Faith, Hope and Charity are infused into our souls. What is infused is an embryo, a living and growing thing. It needs our care and cooperation throughout life to preserve it and to bring it to fruition. But the reality is already there.[22]

The Catechism continues:

Q257 **Baptism also forgives actual sins, with all punishment due to them, when it is received in proper dispositions by those who have been guilty of actual sin.**

If a baptized infant dies, we think of him as at once being admitted into the Divine Presence. Such a child is in a state of grace and, having no sins to expiate, he comes immediately into the beatific vision.

Only the last of the next group of answers requires comment:

> **The ordinary minister of Baptism is a priest; but anyone may baptize in case of necessity, when a priest cannot be had.** Q258
>
> **Baptism is given by pouring water on the head of the child, saying at the same time these words: "I baptize thee in the name of the Father and of the Son and of the Holy Spirit."** Q259
>
> **We promise in Baptism to renounce the devil and all his works and pomps.** Q260
>
> **Baptism is necessary for salvation, because Christ has said: "Unless a man be born again of water and the Holy Spirit, he cannot enter into the Kingdom of God."** Q261

I think it is relevant at this stage to consider the absolute necessity for Baptism and the exclusive nature of Christ's claims. I say this because it is so widely believed today even among Christians that all that is needed is to lead a good life and then all will be well. This view ignores Christ's claims that He is the one and only Redeemer and that He has left us the Church as the covenanted means of benefiting by that redemption.

We considered Christ's claim to be the only Redeemer when we were talking about the Church's claim to be the one and only means of salvation. We saw that the Church's claim has meaning only if we equate Christ with her. Just as He is the one and only Redeemer, so she claims to be the only covenanted means of communicating that redemption to us. Every single person is saved through acting in accordance with such lights as he has, because of Christ's redemption, even though he does not know what is giving his virtuous life its value. A good life of itself, were it not complementary to the redemption of Christ, would be ineffective as a means to attain our supernatural end. Christ's redemption is essential. No one is saved outside it. This is the first thing to get clear: people are saved by what Christ has done even though they may not know what is giving their lives their supernatural value.

Further, Christ has left us the Church and the Sacraments as the covenanted means for communicating His redemption to us. But, just as many people are saved though they are unconscious of what is saving them, so likewise God Himself is not tied to His convenanted means to salvation, the Sacraments. There is a theological phrase or tag which I quoted earlier: *Deus non alligatur Sacramentis*—"Almighty God is not tied to the Sacraments." No: He can work outside His divine scheme for salvation. But on our part, only our ignorance can excuse us for not using the divine means to our salvation. The Church, though she has always believed and taught our Blessed Lord's own teaching that Baptism is essential for salvation, has always recognized equivalent forms.

For example, in the early days of the Church catechumens were kept under instruction for long periods, even during times of persecution. Those catechumens who, as not infrequently happened, were martyred during their period of instruction, never having received the Sacrament of Baptism for which they were being prepared, were always recognized as having received what is called the Baptism of Blood. They were therefore regarded as having been effectively baptized by their own martyrdom. In the same way, people who died as catechumens were considered to have received what is technically called Baptism of Desire.

It is generally also believed that those who are willing to do God's will in so far as they understand it are in that condition. But I believe that it is very important that in days like the present, when popular opinion constantly minimizes the absolute necessity of the Redemption, we should be reminded that our Blessed Lord Himself was insistent on the exclusiveness of His claim to be the one and only way for mankind to come to Almighty God our Heavenly Father. We can be excused from using the covenanted means to salvation by our own ignorance, and Almighty God can act outside them. What we may not do is to acknowledge the means and then refuse them.

We now come to the Sacrament of Confirmation. In view of the present practice of administering the Sacrament of Confirmation several years after the Sacrament of Baptism, it may rather surprise you if we consider the one immediately after the other. But you will see that the purpose of Confirmation is the fulfillment, the confirming and driving home, the consolidating, of that life of grace which began with Baptism. Confirmation should therefore be considered in connection with Baptism.

Confirmation is a Sacrament by which we Q262
receive the Holy Spirit in order to make us strong and perfect Christians and soldiers of Jesus Christ.

Q263 **The ordinary minister of Confirmation is a Bishop.**

Q264 **The Bishop administers the Sacrament of Confirmation by praying that the Holy Spirit may come down upon those who are to be confirmed; and by laying his hand on them and making the Sign of the Cross with chrism on their foreheads, at the same time pronouncing certain words.**

Q265 **The words used in the Confirmation are these: "Be sealed with the gift of the Holy Spirit."**

Confirmation is the Sacrament by which we receive the Holy Spirit in order to make us strong and perfect Christians. We have already received the Holy Spirit at our Baptism. All the Sacraments convey the Holy Spirit, the Third Person of the Blessed Trinity, to our souls. Being in a state of grace means, in St. Paul's wonderful words, that we are already temples of the Holy Spirit (*1 Corinthians* 6:19). God, the Third Person of the Blessed Trinity, dwells in our souls so long as we are in a state of grace. What the Sacraments do is to strengthen that life of grace. Confirmation does so in a special way.

First, Confirmation confirms the initial coming of the Holy Spirit into our souls in Baptism. That initiation, the Sacrament of Baptism, makes us Christians. We are Christians from that moment when the three theological virtues, Faith, Hope and Charity, are infused into our souls. Confirmation complements Baptism by making us strong and perfect in the faith. The word "Confirmation" means, of course, "making strong."

The significance of the last phrase of answer 262,

"soldiers of Jesus Christ," is that Confirmation is always considered as being the Sacrament that gives us the grace to profess Christ before men. It is as though Baptism were in a sense a private thing, the bringing of the Holy Spirit into our hearts. Confirmation is what enables us and gives us the strength publicly to profess our faith, in all the circumstances which make it difficult, from persecution to social pressure. It enables us to fulfill the constant obligation which falls upon a Christian to bear witness to the message of Christ.

The Holy Spirit still has that power which He manifested at Pentecost. Almighty God's arm is not shortened and His power is not lessened by the passage of time. The Holy Spirit comes down upon us in Confirmation in order to perform in our souls a mission parallel to that of the first Pentecost, thereby giving us the strength to confess Christ before all men.

Since Confirmation is primarily a strengthening Sacrament, it is symbolized by the anointing with oil, which is a symbol of strength, because it was used by athletes in antiquity.

CHAPTER 15

The Central Sacrament: The Holy Eucharist

WE NOW come to what is the central Sacrament of them all: the Holy Eucharist.

The Sacrament of the Holy Eucharist is the true Body and Blood of Jesus Christ together with His Soul and Divinity under the appearances of bread and wine. Q266

The bread and wine are changed into the body and blood of Christ by the power of God, to Whom nothing is impossible or difficult. Q267

The bread and wine are changed into the Body and Blood of Christ when the words of consecration, ordained by Jesus Christ, are pronounced by the priest in Holy Mass. Q268

Christ has given Himself to us in the Holy Eucharist to be the life and the food of our souls. "He that eateth Me, the same also shall live by Me" (*John* 6:57); **"he that eateth this bread shall live for ever."** (*John* 6:51). **Christ is received whole and entire under either kind alone.** Q269

Q271 **In order to receive the Blessed Sacrament worthily it is required that we be in a state of grace and keep the prescribed fast; water does not break this fast.**

Q272 **To be in a state of grace is to be free from mortal sin, and pleasing to God.**

Q273 **It is a great sin to receive Holy Communion in mortal sin, "for he that eateth and drinketh unworthily eateth and drinketh judgment to himself."** (*1 Corinthians* 11:29)

And then lastly for our present purposes,

Q274 **The Blessed Sacrament is not a Sacrament only, it is also a sacrifice.**

The first thing to consider is that the Holy Eucharist is completely different from all the other Sacraments in two very important respects. First, in all the other Sacraments we believe that grace is conveyed to us by a means which has no power to do so of itself. Water of itself has no power to wash away our sins. Oil and the laying-on of hands have no power in themselves to confer the Holy Spirit, and so on. And all the outward forms of the Sacraments are of themselves impotent. They derive their power only from the fact that Jesus Christ our Lord, Who is very God, took those material things and made of them the channels of grace for us. The Holy Eucharist is different from all the other Sacraments. We believe that this Sacrament alone conveys grace to our souls not as a material thing of no value but as the real and bodily Presence of Jesus Christ Himself, God and Man, whole and entire, Body, Blood, Soul and Divinity. That plainly makes the Holy Eucharist unique.

Secondly, the Holy Eucharist is not a Sacrament only; it is also a sacrifice. We will consider this point in more detail later.

It is indeed Jesus Christ Himself who conveys grace to us in the Blessed Sacrament. The Holy Eucharist should be seen as the Incarnation continued. The Incarnation, which is the central mystery of all that we believe, is continued in two very remarkable ways, each as mysterious as itself: one, its continuation in the Church, we have considered already. The Church is in a real sense the Incarnation continued: the millions upon millions of people who belong to the Catholic Church here on earth form one body in which Almighty God dwells. The Incarnation is continued in and through that body, the mystical body of Christ Himself. No less surely do we believe that the Incarnation is continued in the Holy Eucharist.

I want to emphasize both these points because it is so surprising to us that non-Catholic Christians who profess belief in the Incarnation often appear to think that this staggering event could have taken place without setting up consequences or repercussions as remarkable as itself. To think of the Incarnation as being something done once and for all, and then finished with, would seem to negate the whole of God's purpose.

I remember seeing in a bookseller's window some years ago one of the several books which I leave unread on the strength of the title alone. The title was When God was Man, implying that the Incarnation ceased at some point. Since I never read the book, I do not know whether the author considered that Christ laid down His human nature on Calvary or at the Resurrection or at the Ascension. But the whole idea of "when God was man" is incompatible with the concept of the Incarnation as a continuing reality.

The Incarnation continues in our Blessed Lord's own risen and glorified body now in Heaven: man is seated at the right hand of the Father. The Incarnation continues again, in a corporate fashion, in the Church. Furthermore, God Incarnate is still with us in the tabernacle of every Catholic church. God has entered His own creation and the GodMan, Jesus Christ, is present on our altars. That is what we mean by the Real Presence of Christ in the Holy Eucharist.

I stressed when going through the Creed that all the other articles are best understood and seen as a preparation for, or as a consequence of, the Incarnation; they are, in a sense, the frame round this central mystery. Now, just as the center of the system of the Faith is the Incarnation, so the center of the Sacramental system is the Holy Eucharist.

The Holy Eucharist is the Sacrament for which, in a sense, all the other Sacraments exist. You can say that people are baptized and confirmed and forgiven their sins in the Sacraments of Baptism and Confirmation and Penance so that they may receive the Sacrament of Sacraments, the Holy Eucharist. Priests are ordained so that the Holy Eucharist may be perpetuated until the Second Coming of Christ. We may even say that people are married to bring children into the world so that there may be people to receive and perform the Holy Eucharist. So the Holy Eucharist is the central fact of the whole Christian life.

The centrality of the Holy Eucharist has often been represented in art. You have probably seen the often-reproduced fifteenth-century Flemish picture by Roger van der Weyden, showing the interior of a Gothic church with the Mass being celebrated at the High Altar and the other Sacraments being administered all around. I remember seeing in the Prado a Flemish picture of about the same period, a great six-petalled rose with the Holy Eucharist being offered in the center, the six petals each containing representations of the other Sacraments being administered.[23]

That the one adequate worship of Almighty God may be continued to the end of time is the central inspiration of the whole of the Christian life; it is the reason for which the Church exists. That is precisely why we shall soon be considering the Eucharist as a Sacrifice, the worship of God by God, the sacrifice which Christ offered to the Father for the redemption of mankind.

Let us now consider the first aspect of the Holy Eucharist, the Real Presence. We believe that by the words of consecration the elements of bread and wine become the real, living Presence of Jesus Christ, God and Man.

Remember always that the central Catholic doctrine is that of the Real Presence. Transubstantiation, which many people wrongly think is the Catholic doctrine, is a way of explaining the Real Presence. Such people then build criticism on that error, saying quite correctly that transubstantiation is a word which is not found in the early centuries of the Church's history, and which depends upon a philosophy that is not part of divine revelation.

No scheme of philosophy is part of the divine revelation. Divine revelation is concerned with those supernatural truths revealed to us by Jesus Christ our Lord. The Church ponders those truths and uses the disciplines of other sciences and philosophies to express them. What she is effectively saying when she uses a word like "transubstantiation" is, "Here is a wonderful way of explaining what we have always believed: that Jesus Christ, God and Man, is truly present under the appearance of bread and wine. The appearance, the touch and the taste remain the same but the substance is changed to the Body, Blood, Soul and Divinity of our Lord and Saviour Jesus Christ."

The bread and wine are not empty symbols. When Christ at the Last Supper took bread, He said, "This is My body." (*Mark* 14:22). Those were constitutive words: our Blessed Lord was making the bread His body. When He said, "This is My blood" (*Mark* 14:24), He was not speaking figuratively. He meant what He said. He was making the wine His blood.

The Scriptural quotations used by the Church to support her teaching that our Blessed Lord intended the words, "This is My body, this is My blood," to have their plain meaning are in the sixth chapter of St. John's Gospel, which begins with an account of the miracle of the feeding of the five thousand and then records a discourse of our Blessed Lord in which He talked about the miracle that He had just performed. His words were prophetic and pointed forward to the Holy Eucharist, which He intended to establish at the Last Supper in order to leave His abiding Presence in this world after His Ascension into Heaven.

This is typical of our Blessed Lord's teaching. Often He uses something immediately at hand to lead us on to a profound and mysterious truth. Just as, passing through the vineyards from the supper-table to the Garden of Gethsemane, He was moved to use the vine as a symbol of the relationship of His followers to Himself, so here the multiplication of bread for the feeding of the five thousand is a symbol of the Eucharist which He intends to establish. Again, as so often in His teaching, He links it up with the Old Testament—in this case, the feeding of the Israelites with manna in the desert.

I would like you to turn now to St. John's Gospel, 6:26-67. This long passage, pointing forward to the Holy Eucharist, is very important and I want you to read it carefully several times. There are many things there for you to ponder:

> Amen, Amen, I say to you, you seek me, not because you have seen miracles, but because you did eat of the loaves and were filled. Labor not for the meat which perisheth, but for that which endureth unto life everlasting, which the Son of Man will give you. For him hath God, the Father, sealed. They said therefore unto Him: What shall we do that we may work the works of God? Jesus answered and said to them: This is the work of God, that you believe in Him whom He hath sent.
>
> They said therefore to Him: What sign therefore dost thou shew that we may see, and may believe thee? What dost thou work? Our fathers did eat manna in the desert as it is written: He gave them bread from heaven to eat. Then Jesus said to them: Amen, amen, I say to you: Moses gave you not bread from heaven, but my Father giveth you the true bread from heaven. For the bread of God is that which cometh down from heaven, and giveth life to the world. They said therefore unto Him: Lord, give us always this bread. And Jesus said to them: I am the bread of life: he that cometh to me shall not hunger, and he that believeth in me shall never thirst. But I said unto you that you also have seen me, and you believe not. All that the Father giveth me shall come to me; and him that cometh to me, I will not cast out. Because I came down

from heaven, not to do my own will, but the will of Him that sent me. Now this is the will of the Father who sent me: that of all that he hath given me I should lose nothing, but should raise it up again in the last day. And this is the will of my Father that sent me: that every one who seeth the Son and believeth in Him may have life everlasting, and I will raise him up in the last day.

The Jews therefore murmured at Him, because He had said: I am the living bread which came down from heaven. And they said: Is not this Jesus the son of Joseph, whose father and mother we know? How then saith He, I came down from heaven? Jesus therefore answered and said to them: Murmur not among yourselves. No man can come to me except the Father, who hath sent me, draw him: and I will raise him up in the last day. It is written in the prophets: And they shall all be taught of God. Every one that hath heard of the Father and hath learned cometh to me. Not that any man hath seen the Father, but he who is of God, he hath seen the Father. Amen, amen, I say unto you: He that believeth in me hath everlasting life. I am the bread of life, Your fathers did eat manna in the desert, and are dead. This is the bread which cometh down from heaven; that if any man eat of it, he may not die. I am the living bread which came down from heaven. If any man eat of this bread, he shall live for ever, and the bread that I will give is my flesh for the life of the world.

The Jews therefore strove among themselves saying: How can this man give us his flesh to eat? Then Jesus said to them: Amen, amen, I say unto you: Except you eat the flesh of the Son of man and drink His blood, you shall not have life in you. He that eateth my flesh and drinketh my blood hath everlasting life, and I will raise him up in the last day. For my flesh is meat indeed, and my blood is drink indeed. He that eateth my flesh and drinketh my blood, abideth in me, and I in him. As the living Father hath sent me, and I live by the Father, so he that eateth me, the same also shall live by me. This is the bread that came down from heaven. Not as your fathers did eat manna, and are dead. He that eateth this bread shall live for ever.

These things he said teaching in the synagogue in Capharnaum. Many therefore of His disciples hearing it, said: This saying is hard, and who can hear it? But Jesus knowing Himself that His disciples murmured at this, said to them: Doth this scandalize you? If then you shall see the Son of Man ascend up where He was before? It is the spirit that quickeneth: the flesh profiteth nothing. The words that I have spoken to you are spirit and life. But there are some of you that believe not. For Jesus knew from the beginning who they were that did not believe, and who he was that would betray him. And he said: Therefore did I say to you, that no man can come to me unless it be given him by my Father.

After this many of his disciples went back and walked no more with Him. (*John* 6:26–67).

In this chapter of St. John, you can see the very close parallel which our Blessed Lord draws between the Incarnation and the Real Presence. And you see what a difficulty both were to His hearers. When he said first, "I am the living bread which came down from heaven" (*John* 6:41), they said, "Is not this Jesus the son of Joseph, whose father and mother we know? How then saith he, I came down from heaven?" (*John* 6:42). Their first doubt is about the divinity of Jesus Christ our Lord. And the same people, ten verses on, dispute among themselves, saying, "How can this man give us his flesh to eat?" (*John* 6:52). Their doubt is about the Real Presence. The two mysteries—the divinity of Christ the God-Man and His real Presence under the appearances of bread and wine in the Holy Eucharist—are really one and the same. One is a continuation of the other. And those who reject the one reject the other.

What I want you to observe particularly is how our Blessed Lord reacts to those who say, "This saying is hard, and who can hear it?" (*John* 6:60). "Jesus was aware that his followers were complaining about it and said, Doth this scandalize you? If then you shall see the Son of Man ascend up where He was before?" (*John* 6:61–62). In popular parlance, our Blessed Lord is saying,

"If you reject this, what are you going to say when you see Me ascending into Heaven?" His hearers found the idea of the Real Presence hard to believe—indeed, it is impossible without the gift of faith. But does He then explain it away and say, "You have taken literally what I meant figuratively"? Not at all. He just emphasizes it. And not only does He emphasize it but He goes on to link it up at once with His claim to divinity.

Now I want to contrast that passage in St. John's Gospel with an earlier passage, the opening of the third chapter:

> And there was a man of the Pharisees named Nicodemus, a ruler of the Jews. This man came to Jesus by night and said to him: Rabbi, we know that thou art come a teacher from God: for no man can do these signs which thou dost, unless God be with him. Jesus answered and said to him: Amen, amen I say to thee, unless a man be born again, he cannot see the kingdom of God. Nicodemus saith to him: How can a man be born when he is old? Can he enter a second time into his mother's womb, and be born again? Jesus answered: Amen, amen I say to thee, unless a man be born again of water and the Holy Ghost, he cannot enter into the kingdom of God. (*John* 3:1–5).

You see the contrast with the previous passage. In this one, our Blessed Lord had been misunderstood and taken literally when He meant to be taken figuratively. And of course He at once enlightens His hearer. In the passage I quoted earlier, He is taken literally and knows the disciples are leaving Him because they cannot accept His teaching. But He does not call them back and say, "You have misunderstood Me—you have taken literally what I meant figuratively." Why not? Because He did mean His words literally. He did mean that the Holy Eucharist that He would establish at the Last Supper would contain, as we believe it does, the real, living Presence of Jesus Christ, God and Man.

By God's grace we believe in the objective Presence of Jesus Christ, God and Man, Body and Blood, Soul and Divinity, under the appearances of bread and wine. Now, the Church's way of explaining this profound mystery—and remember that every doctrine in which we profess our faith is a mystery, "a truth which is above reason but revealed by God" (q28)—is by using Aristotle's categories of substance and accidents.

The philosophy of substance and accidents is roughly this. All the material things that we know impinge upon us only by their external "accidents"—their color, their taste, their weight, their shape and so on. None of these accidents which our senses can perceive is the thing itself. All these accidents are manifestations of the very essence of the thing itself, which we can never get at directly. We know every single thing by its accidental qualities, many of which can be changed without altering the essence of the object in question. The color, weight, taste and so on may change, but the actual object itself does not change but remains the same substance. The accidents, or physical characteristics, are the way by which the object itself is made known to us.

Given the philosophy of substance and accidents, this is the way in which you must understand the Real Presence: the accidents of bread and wine—their appearance, their taste, their feel—remain, but the substance of the bread and wine gives place to the substance of Jesus Christ Himself.

One objection which is often raised is this: "How can a purely human philosophy be an essential part of divine revelation? And if it is not, how can a Christian be bound to accept it?" We have met this point before. The answer, as we have seen, is that while a purely human philosophy is not part of divine revelation, nevertheless the Church, developing as a person develops in her understanding of herself and of her teaching, may find that new ideas in moral or natural philosophy supply the very vocabulary with which she may explain, more clearly and precisely than before, what she has always believed.

Now, Aristotle's philosophy of substance and accidents is a purely natural approach to natural phenomena. It has no divine authority behind it. But taking that as a working philosophy the Church says, "This is a great help. We can see how the accidents of the bread and the wine continue. They do not look, taste, weigh, measure or feel any differently after the words of consecration. The accidents appear the same, but with this literally mysterious change: that the substance of what was bread and wine has given place to the real, living Presence of Jesus Christ, God and Man. What we sense are the accidents of bread and wine. What we receive is Jesus Christ, Body, Blood, Soul and Divinity—the living God Himself."

That, very briefly, is what we mean by transubstantiation. It is a way of expounding the doctrine of the Real Presence, but it is not the doctrine itself. The Church, on the strength of our Blessed Lord's own words, consecrating the bread as His flesh and the wine as His blood, has always believed in the Real Presence. Her present way of explaining it, by means of the concepts of substance and accidents, was in its fullest form largely worked out in the thirteenth century by St. Thomas Aquinas, the great Dominican theologian. There is a perfect expression of the doctrine in his great Eucharistic hymn *Lauda, Sion*, which was written for the feast of Corpus Christi.

The feast of Corpus Christi, which commemorates the institution of the Holy Eucharist, was established at the beginning of the thirteenth century. The day on which our Blessed Lord instituted the Holy Eucharist is Maundy Thursday, which, however, is in the middle of Holy Week and is overshadowed by thoughts of the Passion and Death of our Blessed Lord. The Church therefore established this special feast of the Holy Eucharist, set apart from all the sad associations of Holy Week, so as to be able to celebrate without any overtones of sadness the institution of the Sacrament of our Blessed Lord Himself. It is said that when the feast was instituted the Pope commissioned St. Thomas Aquinas and St. Bonaventure, who was the great Franciscan theologian of the period, to compose an office for the new feast. And when St. Bonaventure saw what St. Thomas had composed, which is what we now use, he destroyed his own version, thinking that nothing could compare with that of his Dominican friend.

The hymn *Lauda, Sion*, from the office composed by St. Thomas, is worth close study. Let me construe verses 6 to 10, which are very closely philosophical and theological. The Latin is very straightforward and, if you can work your way through it, you will find the most perfect and lucid statement of the doctrine which I have been putting so clumsily:

Dogma datur Christianis
Quod, in carnem transit panis
Et vinum in sanguinem.

Dogma datur Christianis—the truth is given to Christians, *quod in carnem transit panis*—that the bread is changed into flesh, *et vinum in sanguinem*—and the wine into blood.

Quod non capis, quod non vides,
Animosa firmat fides
Praeter rerum ordinem.

The subject of this sentence is *animosa fides*—a lively faith, *fir*—confirms, *quod non capis, quod non vides*—what you can neither grasp nor see, *praeter rerum ordinem*—beyond the nature of things.

Sub diversis speciebus,
Signis tantum, et non rebus,
Latent res eximiae.

The subject is *res eximiae*—outstanding things, *latent*—lie hidden, *sub diversis speciebus*—under diverse species, which are the species of bread and wine, and they lie hidden, *signis tantum*—by the signs or accidents only of bread and wine, *non rebus*—not by the bread and wine themselves.

Caro citrus, sanguis potus:
Manet tamen Christus totus,
Sub utraque specie.

Caro cibus—the food is flesh, *sanguis potus*—the drink is blood, *manet tamen Christus totus*—Christ whole and entire, *tamen*—nevertheless, *manet*—continues, *sub utraque specie*—under either species, bread alone or wine alone.

A sumente non comisus,
Non confractus non divisus,
Integer accipitur.

Integer accipitur—He is received whole, *a sumente*—by the recipient, *non concisus, non confractus, non divisus*—not diminished or broken or divided.

Sumit unus, sumunt mille:
Quantum isti, tantum ille;
Nec sumptus consumitur.

Sumit unus, sumunt mille—whether one receives or one thousand receive, *quantum isti, tantum ille*—the one receives as much as they all receive, *nec sumptus consumitur*—nor being received is He consumed.

Sumunt boni, sumunt mali:
Sorte tamen inaequali,
Vitae vel interitus.

Sumunt boni, summit mali—the good receive and the evil receive, *sorte tamen inaequali*—and the outcome for each is different, *vitae vel interitus*—life for the good and death for the bad.

Mors est malis, vita bonis:
Vide paris sumptionis
Quam sit dispar exitus.

Mors est malis, vita bonis—death is for the evil, life for the good, *vide*—see, *quam sit dispar exitus*—how different is the outcome, *paris sumptionis*—of a like reception.

Fracto demum sacramento
Ne vacilles, sed memento
Tantum esse sub fragmento
Quantum toto tegitur.

Fracto demum sacramento—when at last the Sacrament is broken (as the Host is broken by the priest at Mass), *ne vacil les, sed memento*—do not hesitate but remember, *tantum esse sub fragmento, quantum toto tegitur*—there is as much under the fragment as is covered by the whole.

The next four lines form the high point of the whole. You see, what St. Thomas is emphasizing all the time is that the reality of the Real Presence cannot be broken or divided. And he explains it so perfectly in these lines:

Nulla rei fit scissura;
Signi tantum fit fractura,
Qua nec status nec statura
Signati minuitur.

Nul la rei fit scissura—no division is made of the thing itself, *signi tantum fit fractura*—the breaking is of the sign only, *qua nec status nec statura*—by which neither the condition nor the dimensions, *signati minuitur*—of the reality are diminished.

The whole of the consecrated elements alike, or bread alone or wine alone, all equally enshrine the Real Presence of our Blessed Lord quite independent of the quantity of the consecrated bread or the consecrated wine. The Presence of Christ is as much in the tiniest particle or crumb of bread from the consecrated Host as it would be in a full ciborium.

That again explains how we believe that we are not disobeying or acting contrary to Christ's commands when Communion is given only in one species. What is commanded to be given to the communicant is the Real Presence. The custom, widespread in the west—though there have recently been considerable modifications—of giving Communion in the one kind alone began as a purely practical convenience to avoid the risk of spilling the wine and the risk of contagion. But as soon as the practice is challenged, as it was by heretics saying, You are not doing what our blessed Lord commanded by giving one kind only, the Church replies with the dogmatic justification for what began as a purely practical measure: that in receiving either of the consecrated species one receives Jesus Christ's Body, Blood, Soul and Divinity, "whole and entire" (q270).

You may remember that at the beginning of our consideration of the Sacraments I emphasized two ways in which the Blessed Sacrament is unique, the first being that in It alone we have the Real Presence of our Lord and Saviour Jesus Christ; and the second, to which we now turn, being that It alone of all the Sacraments is also a Sacrifice. As always, we start with a definition—and once again a very good one:

Q275 **A sacrifice is the offering of a victim by a priest to God alone, in testimony of His being the Sovereign Lord of all things.**

We see once again how completely whole and homogeneous the Christian revelation is: once again we go back to something we have met before. The whole idea of sacrifice goes back to one of the very first ideas which we considered, and one which has come up again and again: that God is alone and uniquely the one necessary Being. All other beings exist only because He calls them into being and keeps them in being, and only so far as He exercises His creative and conservative power in their regard. He alone exists of Himself.

Sacrifice would seem to be a ritual expression of that fact. The idea of sacrifice is widespread throughout the human race. It runs all through the Old Testament and through the religions of ancient Greece and Rome, and is even more widespread than that. The idea which inspires it is that of taking a material thing, the best possession one has, the best sheep of the flock, the best fruits of the earth, and offering them to Almighty God in recognition of His complete dominion over everything, and destroying them as though to return their being to Him whence it came. It seems to be something instinctive in mankind to give back to Almighty God the best thing we have in recognition of our complete dependence upon Him.

Q276 **The Sacrifice of the New Law is the Holy Mass.**

The Holy Mass is the Sacrifice of the Body and Blood of Jesus Christ, really present on the altar under the appearances of bread and wine, and offered to God for the living and the dead. Q277

The Holy Mass is one and the same Sacrifice with that of the Cross, inasmuch as Christ, Who offered Himself, a bleeding victim, on the Cross to His heavenly Father, continues to offer Himself in an unbloody manner on the altar, through the ministry of His priests. Q278

The Sacrifice of the Mass is offered for four ends: first, to give supreme honor and glory to God; secondly, to thank Him for all His benefits; thirdly, to satisfy God for our sins and to obtain the grace of repentance; and fourthly, to obtain all other graces and blessings through Jesus Christ. Q279

Christianity, which we believe to be the complete and final revelation of God to mankind, here expresses completely and fully what so many other religions are striving after. We have as the center of our worship the Sacrifice of the Mass, in which bread and wine are offered to Almighty God and then by the words of consecration transformed into very God Himself, so that we are offering to the supreme Being the only worship commensurate with Him, the only worship worthy of Him—the worship of God by God.

We believe that the Mass is nothing less than the continual pleading of the Sacrifice of Calvary, the act of worship of the Father by the Son, the Son doing the complete will of the Father and thereby giving satisfaction for all the sins of the world and wiping them out. In spite of the complete visual difference between the appalling sight of Jesus Christ, God and Man, being tortured to death on the Cross and the ordinary appearance of the celebration of Mass in a Catholic Church, we believe that the sacrifice of the Mass is identical with the sacrifice of Calvary because of the complete identity of priest and victim in both.[24]

That Christ is the Victim at Mass is the consequence of our belief in the Real Presence. And Christ is the Priest because the human priest whom you see standing at the altar is really the means through which Christ our Lord acts. We believe that in every Sacrifice of the Mass it is He Who is offering the sacrifice, but that, since He has ascended into Heaven, He no longer has limbs here on earth to effect the Sacrifice of the Mass. So He deigns to use the hands and the tongue of one of His creatures, and to plead that sacrifice continually through him. Our Blessed Lord is the only Priest, as He is the only Victim. The priest standing at the altar is merely empowered to lend his limbs for Jesus Christ to act and work through.

No less surely is the priest lending his limbs to the mystical body of Christ, the Church. We believe, as you know, that in the Church there is a common priesthood, uniting the faithful with their heavenly King. "Ye are a royal priesthood." (*1 Peter* 2:9 AV). Those who are reborn in Baptism join in the offering of the Holy Eucharist by virtue of that royal priesthood, made effective through the celebrant.

But the Church needs an essentially different participation in Christ's priesthood in order to act in the person of Christ as He did at the Last Supper, consecrating the bread and wine into His own Body and Blood. Without this ministerial priesthood, those who possess the royal priesthood by Baptism would not have the Victim of Calvary to offer in the Mass. For this altogether unique participation in the priesthood, our Blessed Lord gave his Church the Sacrament of Holy Order, which we shall discuss in Chapter 17.

The identity between the Sacrifice of Calvary and the Sacrifice of the Mass is most beautifully set out in the preface that Adrian Fortescue wrote to his edition of the Missal, first published in 1912:

> The Church of Christ knows only one sacrifice, that of the Body and Blood of our Lord, offered for us, once only, on the Cross. The Jews had many sacrifices and many High Priests. We have one High Priest, Christ, and a better tabernacle, not made with hands. He went up once not with the blood of goats and calves, but with His own Blood, into the holy place, and found for us eternal redemption. (*Hebrews* 9:11). The Cross is the only sacrifice Christians know.
>
> Yet we are told that, in the kingdom of the Messiah, "in every place a sacrifice is made and a pure oblation offered to My name, says the Lord of Hosts." (*Malachi* 1:11). We have an altar, that is, a place of sacrifice, of which we only may eat. (*Hebrews* 13:10). In what sense can we be said to eat of the sacrifice of the Cross? We do so when we receive the Holy Eucharist. For in the Eucharist our Lord gives us not merely His Body and Blood, but the Body broken for us, the Blood shed for us (*1 Corinthians* 11:24; *Matthew* 26:28), that is His Body and Blood sacrificed.
>
> The Holy Eucharist, then, is a true sacrifice, the same sacrifice as that of the Cross. It is the

> same Victim, offered by the same High Priest, it is the same offering. It adds nothing to the one sacrifice offered once for all; it is that sacrifice. Christ, our High Priest Who lives ever to make intercession for us (*Hebrews* 7:25), continues in the Eucharist the act of oblation begun on the first Good Friday.
>
> In every sacrifice there are two elements, the slaying of the victim and the act by which this victim is offered to God. The slaying of the victim is in no sense repeated; if it were, there would be some ground for looking on the Mass as at least a repetition of the sacrifice. But the victim, our Lord was slain once only on the Cross, that can never be repeated: "Christ risen from the dead dies no more; death has no more power over him." (*Romans* 6:9). What continues now is the offering of that Victim, slain once outside the city in the reign of Tiberius. Nor is the Eucharist a repetition: it is a continuation of the same act of oblation. Our Lord offered Himself for us on the Cross, He did not cease to make that act of offering when the soldier pierced His side; living always as Priest to intercede for us, He still offers to His Father, through the ministry of His priest, the body broken, the blood shed once for all then.

There used always to be a crucifix standing over the altar where the sacrifice of the Mass was being offered, to remind us that the slaying took place once and for all at Calvary, though the pleading of that sacrifice continues. Every celebration of the Mass has, so to speak, a foot in the church in which it is being offered and a foot on the hill of Calvary.

The Mass is also a memorial of the Passion and Death of our Lord, for Christ at His last supper said: "Do this for a commemoration of Me." Q280

That is one more example of the fact that the Catechism was largely written in order to correct Protestant errors. In the great revolt of the sixteenth century the tendency was to jettison the whole concept of the Mass as a sacrifice and to concentrate on its being nothing more than a memorial of the Passion and Death of our Blessed Lord.

A memorial it cannot help but be. It does carry out our Blessed Lord's command, "Do this in memory of Me." (*Luke* 22:19). But the point that the Catechism has been concerned to emphasize is that the Mass is much more than a memorial. A memorial need be no more than an ineffective thing, whereas the sacrifice of the Mass is an effective pleading of the Sacrifice of Calvary. That is why the Church lays such emphasis on it as the central act of worship and is so insistent that you should try to attend it every Sunday at the very least.

That explains the Catholic tendency to enshrine in the Sacrifice of the Mass all the most important acts of our lives, so that the consecration of Bishops and the ordination of priests take place in the course of the celebration of the Mass, as did the coronations of kings in the past. The important act that is taking place is thus caught up into the supremely important act of the worship of God by God. Coming down to domestic matters, the celebration of a Catholic marriage is ideally enshrined in the celebration of the nuptial Mass. Everything of consequence that takes place in the world should be caught up into the supreme act of worship of Almighty God and made one with it.

We have now finished our consideration of the Holy Eucharist. And just to remind you of it in outline again, we started by considering the two respects in which the Holy Eucharist is unique among the Sacraments: first, that it contains the living Presence of Christ Himself, the author of grace, and secondly, that it is not only a Sacrament but also a sacrifice. We started by considering the objective nature of the Real Presence, particularly as foreshadowed in the sixth chapter of St. John. We then went on to see how that concept of the objective reality of Christ's Presence is explained by the Church in terms of transubstantiation; and, as a very convenient summary of that explanation and of its consequences, I recommended to you the *Lauda, Sion* of St. Thomas Aquinas, who explains them so lucidly.

We then went to consider that the Holy Eucharist is unique in another respect—that it is also a sacrifice. We considered a sacrifice as being an instinctive reaction on the part of mankind seeking to express in liturgical or ritual form the realization that all things depend upon Almighty God for their very being. Men have, throughout the ages, taken the best thing they have and offered it in sacrifice to Almighty God as a symbol of His complete sovereignty and dominion and have then destroyed it, thereby symbolizing the return of the created thing to the Creator. We believe that what so many religions seek to express is fulfilled completely in the Sacrifice of Calvary, the only completely satisfying worship of Almighty God. For Calvary is the worship of God by God, the complete submission and surrendering of the Son to the Father in fulfillment of the Father's will.

CHAPTER 16

The Sacrament of Penance

NOW we are going on to the Sacrament of Penance, commonly called Confession. Once again we start with a definition:

> **Penance is a Sacrament whereby the sins, whether mortal or venial, which we have committed after Baptism are forgiven.** Q281

God's forgiveness is clearly paramount, so it is not surprising to find that the Church now refers to this Sacrament as "the Sacrament of Reconciliation."

Once again we see the consistency and the coherence of the whole of the Christian revelation as propounded by the Catholic Church. The necessity of the Sacrament of Penance or Reconciliation depends on the possibility of our committing sin after Baptism. Baptism is our initial integration into Christ, but it leaves the will free. Even after we have been integrated into Christ in the Sacrament of Baptism, we still have free will and can divert our will from the will of Christ thereby separating ourselves from Him.

The sixteenth-century Protestant tradition rejects the concept of Confession and the Sacrament of Penance altogether, partly through being misled by a view of the priest as standing between Creator and creature—Catholics, of course, see the priest as a channel for God's grace, not an obstacle to it—and partly for a reason that is fundamentally philosophical rather than theological. The divergence stems from differing ideas about free will. The Catholic Church teaches that our wills are free and remain free, however conditioned, for the whole of our lives. Until our dying day we can bring our will to the will of Almighty God or we can divert it from His will. That diversion is what sin is—the turning of the will and mind away from the will and mind of the Creator. But in the extreme Calvinist view, the man who has accepted Christ's salvation, and is saved, not only will not but cannot sin again. If he does sin again, it is explained by the fact that his conversion cannot have been genuine. Thus, if you hold the doctrine of justification by faith alone, first stated by Luther and developed by Calvin, and if you believe that in a moment of conversion your will is fixed unalterably in Christ, you will see no need for any remedial Sacrament to restore you to God's grace.

The main object of the Sacrament of Penance is to restore us to God's grace when by willful sin we have forfeited it. Penance is the means whereby our mind and will is reconciled with the mind and will of Almighty God, so that we are restored to the life of grace and reintegrated into Christ's mystical body. But over and above that principal object of Christ's institution of the Sacrament of Penance, there is the secondary object of increasing the grace of God in the soul.

The Catechism continues:

The Sacrament of Penance increases the grace of God in the soul, besides forgiving sin; we should, therefore, often go to Confession. Q282

All the Sacraments can be said to have two objects. They each have a principal object—the immediate and obvious one of Baptism is to integrate us into Christ, of the Holy Eucharist to feed us with Christ, of the Anointing of the Sick to strengthen us when we are ill and to prepare us for the passage from time to eternity. And they each have a secondary object—to increase the grace of God in the soul. The two Sacraments which we can and should go on receiving constantly are the Holy Eucharist and the Sacrament of Penance. A phrase which you may have heard Catholics using is "going to the Sacraments," by which, of course, they mean those two. Our life in Christ depends principally on our reception of them and on the frequency and fervor with which we receive them. So the Catechism, in its answer to Question 282, very properly emphasizes that "the Sacrament of Penance increases the grace of God in the soul, besides forgiving sin; we should, therefore, often go to Confession."

You hear people say—sometimes even Catholics—that whereas in earlier ages people went to Confession only to have grave sins forgiven, there is a tendency today to go to Confession too frequently as a matter of rote. It always amuses me to see how critics of that type claim what they call "insights" for themselves, never allowing insights to earlier periods of the Church's development. No doubt the Sacrament of Penance was received less frequently in earlier ages than has been the case for many centuries. But the Church is constantly seeing more and more in the truths she has always held, and is constantly making more and more use of them. Over the centuries she has come to see the enormous value of the Sacrament of Penance for its secondary object—to increase the grace of God in the soul. So the practice among fervent Catholics, even if they are leading exemplary lives, of going to Confession once a week is one to be encouraged.

I always urge people when they start leading Catholic lives never to let a month go by without going to Confession. People in their first fervor often think that the practice I am suggesting makes only very moderate demands. I believe firmly in the value, at the beginning of a Catholic life, of setting oneself the ideal of unwavering adherence to a moderate practice which one will be able to follow throughout life. Add to that practice as much as your fervor prompts you to, but never, never depart from it At all times do as much as you can for the deepening of your spiritual life, but always with the safety net of a firm but not too demanding commitment. Therefore start with the fixed resolution of going to Confession and receiving Holy Communion, say, on the first Sunday of every month. Do not be discouraged by the critics who say that doing anything by rote is mechanical and valueless. Things that you leave to the inspiration of the moment are very likely to be neglected.

This is particularly true of Confession. If you go absolutely regularly it does not become the bugbear that it may become for some people, especially for those who leave it until they are conscious of having committed a mortal sin. It is much more difficult to go then—rather like a visit to the dentist. If you go regularly, there is seldom anything dramatically serious to be done.

In *The End of the House of Alard* by Sheila Kaye-Smith (London: Cassell, 1923; page 163 of the 1925 Uniform

Edition), Miss Jenny Alard, daughter of the local squire, is talking to a yeoman farmer:

> She looked at his hands. . . . They were clean, but not as Peter's or Jim's or her father's hands were clean; they suggested effort rather than custom—that he washed when he was dirty in order to be clean rather than when he was clean in order to prevent his ever being dirty.

She might have been describing the value of regular Confession. The Catechism continues:

> **Our Lord instituted the Sacrament of Penance when He breathed on His Apostles and gave them power to forgive sins, saying: "Whose sins you shall forgive, they are forgiven."** Q283
>
> **The priest forgives sins by the power of God, when he pronounces the words of absolution.** Q284
>
> **The words of absolution are: "I absolve you from your sins, in the name of the Father, and of the Son, and of the Holy Spirit."** Q285
>
> **Three conditions for forgiveness are required on the part of the penitent—Contrition, Confession and Satisfaction.** Q286

The Catechism treatment of this section always strikes me as a little surprising in that it gives the three conditions required on the part of the penitent, without mentioning those conditions required on the part of the priest. On the part of the penitent they are Contrition, Confession and Satisfaction. It is unfortunate that those words, like so many of the technical words used in the Catechism, have very different meanings in ordinary speech.

Contrition, with which we begin, is the basic condition:

Q287 **Contrition is a hearty sorrow for our sins, because by them we have offended so good a God, together with a firm purpose of amendment.**

I prefer the use of the word "sorrow" rather than "contrition," which is a remoter word than "sorrow."

Q288 **A firm purpose of amendment is a resolution to avoid, by the grace of God, not only sin but also the dangerous occasions of sin.**

Q289 **We may obtain a hearty sorrow for our sins by earnestly praying for it, and by making use of such considerations as may lead us to it.**

There appears to be a slight stylistic difference at this point in the Catechism, which for the most part is extraordinarily simple and straightforward in its language. Answer 289 lacks the vigor of the language of the rest of the Catechism.

Q290 **This consideration concerning God will lead us to sorrow for our sins: that by our sins we have offended God, Who is infinitely good in Himself and infinitely good to us.**

Q291 **This consideration concerning our Saviour will lead us to sorrow for our sins: that our Saviour died for our sins, and that those who sin grievously "crucify again to themselves the Son of God, making Him a mockery."** (*Hebrews* 6:6)

Q292 **Sorrow for our sins, because by them we have lost heaven and deserved hell, is sufficient when we go to Confession.**

Now, all those questions are concerned with sorrow for sin, or, as the Catechism calls it, "contrition." It is important to stress that, though the Catechism gives the reasons for sorrow which may move your feelings, we are in this matter not really concerned with feelings at all.

Sorrow for sin is an act of the will. I have already emphasized that on the last day we shall each be judged only by the use we have made of our own mind and our own will, the two things we can control. We can control our feelings only very slightly and at most indirectly. We are never bound to feel anything at all. Plainly it is infinitely easier to will what you also feel, and so, as I have mentioned earlier, you will find in the Missal a prayer for the gift of tears. Such a feeling of sorrow is a great help to being sorry. But being sorry is an act of the will: you bring back your will to the will of Almighty God and determine never again to abuse that supreme gift of free will that He has given you. You are determined to use your will for ever after in the promotion of His will and purpose.

So in Contrition we are concerned with bringing back our will to the will of Almighty God. By all means ask to have feelings corresponding to that resolution, for plainly it is very much easier to will what you also feel. The great thing is to will what Almighty God wills.

Such a resolution inevitably includes what the Catechism calls a "firm purpose of amendment." Unless you really mean to avoid sin in the future, you cannot be said to be bringing your will back to the will of Almighty God. But remember that we are not required to prophesy for the future but to will in the present moment. We are not saying, when we make an act of Contrition,

"I shall never sin again." Who knows, seeing how weak

we are? No, what we are saying is, "I will never sin again." What matters is the fixed resolution of my will here and now never to offend Almighty God. And by His grace I am determined not to offend Him again. I am not saying it will never happen; so if by weakness I fall into sin again it does not mean my act of will at this moment was insincere.

Remember that when critics say, as they often do, "When you have fallen into sin again, what reality was there in your former sorrow?" it is like asking a man who has fallen sick, "Of what value was your determination to preserve your health?" The parallel is inexact, as illness is hardly voluntary.

The Catechism now goes on to distinguish between perfect and imperfect contrition:

Q293 **Perfect contrition is sorrow for sin arising purely from the love of God.**

Q294 **Perfect contrition has this special value: that by it our sins are forgiven immediately, even before we confess them, but nevertheless, if they are serious, we are strictly bound to confess them afterwards.**

Therefore you should make an act of perfect contrition every single night of your life before you go to bed. Examine your conscience, cast your mind back over the day and try to make an act of perfect contrition purely for the love of God, because He is perfection and goodness itself and we would do anything rather than offend Him. Do not let twenty-four hours pass with your being out of the love and friendship of Almighty God.

Of course, such an act of sorrow for sin implies doing what Almighty God wants you to do—to submit your sins to

Sacramental absolution. Let me stress again the importance of habit. If a day comes on which you have greatly offended Almighty God, which God forbid, and you are in the habit of making nightly an act of perfect contrition, you will have no difficulty in doing so. If you have not formed that habit, then when the time comes when you positively need to make an act of perfect contrition, you will find it more difficult.

The Catechism now turns to the second condition of the three required on the part of the penitent:

> **Confession is to accuse ourselves of our sins to a priest approved by the Bishop.** Q295

Implicit in that answer are the three conditions required on the part of the priest. First, he must be a validly ordained priest, with that power to forgive sins which Christ gave to His Apostles and which is conferred by the Sacrament of Holy Order. The Sacrament which makes a man a priest and empowers him to offer the Sacrifice of the Mass also gives him the power to forgive sins.

Secondly, the power which comes to a priest through ordination, which we shall discuss more fully in the next chapter, is, so to speak, held in suspense until he is licensed to exercise that power in a particular part of Christ's vineyard. This granting of jurisdiction, which is colloquially referred to as "having faculties," is the second condition for effective absolution.

There is a chain of command in the Church: the Pope has universal jurisdiction over the whole Church; a diocesan Bishop has jurisdiction in his own diocese; and he empowers priests to hear confessions and to preach within his diocese. These faculties are now given very much more widely than they were. When I was ordained, it was very exceptional to have faculties to hear confessions outside your own diocese. If you went out of the diocese and were asked to hear Confessions, you had to ask for faculties to do so. Now they are given much more widely; in our case on a national basis. But a priest going to another country or passing out of the jurisdiction where he has faculties has to obtain them from the local Ordinary. In case of necessity the Church supplies that jurisdiction which has not been formally granted.

The third condition is implied by the word "confession": that is, the priest must have knowledge of what he is forgiving.

The Catechism says:

Q296 **If a person willfully conceals a serious sin in confession he is guilty of a great sacrilege, by telling a lie to the Holy Spirit in making a bad confession.**

Christ's commission is to forgive and to retain or withhold forgiveness: "Whose sins you shall forgive, they are forgiven them: and whose sins you shall retain, they are retained." (*John* 20:23). A priest is not just a forgiving machine, turning out absolutions. He is a judge of the gravity of the sin, the personal responsibility of the sinner. This is an office he can exercise only with knowledge, and no one can provide the knowledge but the penitent. In cases when a person is dying or is the victim of an accident the priest gives absolution without first hearing Confession. This is called "conditional absolution" because it is given on the implicit condition that the person is in the right disposition to receive it. Absolution on the part of the priest needs corresponding contrition on the part of the penitent in order to be effective.

So the three conditions on the part of the priest are that he should be validly ordained, that he should have faculties and, normally, that he should have that knowledge with which the penitent alone can furnish him.

> **We have four things to do in order to prepare for Confession: first, we must heartily pray for grace to make a good Confession; secondly, we must carefully examine our conscience; thirdly, we must take time and care to make a good act of contrition; and fourthly, we must resolve by the help of God to renounce our sins and to begin a new life for the future.** Q297

That answer needs no comment beyond remarking, as I did when discussing Answer 294, that the fourth requirement is contained in the third. We now come on to the last condition required of the penitent:

> **Satisfaction is doing the penance given us by the priest.** Q298

In ordinary speech, "satisfaction" hardly means that. Here it is used in its original sense of "making good," which comes from the Latin word *satisfacere*.

It is curious that the distinction between the guilt of a sin and the violence which it has done to the balance of justice is a distinction which people make constantly in the conduct of ordinary life—as I remarked when we were discussing the doctrine of Purgatory in Chapter 9—but which they often fail to make when it comes to the things of God.

In ordinary life, as we know, if a man does something to hurt, offend, damage, wound or impoverish you, you may forgive him wholly and completely for the injury he has done you. But the fact of your having forgiven him and saying, "It is going to be between us as though this had never happened at all; I am going to wipe it out of my mind," is entirely compatible with wanting to be recompensed for the damage done. The forgiveness and the need for restitution or making good are two completely different things.

The same distinction holds in our relationship with Almighty God. Our sins are forgiven wholly, utterly and completely: Though your sins be as scarlet, yet they shall be whiter than snow. (*Isaiah* 1:18). They just are not there. They have gone. There is absolutely no feeling of tension between Almighty God and ourselves. But if He is a God of justice, He cannot say that the consequence of injustice need not be remedied.

So when our sins are forgiven in the Sacrament of Penance we are given a token penance—token indeed, seven Hail Marys or whatever it may be. We are given a prayer to say, or a work of charity to perform, as a token that we need to do something to put the matter right. We cannot just leave our injustices unremedied.

The Catechism now turns to a further way in which we can make satisfaction for our sins:

Q299 **The penance given by the priest does not always make full satisfaction for our sins. We should therefore try to add to it other good works and penances, and try to gain Indulgences.**

We simply have no means of judging how much or how little the token penance we are given is effective.

The present-day critics of the modern disciplinary practices of the Church, who want in many ways to return to the usages of the early Church, never seem to wish to return to the extremely severe canonical penances which used to be exacted, such as standing at the church door in penitential garb. As convicted criminals used to sit in the stocks, so those who had committed sins expiated them publicly. With the gradual abandonment of the discipline of the Church over the centuries, those practices have disappeared more and more. Certainly no one has recently suggested reviving them.

I think the last example of a canonical penance being imposed in the Church of England occurred in the parish of Fen Ditton near Cambridge on Sunday, 6 May 1849, when a man who had slandered the vicar's wife was made to stand in the pulpit. All the bargees came to support him and it ended in pandemonium.

The word "indulgence" is now likely to mislead people. As with "satisfaction," the word now conveys quite a different impression to the ordinary mind from the sense in which the Catechism uses it:

> **An Indulgence is a remission, granted by the Church, of the temporal punishment which often remains due to sin after its guilt has been forgiven.** Q300

So often Catholics make the mistake of thinking that they can expound or defend any Catholic doctrine out of context. To understand the theory and practice of indulgences, one must go back to two underlying doctrines. The first is the infinite merits of Christ. Because He is God, His redemption of the world is of such value that it infinitely outweighs all the sins of mankind. What is called "the treasury of the Church" is the infinite and superabundant merits of Christ. The second doctrine is that this overflowing of merit, like everything else that Christ won for us, is committed to the Church to dispense.

What the Church does in granting us an indulgence is to attach a specific share in the superabundant merits of Christ to a prayer or to the performance of a certain good work. It is nothing to do with the forgiveness of sin: it is the expiation of the injustice of it.

With hindsight it is easy to say that the Church's attempt to measure what she is doing has been open to misunderstanding. She chose, as a scale of value, to refer to the ancient days of canonical penance that I mentioned a moment ago. The phrase "one hundred days" indulgence means, "Let saying this prayer or performing this good work be to you as though you had performed a canonical penance for one hundred days." It does not mean that by saying that prayer you obtain leave to do what you like for one hundred days. Nor does it mean that one hundred days will be deducted from the time you will spend in Purgatory.[25]

We have covered four of the seven Sacraments—Baptism, Confirmation, the Holy Eucharist and Penance. That leaves us with the Sacrament of the Anointing of the Sick, Holy Order and Matrimony. Once again, I make two general observations.

The first concerns the way in which the Sacraments reflect two fundamental principles which lie at the root of all we believe, the twofold nature of man and the doctrine of the Incarnation. The first principle is that man is always moving on two planes at once, the physical and the spiritual. Remember the scholastic tag *nihil est in intel lectu nisi prius fuerit in sensu*—there is nothing in our minds which has not reached them though the gateway of the senses. And on the other hand the actions of the mind and the will need the senses for their expression. The Sacraments echo that fundamental nature of our being, since they are external signs carrying invisible and spiritual grace.

Again, the Sacraments echo the fundamental mystery of the whole Christian revelation, which is the Incarnation of our Lord and Saviour Jesus Christ. The characteristic of a Sacrament is that Almighty God uses material means, of themselves incapable of achieving the purpose for which He has designed the Sacrament, and only Almighty God can make them fulfill that purpose. In that sense the Incarnation will be seen as the supreme Sacrament, in that the Word, the Second Person of the Blessed Trinity, takes our nature and works our redemption in it and through it.

The other general observation is that I think it helpful to see all the Sacraments centering round the Holy Eucharist and forming its framework. The Holy Eucharist is as central to the whole sacramental system as the Incarnation—of which it is properly seen as the continuation—is to the whole dogmatic system.

CHAPTER 17

The Sacrament of the Sick, Holy Order and Matrimony

WE NOW come on to the last three of the seven Sacraments of the Church. The first of these is the Sacrament of the Anointing of the Sick:

This Sacrament is the anointing of the sick with holy oil, accompanied by prayer. Q301

The Sacrament of the Anointing of the Sick is given when we are in danger of death by sickness. Q302

The effects of the Sacrament of the Anointing of the Sick are to comfort and strengthen the soul, to remit sin and even to restore health, when God sees it to be expedient. Q303

The authority in Scripture for the Sacrament of the Anointing of the Sick is in the Fifth Chapter of St. James, where it is said: "Is any one sick among you? Let him bring in the priests of the Church and let them pray over him, anointing him with oil in the name of the Lord. And the prayer of faith shall save the sick man, Q304

and the Lord shall raise him up; and if he be in sins they shall be forgiven him."

Once again, you will notice in that Sacrament the common characteristic of all, that the means whereby the Sacrament is administered, the holy oil, is a material means.

The first object of the Sacrament of the Sick is to strengthen the soul for the awful passage from time, which is familiar to us, to eternity, which is wholly unknown. As with all the Sacraments which denote spiritual strengthening, the outward sign of it is anointing. We have seen this already in Confirmation and we shall see likewise how in Holy Order oil is used, though it is not the principal outward sign of that Sacrament. In the Anointing of the Sick the senses are anointed, with prayers that by this anointing we may be forgiven the sins we have committed through the abuse of those senses through using the gifts of Almighty God in a way that is contrary to His design and purpose.

The secondary object of the Sacrament of the Sick is to forgive sins. In the case of people who die unconscious or who are for some other reason unable to make their Confession, anointing carries with it the forgiveness of sins to those who are in a proper disposition to receive such forgiveness.

The third object of the Sacrament is the possible restoration to health or improvement in health of the recipient. Anyone with any pastoral experience will remember occasions when the Sacrament of the Sick has had this effect of improving the recipient's health. A skeptic may attribute this to the psychological effect of composing the mind of the sick person to give all his strength to seeking recovery;

but whatever the reasons, natural or supernatural, it is not an uncommon phenomenon to see people improving very markedly as a result of receiving the Sacrament.

For that reason it is important to receive anointing early in an illness and not just at the last gasp. In that respect the old name for the Sacrament—Extreme Unction—does rather suggest that it should be received in extremis, at the very last moment of life, whereas it should really be received as soon as there is, as the Catechism says, "danger of death by sickness." And the Sacrament is also given to those who are permanently sick or disabled in some way. So the name now used, the "Anointing of the Sick," is probably a better one.

As soon as the doctor shakes his head and says, "I don't like the way things are going," that is the time to call in a priest to anoint the sick person. And if you are in such a position yourself, that is the time for you to ask for the Sacrament of the Sick.

Plainly the possible consequence of restoring health is far more likely to be effective earlier in the illness than at the last moment of one's life.

The Sacrament of the Anointing of the Sick cannot be received before going into battle, however likely or certain the prospect of death, nor before being executed. It can only be received when the recipient is actually sick. Because it is sometimes the case that apparent death is not coincident with actual death, people are generally anointed immediately after death in an accident, in battle or even on the scaffold.

So much for the Anointing of the Sick. With that we finish our consideration of the five Sacraments which, we believe, are by God's intention and design of universal application. Everyone, in God's intention and design, should be baptized and confirmed, should receive our Blessed Lord in the Holy Eucharist, should have his sins forgiven in Confession and should receive the Sacrament of Anointing when he is sick and in danger of death.

We now turn to the first of the two Sacraments of special states of life:

Q305 **Holy Order is the Sacrament by which bishops, priests and other ministers of the Church are ordained and receive power and grace to perform their sacred duties.**

We have considered already that, in the celebration of the Holy Eucharist, an ordained priest is necessary. The sacrifice can be offered only by a person empowered to do so. And we have seen in our quotation from Dr. Adrian Fortescue in Chapter 15 that in the Holy Sacrifice of the Mass the priest and victim are both Christ Himself. It is that fact which gives the Holy Eucharist its complete identity with Calvary. The victim is plainly our Blessed Lord Himself under the appearance of bread and wine. The priest is no less surely our Blessed Lord Himself, deigning to exercise His priesthood through the hands and lips of one of His own creatures. So the priest standing at the altar is there as the human means through which Christ exercises His priesthood.

There is, as we have seen, a general priesthood in the whole Christian people, precisely because we are all, by our membership of the Church, incorporated into Christ, the great High Priest. All the baptized share in the priesthood of Christ. They offer, as He did, prayers and supplications, even the sacrifice of the Mass "in Him, with Him, through Him." But only ordained priests offer "with Him, in Him and through Him" at Mass by consecrating the victim. This is theirs through sharing Christ's priesthood for a different kind of purpose. The Sacrament of Holy Order empowers a priest to offer the Holy Sacrifice of the Mass on behalf of the whole Christian people. He is, so to speak, their mouthpiece, through whom the priesthood is effectively exercised, as well as standing in the place of Christ Himself, sharing His effective priesthood.

The Sacrament in which the priest receives his priestly power is what we call the Sacrament of Holy Order. I mentioned that in this Sacrament holy oil is used to anoint the hands which are to be used to hold very God Himself, but that anointing is not the means by which the Sacrament is bestowed, nor even is the handing of the chalice to the priest in the course of ordination. The Sacrament of Holy Order is conveyed by the laying-on of hands by a Bishop.

Alone among priests, Bishops have the priesthood in a form which allows them to communicate that power. The episcopate is therefore rightly referred to as "the fullness of the priesthood." The Church teaches that the Apostles were all Bishops. It would appear that from very early times the priesthood was transmitted sometimes in its fullness, sometimes in that limited form which does not convey the power of transmission, and that the distinction between the episcopate and the priesthood lies in that limitation. But the limitation must not be thought of as merely an administrative convenience—as anyone might think who remembers Dr. Fisher, when he was Archbishop of Canterbury, urging Dissenters "to take Episcopacy into their system." It enshrines a profound theological truth, that the Bishops are the successors of the Apostles. To them, as to the Apostles, is committed the awful responsibility of proclaiming and safeguarding the Divine Revelation. They are the *Ecclesia*

Docens, the teaching Church. All others, priests and laity alike, are the *Ecclesia Discens*, the learning Church. That is why, as we have considered earlier, they enjoy a corporate or collegiate infallibility. That is why Catholics think it important that a book which purports to expound the Church's teaching should have—as this book has—an episcopal imprimatur. There is a real sense in which the Bishops are the Church. The Church could exist without the Pope—as she does between the death of one Pope and the election of his successor. If some worldwide cataclysm were to wipe out the entire clergy she would not cease to be. But if a cataclysm were to destroy the entire episcopate, she would cease to be. She would have lost the power of fulfilling her two essential functions—that of proclaiming Revealed Truth, and that of communicating God's grace through the Sacraments.

We now come on to the Sacrament of Matrimony. At the outset I want to stress that there is a very close parallel between the Sacraments of Matrimony and of Holy Order—the two Sacraments of states of life.

The priesthood is established as a means through which the grace earned by Christ for us is sacramentally communicated to men. Priests are the channels for that grace: the high function of every priest is to offer the Holy Sacrifice of the Mass and through it to bring down grace and salvation to the souls of men, pouring out that grace through the other Sacraments as well as through the Holy Eucharist itself. You see once again how the other Sacraments are related to the Holy Eucharist: they can be considered as further channels through which the Eucharistic power and grace is communicated to men.

As the priest is empowered by the Sacrament of Holy Order to communicate the supernatural life, so the communication of natural life is sanctified by the Sacrament of Matrimony. With that parallel between the priesthood and the married state in mind, we go on to the Catechism definition of Matrimony:

> **Matrimony is the Sacrament which sanctifies the contract of a Christian marriage, and gives a special grace to those who receive it worthily.** Q306
>
> **The Sacrament of Matrimony gives to those who receive it worthily a special grace, to enable them to bear the difficulties of their state, to love and be faithful to one another and to bring up their children in the fear of God.** Q307

Matrimony is not of Christian institution. It is that universal institution whereby a free man and a free woman freely bind themselves to live together as man and wife for the rest of their natural lives. So there are perfectly valid marriages outside the Christian tradition. Where a free man and a free woman so bind themselves they have contracted a valid marriage which has, or should have, binding consequences for the rest of their natural lives. They have entered upon a contract which no human power can undo. That is essentially what marriage is.

Our Blessed Lord takes this institution and, in effect, says, "Now, to My children this contract, this exchange of vows and promises, is a Sacrament. I am working in it and through it." Matrimony thus becomes a Sacrament and conveys grace to those who receive it, just as surely as the other Sacraments which our Blessed Lord has instituted.

With one possible exception, Matrimony is unique among the Sacraments in being the only one in which Christ takes a preexisting institution, something earlier than the

Christian revelation and as old as the human race, and makes it into a Sacrament by attaching to it the power of conveying the grace which He won for us on Calvary. The apparent exception is Baptism, which was foreshadowed by St. John the Baptist. In all the other Sacraments Christ takes something which had no effective significance before his time.

There is a second respect in which Matrimony is unique among the Sacraments: it is the only one in which the recipients administer the Sacrament to each other. The parish priest, or his deputy, is there merely as the Church's official witness. He does not confer the Sacrament as he does in, shall we say, Penance and Extreme Unction, or as a bishop does in Holy Order. In Matrimony the partners themselves are the ministers of the Sacrament. Each stands in a Christ-like relationship to the other; each is the channel through which the grace of Almighty God reaches the other. The husband is the minister of the Sacrament to the wife, the wife to the husband.

The main object of the institution of marriage is, of course, the procreation of the human race. The Sacrament of Matrimony sanctifies that activity by which men and women share with Almighty God the sublime work of creation, the transmission of life.

But procreation must never be separated from education. Many of the lower animals, as we know, conceive and bear their young and, within a very short time—months, days or even hours, leave them to fend for themselves. Not so with human beings. They positively need their parents for the first decade or more of their lives in order to have food, shelter and upbringing. The indissolubility of marriage comes from the absolute necessity of children having this complete security, psychologically, physically and educationally. The stability of the marriage of their parents is the fundamental thing that children need. It should be something as little open to question as that the sun will rise tomorrow; it should be something which is the background to their lives, which is never questioned at all, which comes not from their receiving an assurance that their parents will not separate, but from the very possibility never even crossing their minds.

Thus the indissolubility of marriage is not the consequence of ecclesiastical legislation but is in the very nature of things. You hear people saying, "Oh, Catholics are not allowed to divorce," as though ecclesiastical law had forbidden it. But no one who is validly married can divorce. The bond is still there in the sight of Almighty God. The bringing of children into this world must never be separated from bringing them up in the love and knowledge of Almighty God. These are both aspects of one activity.

And here a much earlier consideration affords a parallel. We saw that the creative and the conservative activity of Almighty God are really two exercises of the same power. It requires the creative power of Almighty God to bring things into being; and it requires no less His conservative power to keep them in being. Things do not become necessary in the philosophical sense merely through having been created. Just as the act of begetting is, so to speak, a sharing in the creative activity of Almighty God, so can the educational role of parents be taken as a reflection of His conservative activity.

Some people say, "Well even granted that," which they are reluctant to do, "why should a childless marriage not break up?" The reason is that once you concede a false principle it is impossible to control its consequences. Hard cases make bad law. Once you start saying that childless marriages can be dissolved, there is a likelihood of people postponing the begetting of children until they feel sure that their marriage is "a success," thereby militating against its success. Even worse, it is not hard to imagine that this false principle would be a powerful temptation to infanticide.

Christ took the existing institution of marriage and made it a Sacrament. His Church therefore controls and legislates for marriage in regard to her own children. We now consider those regulations:

Q308 **It is a sacrilege to contract a marriage in serious sin or in disobedience to the laws of the Church and, instead of a blessing, the guilty parties draw upon themselves the anger of God.**

Q309 **A "mixed marriage" is a marriage in which only one partner is a Catholic.**

Q310 **The Church does not encourage mixed marriages and considers them dangerous.**

Q311 **The Church sometimes permits mixed marriages by granting a dispensation, and under special conditions.**

Q311a **The Catholic partner of a mixed marriage promises to do everything possible to preserve the faith and to have all children of the marriage baptized and brought up in the Catholic religion**

and, I would add, to bring the non-Catholic partner to a knowledge of the truth.

Now, I want to emphasize how in all these matters where the Church is making laws for her own children they are laws which she makes and can alter. In very recent times she has certainly made much easier the conditions surrounding mixed marriages: in earlier editions of the Catechism they were described as "unlawful and pernicious." She always, and rightly, thinks that they can be dangerous; dangerous not so much to the faith of the Catholic partner as to the faith of the children. How can a child have that absolutely firm, unquestioning faith when he sees his parents disagreeing about the most important thing in life? If he sees his father going one way and his mother going the other he cannot but have a divided mind himself.

The regulations have been made very much easier with regard to the place of marriage. Until the recent easing of the law, all marriages of Catholics had to take place in a Catholic church before the parish priest or his deputy. Now the Church, in certain circumstances, allows marriages to be performed by non-Catholic ministers in non-Catholic churches. This is a purely practical piece of legislation dictated by expediency, leaving the underlying theology unaffected. This needs to be emphasized because many Catholics are distressed and bewildered by the change, fearing that such marriages are invalid, as indeed they were before the change in legislation.

It is in the Church's power to legislate for her own children with regard to the Sacraments and then to dispense them from that legislation or to vary it. That is why I emphasized that marriage is not a Christian institution but that, since Christ has taken marriage and has made it a Sacrament for Christians, the administration of the Sacrament is controlled by the Church.

As we have seen, permanence is not merely a Christian ideal to be aimed at—it is of the very essence of marriage. The only way in which what appears to be a marriage can be dissolved is by finding some flaw in the actual contract itself.

Q312 **No human power can dissolve the bond of marriage, because Christ has said: "What God has joined together, let no man put asunder."**

PART III

CHARITY

CHAPTER 18

The First Three Commandments

WE NOW begin our consideration of the third of the three theological virtues, Charity. Let me remind you of the way the Catechism is arranged. The opening seeks to establish the foundation of our faith in natural reason before we come on to the question of revelation. That foundation is summarized as the existence of God, His nature, our own immortality, our free will and our consequent responsibility, and is suggested rather than summarized in the first eight questions of the Catechism. All the rest of the Catechism is concerned with the three theological virtues of Faith, Hope and Charity, which are directed to Almighty God. In practicing them, we have fulfilled the whole duty of man.

We considered Faith as that gift of Almighty God whereby we are enabled to believe in Him and to accept His revelation. Under that heading we went through the Creed. Then we turned to Hope, that gift of God whereby we trust Him to play His part in our salvation if we play our part. Under the heading of Hope we considered the Sacraments, moving them from the place in which the Catechism puts them, because the chief way of obtaining the grace of Almighty God, which is the ground of our hope, is prayer and the holy Sacraments.

That leaves us now with the third theological virtue, Charity:

Q169 **Charity is a supernatural gift of God by which we love God above all things, and our neighbor as ourselves for God's sake.**

Once again we want to emphasize the word "gift" as we did with Faith and Hope. The word "gift" carries with it by implication the need of a free offer on the part of Almighty God, the giver, and a free acceptance on our part as the recipients, so that the virtue of Charity requires an action of the will on our parts, as do the virtues of Faith and Hope. We saw with Faith and Hope that the essence of a gift is free offering and free acceptance. Almighty God offers us the gift of Faith whereby we can accept His revelation. He offers us the gift of Hope whereby we are assured that He will do His part in our salvation. Both of those require an act of acceptance on our part—an act of the will and not of the feelings.

What is true of Faith and Hope is true no less of Charity. In the last analysis, Charity requires an act of the will on our part, by which we love God above all things and our neighbor as ourselves for God's sake. That needs to be constantly emphasized, because Charity, or love—and they are synonymous in the New Testament—is, as you know, nowadays generally spoken of as though it were an intense and passionate form of liking. So we need to distinguish between liking and loving, which are two completely different things.

Liking lies in the feelings, the feelings which we can so little control, or at most control indirectly. We cannot help but like certain persons, things, places and occupations. Liking is an entirely instinctive reaction on our part. Since it is entirely instinctive, there can be no virtue in it. Likewise there is nothing wrong, any more than there is anything right, in liking anything at all. It is an action as instinctive as shutting one's eye if a fly goes into it. We can do something to educate and to change our feelings to some extent, but ultimately liking is an instinctive activity for which we cannot really be held morally responsible.

Now, loving is completely and absolutely different to liking. By love we understand sinking our will in the will of the beloved. That is what love means—to will what the one you love wills. That, of course, is why love is supremely unselfish. Liking has no moral characteristic, but love is the greatest of all virtues. It is quite distinct from liking because it lies in the will, whereas liking lies in the feelings. Plainly, if you can get love and liking to coincide, so very much the easier. It is much easier for us to love the things which we like. But if you cannot get them to coincide, do not worry at all. You and I will never be judged by what we liked or disliked. We shall be judged for all eternity by what we have loved, by the use we have made of our will, by whether we have chosen the object of our love aright when we have sunk our will in the will of another person.

St. Paul tells us, "And now there remain Faith, Hope, Charity, these three: but the greatest of these is Charity." (*1 Corinthians* 13:13). It is the greatest of the virtues because it necessarily includes the other two. It is possible to have Faith without having Hope or Love. It is possible to have Hope, but not to have Faith or Love. But it is quite impossible to have Love without including Faith and Hope. When we love someone and decide to sink our will in the will of that person, we have complete faith and trust in him. Love takes up the other two virtues within itself and is the greatest of them.

Now, if loving is sinking your will in the will of another, there is only one person whom we can love without any qualification at all—Almighty God. With all creatures, when we love them it must always be with a qualification, with a condition that the creature concerned will never will us to do anything that we should not do. It is true that the more highly you revere another person the more completely can you say, "It is inconceivable that this person will ever wish me to do what is evil." But still, with a human being there must always be that qualification. With God, and God alone, there is absolutely no qualification of our love for Him. That is what we mean by loving God above all things. It is nothing to do with liking. There is hardly a sense in which we can attach any meaning to "liking" Almighty God. We can only like the things we experience, but we can love Almighty God with complete abandon, knowing that He is the highest good, the very Good itself; that he is, as St. John tells us, Love. The Catechism puts it,

Q170 **We must love God because He is infinitely good in Himself and infinitely good to us.**

And with Him we can say, "Dear God, I want to sink the whole of my will in your will, willing what You will." We say in the Our Father, "Thy will be done on earth as it is in heaven." Every power of mind and will that I can control is sunk in the will of Almighty God, which is its proper end and object. And that is what loving is all about—sinking our will in His.

What we do when we love a creature is to will for that person the highest possible good, which is what Almighty God wills for him. So the love of any person, properly understood, can never be in opposition to the will of Almighty God, nor in opposition to the love we owe to any other person. We are bound to love all persons precisely because we love Almighty God. And He has brought them into being because He loves them and He wills for them the greatest possible happiness for all eternity, a happiness beyond our power to conceive. What we are bound to do is to will the same for them. Plainly the degree of intensity with which we will happiness for them will depend on how close they are to us. You are bound to love those who are obviously allied to you—your wife, your children, your parents. You are bound to will for them what you will for everyone, but with a greater degree of intensity. But what you will for them is the same. That is why there cannot be any contradiction between any real love and any other real love.

People talk as though there may be a tension between different sorts of love, so that we have to strike a balance between them. But no, if you start at the right end—the love of Almighty God—all other love is seen to flow out from it. All other love cannot help but be compatible with the love of Almighty God. And whenever there seems to you to be a tension between one love and another, be very sure of this, that one or the other cannot really be love. It may be vanity or lust or infatuation or a hundred and one other things masquerading as love, but love it cannot be. There cannot be any stress, strain or incompatibility in your willing for every human being what Almighty God wills for them.

So by love we mean the complete sinking of our will in the will of Almighty God and the willing of what He wills—first for ourselves because our soul is the tiny part of creation committed to us, and then for all others.

We have remarked earlier how the names of the virtues have been so debased in ordinary speech that their meaning is in great danger of being transformed. We saw how Faith is often taken to mean believing something for no particular reason, whereas we mean by it believing something for the best of all reasons; that we believe Almighty God has revealed it. And Hope is often spoken of as though it were nothing stronger than "wish," whereas we mean by it "sure and certain hope," a trust that Almighty God will do His part in our salvation if we do ours.

So it is with Charity. In ordinary speech, Charity has come down to meaning the corporal works of mercy, and is often used in an invidious sense, as when people say, "I don't want your charity"—terrible when you think of what Charity really means! How can you not want that love from all other people which I have been describing—namely, that they should will for you what Almighty God wills for you? Further, "love" in ordinary speech has often come to mean nothing but lust, from which we have seen it differs entirely. Lust is the most selfish and Love the most unselfish thing there is in life.

I hope that has helped to make clear that the word "love" has a coherent meaning very different from its current use. The Catechism, having told us what love is and how we must love God, then asks, "How do we show that we love God?" (q171). To those who think of love as an intense and passionate form of liking, the answer must come as quite a shock:

We show that we love God by keeping His commandments: for Christ says, "If you love Me, keep My commandments." Q171

Those who are surprised at our considering the Commandments under the heading of love have an entirely mistaken approach to them, thinking of them as irksome prohibitions, whereas though they are for the most part cast in the form of prohibitions—they are precise warnings against things that detract from our complete integrity and self-fulfillment. They are prohibitions only in the sense in which a warning against taking poison is a prohibition made in order to preserve life.

But the way in which we do fulfill ourselves is precisely by fulfilling the will of our Creator. He alone knows why He has brought us into the world. He alone can ultimately fulfill our every longing and desire, as a result of our having fulfilled His purpose in this life as far as we can. So it is under this general heading of charity, or love, that we consider the Ten Commandments, regarding them not as something restrictive but as something fulfilling. In the moral order, we fulfill ourselves by fulfilling the purpose for which we were brought into being. The only criterion of success or failure for a creature, is whether he has sought to fulfill or has endeavored to oppose the end for which the Creator created him. There can be no other.

The Catechism now lists the Ten Commandments and discusses each of them individually:

There are ten Commandments. Q172

Q173 **I am the Lord thy God, who brought thee out of the land of Egypt and out of the house of bondage.**

1. **Thou shalt not have strange gods before Me. Thou shalt not make to thyself a graven thing, nor the likeness of any thing that is in heaven above or in the earth beneath, nor of those things that are in the waters under the earth. Thou shalt not adore them nor serve them.**
2. **Thou shalt not take the name of the Lord thy God in vain.**
3. **Remember that thou keep holy the Sabbath day.**
4. **Honor thy father and thy mother.**
5. **Thou shall not kill.**
6. **Thou shalt not commit adultery.**
7. **Thou shalt not steal.**
8. **Thou shalt not bear false witness against thy neighbor.**
9. **Thou shalt not covet thy neighbor's wife.**
10. **Thou shalt not covet thy neighbor's goods** (*Exodus* 20:2–17)

The numbering makes it clear that the first sentence though it is confusingly included in the First Commandment by the Catechism in Answer 175, is not part of a Commandment but is the common preface to them all.

The Protestant numbering differs from that just given by dividing the first Commandment into two, one forbidding strange gods and the other forbidding graven images. Our version puts those two together because they are both concerned with one thing only: the sin of putting anything in the place of Almighty God; that is, the sin of idolatry. The Protestants also combine the Ninth and Tenth Commandments. Our numbering allows a parallel to be drawn between the Sixth and Ninth and between the Seventh and Tenth Commandments. The Sixth and Seventh are concerned with sins of action and the Ninth and Tenth with the sins of thought which give rise to them.

God gave the Ten Commandments to Moses in the Old Law, and Christ confirmed them in the New. Q174

That is perfectly true, but it may mislead you into thinking that the Ten Commandments date from their being given to Moses rather than that they are absolutely rooted in the nature of Almighty God and could not be other than they are. They do not depend for their sanction on their promulgation. They reflect the unchanging nature of Almighty God Himself, so that He Himself could not have altered or changed them. Had human nature not fallen there would have been no need to promulgate or clarify them. They were as effective and binding on mankind before their promulgation as after it. They are incapable of change and they apply not only to the chosen race or only to Christians but to all mankind. The law of Almighty God is in no wise arbitrary and is in this respect quite different from the laws of men, which so often are.

The Catechism now considers each Commandment individually, beginning with the First Commandment:

Q175 **The First Commandment is, "I am the Lord thy God, who brought thee out of the land of Egypt, and out of the house of bondage. Thou shalt not have strange gods before me. Thou shalt not make to thyself any graven thing, nor the likeness of any thing that is in heaven above, or in the earth beneath, nor of those things that are in the waters under the earth. Thou shalt not adore them nor serve them."**

Q176 **By the First Commandment we are commanded to worship the one, true and living God, by Faith, Hope, Charity and Religion.**

This answer was foreshadowed at the end of Chapter 1: To save my soul I must worship God by Faith, Hope and Charity, that is, I must believe in Him, I must hope in Him, and I must love Him with my whole heart (q8).

The word "religion," coming from the same Latin root as "ligament," means something which binds us to Almighty God. The three great links, of which Religion is the synthesis, are the three theological virtues of Faith, Hope and Charity.

Q177 **The sins against Faith are all false religions, willful doubt, disbelief or denial of any article of faith, and also culpable ignorance of the doctrines of the Church.**

This and the next three answers emphasize how the theological virtues are gifts accepted and maintained by acts of the will. In Chapter 12 I stressed the importance of seeing these gifts of Almighty God as living gifts, like a puppy or a pony, which if neglected will die but if nurtured will develop, rather than dead gifts like a book or a picture, given once and for all and requiring no cooperation from us.

Many Christians outside the Church have that "dead" view of Faith, thinking of it as a rational conviction which has been rationally achieved and which, if lost, can be regained by repeating that rational process. Such people consequently consider that if this cannot be done the original act of faith must have lacked validity.

Our concept of Faith as a gift that may thrive or wither depending on our care is quite different. Having accepted the gift of Faith by an act of the will we can lose it by an act of the will. To keep our faith requires not just the initial act of the will which is acceptance, but a constant cooperative activity. To think of Faith as rationally achieved by a process which, if valid, could be repeated to reach the same conclusion is to misunderstand the nature of the acceptance of the revelation of Almighty God by an act of the will.

A course of instructions in the Catholic Faith, such as this, has to be fitted to the need of the person who is being instructed, for he has to know that what is being offered for his acceptance is compatible with what he already knows. But he also needs to keep his knowledge of the Faith growing in step with an increasing knowledge of other things.

In Answer 177 we read about "culpable ignorance of the doctrines of the Church." Notice once again the emphasis on the will implicit in the word "culpable." Ignorance can be wholly innocent, but it becomes culpable when it is an act of the will: "I will not take the trouble," or, "I cannot be bothered."

Q178 **We expose ourselves to the danger of losing our Faith by neglecting our spiritual duties, reading bad books, and going to non-Catholic services.**

The new edition of the Catechism, in these ecumenical days, has left out "going to non-Catholic services." But a danger remains: our attendance can give the impression that we believe one religion is as good as another or that one presentation of Christianity is as good as another. And that, of course, is precisely what we do not believe.[13, 26]

We believe that the Catholic Church is the one authentic presentation of Christianity and, however close the approximation of the others to what the Church teaches, they cannot be the Church.

Answer 178 also emphasizes the need not only to take an intellectual interest in our Faith but to pray about it: to pray for light, to pray for understanding. To see more deeply into the mysteries of Almighty God is a gift to be asked for. How erroneous is the view that once you have lost your faith you can recover it again and again simply by a rational process! No, the living thing may simply die.

The Catechism now considers the sins against Hope:

Q179 **The sins against Hope are despair and presumption.**

This question might well have been placed in an earlier section of the Catechism, but we are now drawing together the threads of all that we have been saying as we consider the Commandments of God and the Commandments of the Church under the heading of Charity.

Despair is throwing up the sponge and saying, "No, whatever I do, Almighty God will not save me. I am damned." And despair is a very grave sin, because the three theological virtues require that we should respond to the grace of Almighty God throughout our lives, making acts of Faith, Hope and Charity to keep these virtues exercised and alive. Despair is saying, "No, I am not going to make acts of trust in Almighty God."

Presumption is going to the other extreme, making an excessive and therefore unfounded act of trust in Almighty God by saying, "Whatever I do, Almighty God is going to save me in the end. He is going to override my free will and however much I abuse it in life He will save me." That is equally untrue. What is required is that we should trust and continue to trust in Almighty God, doing what we can to justify that trust by our own lives.

The Catechism says,

> **The chief sins against Religion are the worship of false gods or idols, and the giving to any creature whatsoever of the honor which belongs to God alone.** Q180

When we encounter the First Commandment we are inclined to think immediately, "This does not apply to us. Members of the more advanced nations are not tempted to worship false gods or idols. The 'green eye of the yellow god' is not for us." Nothing could be more unfounded. We are effectively guilty of idolatry whenever we make anything that is not God, be it wealth, lust or power, the end or object of our lives:

> Before his senseless stocks and stones
> The heathen offers up his prayers.
> How better far advised are we
> Who worship rather stocks and shares.

A subtler form of idolatry occurs when we put a fellow-creature in the place of Almighty God—subtler because it can be disguised as altruism. A parent who idolizes a child, a child who idolizes a parent, is hoping to get from the object of his worship a fulfillment which only God can give.

Q181 **The First Commandment does not forbid the making of images but the making of idols, that is, it forbids us to make images to be adored or honored as gods.**

This answer is colored by the sixteenth-century controversy which led to a revival of the old heresy of iconoclasm. Images and statues were destroyed because of the possibility of their being worshiped idolatrously.

There is nothing wrong in the making of images. The sin occurs only if one worships an image as being the reality which it represents. The danger of this form of idolatry was a great bugbear to the old Protestant mind, as it is to some people still. But I have yet to find any Catholic, however uninstructed, who thinks that what he is praying to is that bit of plaster on the wall. Of course he is not, any more than when he keeps his wife's photograph on his desk he is expressing his love of that bit of paper. So it is with the images of the saints, of which, as you know, we Catholics made great use until we ourselves were visited by an outburst of iconoclasm.

Q182 **The First Commandment forbids all dealing with the devil and superstitious practices, such as consulting spiritualists and fortune-tellers, and trusting to charms, omens, dreams and suchlike fooleries.**

Plainly such practices dishonor Almighty God, to Whom alone all our faith and trust and love must be directed. All attempts contrary to His will to find out what He has concealed from us are a derogation of the majesty of Almighty God. It is one thing for Almighty God to use a dream for His purpose. It is quite another thing for us to try to interpret a dream as though it were a message from Almighty God.

So, too, with visions: Almighty God may wish, as we believe He has done both in the Old Law and the New, to communicate with His creatures, through a vision—a direct appeal to the senses. In the recent history of the Church there have been many cases of pretended—I use the word in its proper sense of "claimed"—visions, which the Church always examines with extreme caution and occasionally recognizes after examination as authentic, as she does the apparition of the Sacred Heart to St. Margaret Mary Alacoque at Parayle-Monial and the apparition of our Blessed Lady to St. Bernadette at Lourdes. But always, even when she establishes feasts in their honor, the Church says merely that in her judgment these visions or apparitions are authentic. Such judgments are in quite a different category from those truths which we have to accept by Faith. Of course, the majority of Catholics do accept them because the Church has said they may be recognized as authentic. But you would certainly not be committing a sin against Faith if you did not believe in them. In the very nature of things they cannot be part of divine revelation, since that revelation ended with the Apostolic era.

Sacrilege is the treating of any holy person, place or thing without the reverence due to it. If you commit an act of violence against a priest or take his life, the guilt of sacrilege is added to the sin of violence or murder. Sacrilege may also be committed against sacred things—churches, sacred vessels and the like.

Simony is named after Simon Magus, who offered the Apostles money to obtain their power of laying on hands and was roundly cursed by St. Peter for his pains. It is the attempt to buy or sell sacred things not for the material value which they may have but for their sacred character. For example, buying and selling a chalice for the value of its metal or precious stones is not sin at all, but when a price is offered for its sacred character the sin of simony is committed. Likewise the buying or selling of relics, or offering money in return for being ordained or consecrated, is trying to put a price on that which is above price.

Q184 **It is forbidden to give divine honor or worship to the Angels and Saints, for this belongs to God alone.**

Plainly that worship which we owe to God we owe to Him because He is the supreme good and we cannot give that worship to anyone else without idolatry. The uniqueness of the worship which we give to Almighty God goes back to the point which we considered early in Chapter 1—that He is Existence itself. God is the supreme Being Who alone exists of Himself and is infinite in all perfections (q17) and to Him we give an absolute and unqualified adoration.

Q185 **We should pay to the Angels and Saints an inferior honor or worship, for this is due to them as the servants and special friends of God.**

Though we use the word "worship" of the lesser respect we pay to those through whom Almighty God has chosen to work, it is a completely different thing from the adoration we owe to him alone. "Worship" means merely "veneration": it does not mean "adoration." Thus in the old marriage service the bridegroom said, "With my body I thee worship"; we speak of His Worship the Mayor, and quite rightly and properly we speak of worshipping our Blessed Lady, but we do not mean that in "worshipping" or venerating her we are according to her that adoration which is the tribute we pay to Almighty God alone.

We should give to relics, crucifixes and holy pictures a relative honor, as they relate to Christ and His Saints, and are memorials of them. Q186

We do not pray to relics or images, for they can neither see, nor hear, nor help us. Q187

The Second Commandment is, "Thou shalt not take the name of the Lord thy God in vain." Q188

By the Second Commandment we are commanded to speak with reverence of God and all holy persons and things, and to keep our lawful oaths and vows. Q189

The Second Commandment forbids all false, rash, unjust and unnecessary oaths, as also blaspheming, cursing and profane words. Q190

It is lawful to swear, or to take an oath only when God's honor or our own or our neighbor's good requires it. Q191

Perjury is calling Almighty God to witness the truth of what we are saying, when what we are saying is not true. It is hard to imagine a greater irreverence to Almighty God, Who is Truth itself, than to call upon Him to witness to the truth of a lie. Clearly that is a most heinous sin. What we ordinarily speak of as swearing and cursing is hardly to be thought of in that light. Generally with us it is little more than a bad habit, so that many people who swear in ordinary speech are not doing anything as awful as what I have just described.

On the whole the sort of perjury that may, alas, still continue is to be found in a court of law. Several times I have acted as chaplain to High Sheriffs and sat on the bench and seen witness after witness taking up the New Testament and swearing by Almighty God that what he is going to say is the truth, the whole truth and nothing but the truth—and then appearing to think he can say whatever will further his cause or secure his own acquittal.

We move on to the Third Commandment:

Q192 **The Third Commandment is, "Remember that thou keep holy the Sabbath day."**

Q193 **By the Third Commandment we are commanded to keep the Sunday holy.**

Q194 **We are to keep the Sunday holy by hearing Mass and resting from servile works.**

We are commanded to rest from servile works that we may have time and opportunity for prayer, going to the Sacraments, hearing instructions and reading good books. Q195

Now, the Third Commandment, which is the last of the three Commandments concerned with our direct duty to Almighty God, is the only one of them which has a two-fold aspect. All three are concerned with the moral law. This Third Commandment, over and above its concern with the moral law, also had in the Old Testament a ritual aspect. And we believe that that ritual aspect was completely abrogated, along with all the other ceremonies of the Old Law, by the New Covenant. What remains is our obligation to devote one day of the week to the solemn worship of Almighty God.

There is a certain inconsistency in those "Bible Christians" who contend that the ceremonial observances of the Old Law still have force and ignore the fact that the authority which tells us how to observe the holy day is the very authority that moved that holy day from the Saturday, the last day of the week, the day that is still observed by Jews, to the first day of the week. The Church moved the observance from the last day of the week, when Almighty God rested after the work of completing the Creation, to the first day of the week, when Christ rose from the dead. And it is the Church which tells us now how to make that day holy.

The first obligation imposed by the Church is to attend Mass on Sunday, an obligation that is gravely binding. Over and above that, we should try to devote some part of the day to other religious observances and to reading good books.

I find it very hard to give any exact meaning to "servile works." My interpretation is that the provision of the law which it expresses is directed to employers rather than to those who labor themselves. What is forbidden, as it seems to me, is really the employment of people in the work formerly done by slaves, and it therefore applies to those who employed them. Employers were bound to give their slaves that opportunity for keeping Sunday holy which free men can claim for themselves.

That completes our consideration of the three Commandments concerned with our direct duty towards Almighty God. The remaining seven Commandments are concerned with our duty towards Him as performed through His creatures. All the Commandments, then, are concerned with our duty towards Almighty God—the first three directly and the last seven indirectly—because all love springs from and returns to Almighty God Himself.

CHAPTER 19

The Fourth and Fifth Commandments

AS I HAVE explained before, the whole of the Catechism is constructed on the framework of the three theological virtues of Faith, Hope and Charity, which unite us directly to Almighty God. They are all gifts of Almighty God, required to be offered by Him, required to be received by us. We have recently been considering how "Charity" here means "Love," which in turn means sinking our will in the will of the beloved. The only Person Whom we can love without any reservation or qualification, because He is the very Good Himself, is Almighty God. We show that we love God by keeping His Commandments. We have seen that all the Ten Commandments are concerned with our duty to Almighty God, because we really have no other duty than our duty towards Him, from which our duty to all others is derived. We saw that, of the ten Commandments, the first three are concerned with fulfilling our duty directly to Him; and the last seven, which we are now beginning to consider, are concerned with our duty towards Him through our fellow creatures, so that we have that relationship with our fellow creatures which He wills.

Q196 **The Fourth Commandment is, "Honor thy father and thy mother."**

Q197 **By the Fourth Commandment we are commanded to love, reverence and obey our parents in all that is not sin.**

Q198 **We are commanded to obey not only our parents but also our bishops and pastors, the civil authorities and our lawful superiors.**

Q199 **We are bound to assist our parents in their wants, both spiritual and temporal.**

Q200 **We are bound in justice to contribute to the support of our pastors; for St. Paul says, "The Lord ordained that they who preach the Gospel should live by the Gospel."** (*1 Corinthians* 9:14)

Q201 **The duty of parents towards their children is to provide for them, to instruct and correct them and to give them a good Catholic education.**

Q202 **The duty of masters, mistresses and other superiors is to take proper care of those under their charge and to enable them to practice their religious duties.**

Q203 **The Fourth Commandment forbids all contempt, stubbornness and disobedience to our parents and lawful superiors.**

As we shall find with the Fifth and Sixth Commandments, the Catechism's interpretation of the Fourth Commandment is much wider than the mere words might suggest. Under the heading of "thy father and thy mother," the Catechism is concerned with the whole of our duty towards society and our attitude towards authority, because the family is the basic model of society. A consideration of our duty and an understanding of its full meaning leads us immediately to a consideration of our place in society and the duties that that position involves.

Man alone in the visible universe has a value which transcends time and place and continues for eternity. Each individual man is an immortal expression of the will of Almighty God. For that reason he is worthy of our worship and veneration. In the whole, visible universe every other thing that we know will disappear completely, as though it had never been. But each individual human being will go on for ever and ever. The value of each individual is immeasurable and eternal. And yet the first thing we realize about man is that he cannot exist alone. Man differs completely from the lower animals and from the whole universe of mere objects, as we have already seen, in that he uniquely echoes Almighty God in having a mind and a will. He also differs completely from the lower animals in that he is unable to fend for himself for the first decade or more of his natural life.

We enter the world in a society and a family not of our choosing. Without it we should not survive at all. Man comes into a society and a family and depends upon them for shelter, food, drink and clothing. Man simply would not survive his birth if it were not for a family. Not only does he need his family at the physical level but he also needs it for the growth of his own personality, for love, understanding, communication with others and development of the power of speech. A man who is unable to communicate with others hardly develops at all.

That relationship sets up a whole chain of rights and

duties between us and society. The family has the duty to provide us with such shelter, food and drink as it can, and with love and care. And that duty is morally binding upon our parents. Consequently we have an exactly reciprocal moral duty of obedience to those who provide us with these necessities and who therefore have authority over us. We have a duty of obedience towards those who provide us with the very things we need to grow and develop and realize ourselves.

On both sides, the authority and the duties we have been talking about should be transfigured by love—by that real desire on both sides to sink our will into the will of the beloved, to do what is best for the beloved and to do for the beloved what Almighty God would wish for him. The whole of that relationship is not just a stark matter of authority and obedience, but is transfigured both ways by love.

The fulfillment of the duty of parents to their children and of children to their parents is reinforced by a moral obligation which is something binding on us by the law of Almighty God. The duty we are talking about is a duty to Almighty God, done through His creatures. Just as, though He Himself has created us through His creatures, it is none the less He Who is creating us, so when we seek to fulfill these social duties and obligations we are doing it primarily for the love of Almighty God, because it is His will.

Now, that is the basic pattern of all society, a pattern which we believe was instituted by Almighty God. The authority of the family does not depend on choice or consent but is something in the very nature of our being. But notice this: just because the individual goes on for ever and the family does not, it is plain that the family exists for the individual and not the individual for the family. The family exists precisely to forward the wellbeing of the individuals who compose it. It has no end or object in itself. The family as a family will disappear as surely as will all other material things. The individuals composing the family will never cease to exist. So long as the family exists as a social unit, it exists for the wellbeing of its members, not they for it.

So the whole justification for the exercise of authority in the family is for the wellbeing of the members composing it; it can never be exercised against their true interests. An attempt to exercise authority against the interests of the members of a family has no moral authority at all. Looking further, just as the family exists for the wellbeing of the members and not as an entity for itself, so when those families come together to form a larger society or state that larger society exists for the wellbeing of the families who compose it. You see clearly how these concentric circles go out from the one created thing that can bridge time and eternity—the individual human being.

Now, nearly all our present social thinking leaves out that middle term, the family. Nearly all the arguments and discussions you hear are carried on as though all that we are concerned with are the tensions between individuals and the State. This misses the whole point—that the relationship between individuals and the State is transmitted through the family. The State as such has no direct concern with the individual at all. Its concern is precisely to strengthen and support the family and to perform those functions which the family cannot perform. It is only when the family fails to fulfill its function that society may try to do so.

To think of the State as having a direct responsibility for the individual is, of course, to misunderstand the whole of this concentric system which is the root of all Christian social thinking. The unhappy position has now been reached where the State has taken over nearly all the functions of the family—housing, education, care of the young and care of the old. The family is rapidly disappearing. The State is seeking to perform functions for which it has no authority.[27]

As soon as you leave out the family and remove it from its proper position between the individual and the State, you destroy the whole concept of property, which is very closely bound up with that of the family.

The family exists to try to give the individual what he needs, physically and psychologically, at the start of life. But the family is not just something static in time or for a moment in time: by its very nature it is a continuing organism. It does not exist only for a week or a month or a year, it exists at least until the members of it go out to found other families themselves. The root of the idea of property is the material security that a family needs to fulfill its continuing obligations. The State should guarantee to parents the peaceful possession of what they justly own. The family and the concept of property are both profoundly moral concepts, very closely interlinked.[28]

The State today has an entirely erroneous view of property. It thinks and acts as though there were such a thing as a national income which needs to be equitably divided— "Fair shares for all." But there is no "national income." There is only what individuals have made and achieved. It is not the State's function to possess or control. Its proper functions are two—to repel attack from without and to administer justice within. These are the two functions which individual families are powerless to perform.

The State may accidentally have supplementary

functions, as a matter of expediency, but the defense of the realm and the administration of justice are the only two essential ones. In the exercise of these essential functions, the State has a moral authority and rightly commands our obedience.

You see once again how everything goes back to Almighty God. There is no moral law apart from Him or away from Him. Just as the family has no right to do anything other than to promote the wellbeing of its individual members (but when it does that it is backed by the authority of Almighty God; and we commit sin if we oppose it), so the State, when it exercises its proper function—supporting and buttressing the family—does so with the authority of Almighty God behind it. Once again we commit sin if we oppose it. The State exercises authority and can demand from us obedience in the matter of the defense of the realm and the support of law and order, for there indeed it is fulfilling its proper function. But it is not fulfilling its proper function when it seeks to destroy the family which comes between it and the individual.

Now we are in a position to see the relevance of the last question in this section of the Catechism, which otherwise might have seemed to be a little surprising:

> **It is sinful to belong to any secret society that plots against the Church or State, or to any society that by reason of its secrecy is condemned by the Church; for St. Paul says: "Let every soul be subject to higher powers; he that resisteth the power resisteth the ordinance of God; and they that resist purchase to themselves damnation."** (*Romans* 13:1–2) Q204

You see now that, with the concept of civil society which I have given you, any attempt to overthrow legitimate authority is sinful in itself. Catholics widely believed that the many secret societies which flourished in the eighteenth and nineteenth centuries were directed to such an object and therefore called for ecclesiastical condemnation. Any attempt to paralyze or take undue advantage of society on the part of a particular group in its own interests is an act in opposition to legitimate authority and is also sinful.

Before we move on from the Fourth Commandment to the Fifth I am going to spend a little time drawing your attention to a distinction which is not always properly appreciated nowadays. There is a misconception concerning Christian morality which has become so widespread that it is regarded as a commonplace and is seldom challenged. It is widely assumed that the attitudes to private property expressed in the New Testament lend support to the doctrines of modern socialism. According to this view, Christ was a pacifist socialist and the early Christians were Communists. It is consequently inferred that every Christian should be a pacifist and a Communist and that a Christian who is neither is failing to live up to the principles which he professes.

This misconception arises from a failure to distinguish between the Counsels and the Commandments—a distinction which our Blessed Lord makes in a dialogue which is recorded for us in the Gospels of St. Matthew, St. Mark and St. Luke or, as they are called, the three Synoptic Gospels. Like so many Gospel passages, the story of the rich young man is one of which many people retain a vague and inaccurate memory. When asked to recount the story, nine people out of ten will say that a young man asked our Lord what he should do to inherit eternal life and was given the answer,

"Go, sell all thou hast and give to the poor." But by omitting the central passage of the story they lose the whole distinction which our Lord makes.

The relevant parts of the story, as recorded in *Matthew* 19:16–22, *Mark* 10:17–22 and *Luke* 18:18–23, are practically identical and run as follows:

> And behold, one came and said to him: "Good Master, what good shall I do that I may have life everlasting?" And Jesus said unto him: Why askest thou me concerning good? One is good, God. But if thou wilt enter into life, keep the commandments. He said to him: Which? And Jesus said: Thou shalt do no murder, Thou shalt not commit adultery, Thou shalt not steal, Thou shalt not bear false witness. Honor thy father and thy mother and Thou shalt love thy neighbor as thyself. The young man saith to Him: All these have I kept from my youth, what is yet wanting to me? Jesus saith to him: If thou wilt be perfect, go, sell what thou hast, and give to the poor and thou shalt have treasure in heaven: and come, follow me. And when the young man had heard his word, he went away sad: for he had great possessions.

Here, plainly, is a distinction between what is necessary for salvation—keeping the Commandments—and what pertains to the life of perfection: giving up all one has for the closer following of Christ. The Christian believes that the keeping of the Commandments is mandatory. He believes that they derive their force from the fact that they are a reflection of the perfect and unchanging nature of Almighty God and that they are therefore incapable of alteration or repeal.

He believes that they are of the very nature of things; that they are engraved in the mind and heart of man (however obscured by the consequences of man's Fall); and that, but for the Fall, they would not need to have been promulgated. He believes that no man can be saved who knowingly, willingly and unrepentantly fails to observe them.

Now, the life of perfection of which Christ speaks is in a completely different category. To begin with, it is not mandatory. The young man was in the way of salvation through keeping the Commandments. These he could not disregard without sin. The call to the life of perfection, on the other hand, was an invitation which he was morally free to accept or to refuse. The Gospels make it clear that, even in our Blessed Lord's most intimate circles, there were those who followed such a call and those who neither followed nor probably even received it. Naturally the Gospel story concentrates on those who did follow it. But we must remember that though Peter and Andrew leave their nets, James and John their boat and their father, and Matthew his place at the receipt of custom, Lazarus, by contrast (a friend so close that Jesus weeps at his death), lives a domestic life with his sisters, while Nicodemus and Joseph of Arimathea live, so far as we can tell, the ordinary life of men in the world.

The distinction between what Almighty God commands us to do and what He counsels or advises us to do, which can be seen in the Gospels, is one which the Church has always maintained and which she has increasingly clarified in practice and theory—as when she speaks of "the life of Christians living in the world" and "the life of perfection." All Christians alike, whether living in the cloister or in the world, are called to holiness. While the overwhelming majority of her children are living in the world, the Church has always held up the life of complete renunciation as a higher ideal for those who are called to it and as a source of encouragement and a spur to those who are not. But she has persistently resisted the recurrent attempts to identify the Christian life with the "life of perfection." The reason is plain. Complete renunciation of the good things of this world for the closer following of Christ necessarily involves celibacy, since one can only make voluntary sacrifices for oneself: one cannot make them for others, least of all for those who are dependent on us. Moreover, if celibacy were the necessary condition of the Christian life, Christianity could never be, as we believe it to be in God's intention and design, the universal religion of mankind. It would have died in the first generation.

The life of perfection to which the Church has always believed that some will be called begins with celibacy because it is only when a man has, for the love of God, renounced the supreme natural good of taking a wife and begetting children that he can go on to ask himself whether it would be pleasing to God that he should give up those other natural goods—the possession of property, the exercise of his own will, the right to defend his own life. The married man sins if he refuses to take prudent thought for the morrow or if, when his wife or children are attacked, he turns the other cheek to the smiter.

It is worth remembering that the things renounced by a man who seeks to follow the life of perfection are all good things and that any renunciation of them must be voluntary, whereas the man who keeps the Commandments is eschewing evil things which he is bound to avoid if he is to save his soul. Further, we may observe how completely such a voluntary renunciation of those things to which one has a right differs morally from a deprivation or confiscation imposed by the State.

Many people, when the distinction made by our Blessed Lord Himself is brought home to them, feel that a compromise is being made in which the demanding nature of Christian morality is accommodated to the weaker brethren. This is largely because, in the universal atmosphere of egalitarianism in which we live, man has lost the concept of the absolute uniqueness of his own creation and vocation. He is tempted to measure himself against his fellow man and not against the uncreated Perfection of Almighty God, Who alone gives meaning to his life. He fails to appreciate that man achieves sanctity not necessarily by aspiring to a way of life which is objectively higher in itself, but by fulfilling the unique role which God has given him. St. Louis of France, our own St. Thomas More, St. Benedict Joseph Labre, all achieved sanctity not in a "religious" state but in the highly individual and very different ways of life to which each believed that God had called him.

We come now to the Fifth Commandment. All these Commandments, Fourth, Fifth and Sixth, are extremely topical. They touch the moral matters that are so much debated and so widely misunderstood at the present time. As I pointed out with regard to the Fourth Commandment, there is a very wide misunderstanding of the relationship of the individual to the State which gives rise to the misunderstanding that all tensions exist between these two.

The Fifth Commandment is no less a matter of current debate and current misconception than the Fourth:

Q205 **The Fifth Commandment is, "Thou shalt not kill."**

The Fifth Commandment forbids all willful murder, fighting, quarrelling and injurious words, and also scandal and bad example. Q206

The Fifth Commandment forbids anger and, still more, hatred and revenge. Q207

Scandal and bad example are forbidden by the Fifth Commandment, because they lead to the injury and spiritual death of our neighbor's soul. Q208

Once again we can see that the Catechism's treatment has a much wider scope than the plain words might suggest. If we were to take the words "Thou shalt not kill" literally, without allowing for the teaching and practice of Christians throughout the ages, to say nothing of the Old Testament, we shall be driven to a sectarian position of considering all taking of life to be wrong, whether it be that of a fly or a rat or a human being. People who take such a stand are few in the West, but you would certainly find them in the East. And even in the West some preservationists seem to go pretty far in that direction.

The Christian position is quite different. We start by believing that man has been given dominion over lower animals. Rights and duties are peculiar to rational beings, who, having minds and wills, reflect Almighty God Himself. The lower animals are incapable of moral acts, are innocent of virtues and vices, and have no rights and no duties. We believe that man is given complete dominion over them. He may therefore rightly bring into captivity, domesticate, kill or use for food any of the lower animals.

The dominion of man over the lower creation is limited not by the rights of that creation—for it has none—but by the influence that the abuse of that dominion may have upon man. He must therefore never do anything to animals that is morally harmful to himself. The sinfulness of cruelty lies in the harm it does to man and the very helplessness of the creatures who are the victims of cruelty makes that sinfulness—and therefore the damage to man—all the more grave.

When it comes to the right to take human life, opinion is very confused and misinformed. First of all, if you read the Fifth Commandment in the light of the Old Testament, in which the Ten Commandments are set, you will see that it can never have meant that taking human life was universally wrong, seeing that the moral code of the Old Testament includes the taking of life for a much larger number of transgressions of the law than has been the case in modern times. Furthermore, in the Old Testament, war is not only condoned but positively prescribed. So the Fifth Commandment cannot mean that the taking of human life is always wrong.

For a proper understanding we have to look to Answer 207. The real sin the Catechism is talking about starts in the mind when we hate others and wish evil to them. This is always and in all circumstances wrong. We can never, never, never wish evil to others, seeing that we are bound, as we saw at the outset of our consideration of the Commandments, to love everyone. We saw that the Person we must supremely love without qualification is Almighty God and that we must therefore love all creatures, desiring for them what He desires for them—the eternal enjoyment of Himself.

Such love must be quite compatible with pain, suffering and death, seeing that Almighty God, Who loves His creatures more than we can imagine, ordains pain, suffering and death as the means of their coming to Him.

Plainly, then, there must be circumstances where the taking of human life can be justified. What is universally forbidden is the hating of anyone, the wishing of evil for them: worst of all, wishing their eternal damnation, their eternal separation from Almighty God, which is in a sense the only evil there is. And plainly that is very sinful indeed.

Life is a gift from Almighty God. We have no right to it, as we were not there to have it at the moment it was given to us. The principle on which every justified taking of human life rests is a very simple one. The gift of life carries the duty to maintain yourself in good health and to look after yourself so that your life is not cut short through neglect of God's gift. But more than that, the gift of life carries with it the right to defend life, by violence if need be, against a violent attack.

The right to defend life means that if anyone appears to be attacking you with homicidal intent and the only way you can restrain him is to take his life, you are entirely justified in doing so; there is no sin at all.

So when people use the phrase "the right to life," they really mean "the right to defend life." When Almighty God called you into being, He gave you a right to defend and preserve that life which He gave you.

Now, just as the individual has the right to defend his own life when it is under attack, so the State has the right to defend its own existence because, as we have seen, the life of the State is essential for the wellbeing of those who compose it. The families composing the State cannot effectively defend themselves from aggression from without or from crime from within. The state exists for these functions. And the right which the individual has to defend his own life is enjoyed by the State to defend its own existence. So just as an individual, when assailed by someone with homicidal intent, may take the life of the assailant, the State may take life when its existence is threatened by war from without or crime from within. There lies the whole justification for the taking of human life.

We must now consider in what circumstances we are obliged to defend ourselves against attack and in what circumstances we may, without sin, waive that undoubted right. People often do not distinguish between "the right to life" and "the right to defend life," but are swayed by sentiment in the matter and are liable to ask, "How do you reconcile the right to take life with the counsel 'to turn the other cheek to the smiter'?" It is important to understand the distinction between the Counsels and the Commandments, to which we referred earlier in this chapter. For the moment, let me say that the Commandments are of universal application and that no one can knowingly disregard them without committing sin, whereas the Counsels are counsels of perfection which are not mandatory and are therefore not binding on pain of sin.

An individual who has no one dependent upon him and finds himself the subject of homicidal attack may either take the life of the assailant or turn the other cheek to the smiter, which is a very heroic thing to do. But a man who has others dependent upon him cannot possibly choose to follow the counsels without sin. If you, a bachelor, were going home tonight and someone leaped out at you from a dark doorway, you might, in that split second, say, "I am going to repel this man's attack," or you might say, "I will turn the other cheek." But if you, as a married man, were to come home one day and find your wife being beaten up and your children being killed, you could not morally turn the other cheek. You have a duty to act for their protection. Observe once again that celibacy is the necessary first condition for following the other counsels.

The State may choose not to exercise its right to declare war, as it may choose not to exercise its right to capital punishment. It may on grounds of expediency judge that its subjects will suffer more from offering a possibly ineffective resistance or that public interest is best served by not hanging a murderer. What cannot be said is that the State has no right to take these measures for its defense, because it always has a nation of families dependent upon it for protection. All taking of human life or use of physical sanctions comes back to the simple principle that the gift of life carries with it the right to defend life.

CHAPTER 20

The Sixth and Ninth Commandments

WE ARE now halfway through our consideration of the theological virtue of Charity, which is that gift of Almighty God whereby we love God above all things and our neighbor as ourselves for God's sake (q169). As we saw, our duty towards Almighty God is contained in the Ten Commandments. We have considered the first three, in which we serve Almighty God directly by worshiping Him before all things, by refraining from taking His name in vain and by keeping the Sabbath holy. Of the remaining seven Commandments, in which we worship Him and are united to Him through other creatures, we have considered our duty to our father and mother and consequently to society, our duty to refrain from the unjustified taking of human life; and, under that heading, we considered the circumstances that may justify it. We saw that the Fourth and Fifth Commandments had a far more extended meaning than the plain words might at first lead us to expect.

This is no less true of the Sixth Commandment, to which we now turn, "Thou shalt not commit adultery," which I shall take in conjunction with the Ninth Commandment,

"Thou shalt not covet thy neighbor's wife." Both these Commandments are concerned with sins of lust, the Sixth with lustful acts and the Ninth with lustful thoughts.

As we have considered so often, there is no such thing as a sin in action which has not been preceded by a sin in thought. We inevitably begin with our minds willing evil as a necessary preliminary to doing evil. So I suggest that we consider the sins of the flesh by going through the answers in the Catechism under the heading of the Sixth and Ninth Commandments together:

Q209 **The Sixth Commandment is, "Thou shalt not commit adultery."**

Q210 **The Sixth Commandment forbids all sins of impurity with another's wife or husband.**

Q211 **The Sixth Commandment forbids whatever is contrary to holy purity in looks, words or actions.**

Q212 **Immodest plays and dances are forbidden by the Sixth Commandment, and it is sinful to look at them.**

Q213 **The Sixth Commandment forbids immodest songs, books and pictures, because they are the most dangerous to the soul and lead to mortal sin.**

Q223 **The Ninth Commandment is, "Thou shalt not covet thy neighbor's wife."**

Q224 **The Ninth Commandment forbids all willful consent to impure thoughts and desires, and all willful pleasure in the irregular motions of the flesh.**

The sins that commonly lead to the breaking of the Sixth and Ninth Commandments are gluttony, drunkenness and intemperance, and also idleness, bad company and the neglect of prayer. Q225

As you see from running through these answers, the Catechism treats the Sixth and Ninth Commandments as covering all abuses of our sexual powers and not only sins of adultery.

As always when we come to consider the use of the gifts given to us by Almighty God, we do well to consider at the very outset the reason for those gifts being given to us. We believe that we are given this most powerful of all impulses, sexuality, in order to cooperate with Almighty God in the procreation and the continuation of human life. We have already seen, under the Fourth Commandment, how inseparable those two roles are.

There is nothing more wonderful in the whole of creation than life; nothing more wonderful, nothing more characteristic of Almighty God than the work of creation itself. We refer to Him properly as the Creator: that is—if you can apply human language to Him—His specific role. It is this role that makes the distinction between Creator and creature. Almighty God is the Creator and everything else that exists is brought into being and sustained in being by Him. He is uniquely the Creator: all other things are creatures, realizations of His mind and will.

In giving us the gift of procreation, Almighty God has given us a share in this uniquely and specifically divine role of calling things into being. So the gift of sex is something sublime and sacred. Nothing could be a greater distortion of the Christian view of sex than to consider it something low, degrading and unworthy. It is not; it is something absolutely sublime.[29]

But like every gift which Almighty God has given us, it has to be exercised in accordance with His will and purpose. Rightly exercised, it is something positively sanctifying and is in no way sinful.

This is true of all God's gifts, whether they are gifts of mind or body, intellect or physical strength or beauty. They may all be used according to His will and purpose, in which case our use of them is something that helps to sanctify us, or they can be used contrary to His will and purpose, in which case our use of them takes us away from Him and is the occasion of sin.

That is particularly plain with gifts of the mind. The use of the mind to discover truth, to discover God Himself, is plainly something sanctifying. Its use apart from Him, in opposition to Him, is something which leads to that root of all sins, the sin of pride. It can be used to very evil purpose indeed.

Our sexual and procreative gifts are given to us so that we may bring life into being. Not only that, but when life has been brought into being, we should exercise the conservative role by rearing that life in the knowledge and love of Almighty God. Always remember that you cannot separate procreation from education—the bringing of life into being from the nurturing of that life. It is a double role which cannot be divided any more than the creative and conservative power of Almighty God can be divided.

Used for its proper end and purpose, sex is a holy and a sanctifying thing. Used to the exclusion of its proper purpose—procreation and education, which are so inextricably united—it becomes an occasion of sin. We are using a gift of Almighty God for a purpose other than that for which it was intended.

You will see, if you apply that yardstick, that every sin of a sexual character derives its malice from excluding one or other of those purposes. Plainly masturbation excludes the very possibility of procreation taking place; as do homosexual acts and the practice of artificial birth control. Adultery and fornication exclude the possibility of bringing up the fruits of such a union within the framework of a Christian family and it is only in such a framework that the conservative responsibilities of our sexual gifts can be fulfilled. Every one of the abuses of our sexual gifts derives its malice, as I have said, from excluding the possibility of procreation or the possibility of education within a Christian context. And that is why they are sinful, not because the activity itself is sinful. It is not sinful at all: used properly, it is sanctifying.[30]

That, you see, is where the Catholic attitude towards the gift of sex differs completely from all those purely repressive attitudes which would seem to consider it as though it were something sinful and, on the other hand, from the modern "progressive" view that every sexual act is natural and right and that attempts to control them are psychologically harmful.

The reason for linking the Sixth Commandment to the Ninth in our consideration is that all the sins we have been mentioning inevitably start in the mind, as all sins do. That is true of the last sin we considered—murder, the unjustified taking of life. Sins of violence all start from harboring hateful thoughts. No man has ever committed a sin of violence or murder who does not start by committing a sin of hate.

So, too, in the matter of the use of our sexual gifts.

Physical sins of sex are not committed until we have first given our mind over to a disordered consideration of those sins, to thinking of sensual pleasures beyond the proper and right context of Christian marriage. The sins that are enumerated in Answer 213 are considered heinous because no thoughts can so completely obsess a man's mind as those stimulated by immodest songs, books and pictures.

Almighty God has attached the greatest of all physical pleasures to the exercise of the gift of sex precisely because of the immense responsibility that is entailed in bringing life into this world. If the greatest of all physical pleasures were not attached to the exercise of this gift, who on earth would go to the immense trouble of marrying in the first place, of begetting children, of saddling himself with the responsibility of their clothing and education and carrying the burden of their support at least for the first decade or two? Who would undertake the burden of those responsibilities unless there were attached to the exercise of our sexual powers the greatest physical pleasure known to man? The inducement is exactly in proportion to the responsibility incurred.

There is a parallel in other sensual matters, as in our pleasure in food and drink. Who, if pleasure were not attached to the very necessary task of replenishing our physical powers, would bother to eat? If eating and drinking had no pleasure attached to them, we should inevitably neglect this duty of restoring our physical strength. The pleasure attached to them is less than sexual pleasure, but proportionate to the purpose. It is so much more important that the whole human race be continued than that any single individual should keep himself in good health.

Here is another comparison which may help to make clear the wickedness of getting the pleasure of an act whilst excluding the possibility of the consequence for which that act is intended by Almighty God. The Romans, we are told—though it is hard for us to imagine the mentality that allowed them to act in that way—ate and drank till they could hold no more and then made themselves sick in order to have the pleasure of eating and drinking again.

That is the perfect parallel to what we do when we exercise our sexual gifts and yet exclude the possibility of their resulting in the purpose for which Almighty God has intended them. Food and drink are given to us so that we may replenish our bodily strength. So long as we are not excluding the possibility of its nourishing us, it is right to take pleasure in eating and drinking. There is nothing wrong or sinful about it. When we start eating and drinking solely for pleasure, as in the Roman example I have given you, the attempt to obtain the pleasure while excluding the purpose for which it is given is sinful.

In exactly the same way masturbation, homosexuality and the practice of artificial birth control exclude the very possibility of conception taking place.

CHAPTER 21

The Seventh, Tenth and Eighth Commandments

NOW we come to the Seventh and Tenth Commandments. In the last chapter I took the Sixth and Ninth Commandments together because they were both concerned with sins of the flesh. The Seventh and Tenth are similarly related: the Seventh is concerned with sins against justice in deed and the Tenth with sins against justice in thought. So I think it is probably easier if we take them together, remembering that all sins begin in the mind and that a deliberate, evil thought is a sin even if that thought is not acted upon. The sinfulness of sin lies in averting from Almighty God those faculties in which we most resemble Him—the power to think and the power to will. In the Seventh and Tenth Commandments we are concerned with using those two powers otherwise than in accordance with His will in matters of justice.

The Seventh Commandment is, "Thou shalt not steal." Q214

The Seventh Commandment forbids all unjust taking away or keeping what belongs to another. Q215

Q216 **All manner of cheating in buying and selling is forbidden by the Seventh Commandment, and also every other way of wronging our neighbor.**

Q217 **We are bound to restore ill-gotten goods if we are able, or else the sin will not be forgiven; we must also pay our debts.**

The next answer used to read as follows:

Q218* **It is dishonest for servants to waste their master's time or property, because it is wasting what is not their own.**

In the 1971 version of the Catechism this was altered to:

Q218 **It is dishonest for workers to waste their employer's time or property, because it is wasting what is not their own,**

which causes me wry amusement. Workers presumably must not be considered to be the servants of their masters. It is very sad to consider how the whole concept of service and servants is now held to be a derogatory one. What an impoverishment not only in language but in thought! We ought to consider it a privilege to serve other people. The Pope is described as "the servant of the servants of God." The motto of the Prince of Wales is "I serve." Little boys used to think it a privilege to serve Mass. How sad that "serve" is now a dirty word.

The Tenth Commandment deals with sins of injustice in thought, whereas the Seventh dealt with sins of injustice in deed.

Q226 **The Tenth Commandment is, "Thou shalt not covet thy neighbor's goods."**

The Tenth Commandment forbids all envious and covetous thoughts and unjust desires of our neighbor's goods and profits. Q227

Most people believe that there is something wrong in sins of injustice. Whereas in this "permissive" age thoughts of lust are held to be inescapable and acts of lust all but inevitable, the practice of stealing is still generally frowned upon. You might therefore think that, unlike the Sixth and Ninth Commandments, the Seventh and Tenth require no particular exposition. But it is important to see what we mean by "justice," because in popular speech now, justice is often equated with egalitarianism—the widespread superstition that men are or should be equal in social or economic status or opportunity. There is no foundation at all in Christian thought, morality or practice for the idea that such equality is a Christian concept. Not only is it not a Christian concept, but too often in popular thought and speech it involves a complete denial of a Christian concept. In popular speech it is often suggested that the dignity of man comes only from his being equal to other men in what he has and that, if he is not equal, injustice has been done to him.

This implies a complete denial of the Christian concept that the sublime dignity of every individual human being derives not from his relation to another person or to society as a whole but from the fact that Almighty God has chosen to bring him, a single, particular individual, into being and to keep him in being. What makes every single man so uniquely valuable and important is that he is the individual and absolutely unique creation of Almighty God. Therein lies his whole dignity. Unlike the rest of creation, he is not a means but an end. Whether he is equal in other things to any other man or not is wholly irrelevant. His unique value lies not in his equality to other men but always and only in his relationship to Almighty God. In venerating every one of God's creatures, we are venerating Almighty God Himself, Who has chosen that everyone should exist and continue to exist.

Plainly men are not equal in the gifts that Almighty God gives them or in the circumstances in which He has brought them into this world. We do not each have exactly the same combination of gifts and handicaps. Each man's box of tools is unique. And just as our interior circumstances are special to each of us, so every exterior circumstance of our life is likewise unique.

It follows that each single man has a vocation from Almighty God for which he has the necessary equipment and which he alone can fulfill. The only sense in which he can be a success or failure is in whether or not he carries out that vocation which Almighty God has given to him.

Consequently, the widespread superstition that we are all equal in God's sight runs counter to the whole Christian philosophy of life. Equality is observed nowhere in creation: not only is each man absolutely unique, but every leaf of every tree, every pebble on the beach, every grain of sand on the seashore, is unlike any other. There is no sense in which equality exists between them. Furthermore, not only are our physical conditions unique but also our mental and spiritual conditions. Our gifts and defects of character are peculiar to each single one of us.

To say, as a critic may, that Christianity is therefore in favor of inequality is as meaningless as to say that Christianity is in favor of the Law of Gravitation. Christianity accepts that it is so. All attempts to change the nature of things lead to greater suffering than the evils they seek to avoid. They are a sin against the truth.

Some would say at this point, "Oh but surely we are all equal in the sight of Almighty God: He loves us all equally." This is palpably untrue. You cannot imagine that our Blessed Lady, chosen from all eternity by Almighty God to be the Mother of His only begotten Son, was not more highly privileged than all other members of the human race. She is uniquely and highly favored by Almighty God.

And you can see a hierarchy of love and affection in the human relationships of Jesus Christ, our Blessed Lord, Who is very God Himself. Plainly St. John was more beloved than the other Apostles, and three of the Apostles—Peter, James and John himself—had a closer relationship to Him than the other nine. Furthermore, those twelve were closer to him than the disciples.

The infinite variety in our relationships to Almighty God does not imply that any one of us is a "second-class citizen." Each of us has a unique relationship to Almighty God. The very first step in the spiritual life is to accept that unique relationship and to appreciate that no one else has the vocation that we have. No one else can fulfill our own vocation for us. We run counter to God's plan in seeking a vocation other than our own, even though that vocation may be objectively a higher one. It is our own vocation that we have to fulfill.

Having seen what the Christian concept of justice is not, let us now consider what it is.

Justice means giving to each what is his due. That due varies. The due of every man is the respect we owe to him as being a unique creation of Almighty God. In material things the due of each man is what he has honestly and justly acquired, whether he has earned it by his mental or physical labor or whether it has been lawfully transmitted to him. We have no right to take this from him.

The wickedness of injustice lies in taking away from another person what is justly his. That is generally admitted as being sinful. When we do that, we are guilty of theft or robbery. Our being forgiven for such a sin requires an act of will on our part to rectify the injustice we have done to our victim by restoring what we have unjustly taken from him. We may not always be able to restore what we have taken, but at least the purpose must be there. Without that intention, sin is still in our heart; we still wish to deprive our neighbor of what is justly his.

Another reason why it is necessary to dwell on sins of injustice is that at the present day there is an inclination to consider that all that we possess comes from society. That view is without foundation, since society of itself produces nothing at all. There is no such thing, to use that phrase which is constantly bandied about, as the national wealth, which, the users of the phrase contend, the State has the duty to distribute equitably among its members. A nation of itself can never produce anything. All that there is, is what the individual members of that nation have produced.

Society has the right to take whatever proportion of the achievements of its members is necessary for the fulfillment of its essential functions. When occasionally the burden of taxation is lightened for one class or another, the newspapers are inclined to announce it as "The Chancellor makes a present" to the class concerned. What he is in fact doing is merely saying, "I propose to take less of what you have produced than I have hitherto being taking." He is in no position to give a present to others, having no resources from which to do so, other than what he has previously taken—rightly or wrongly—in tax.

Injustice does not become justice if done by the nation or the State. Robbery is no less robbery if it is committed by the State than if it is committed by an individual. A predatory State undermines honesty and destroys the incentives to achievement.

Much of the view of life which we have been discussing stems from the envy of others to which we are prone as a consequence of the Fall. That takes us on to the Tenth Commandment, which stresses the wickedness of injustice in thought. Envy and jealousy are sins, not virtues, even if they only stay in the mind and are never acted upon. They are often spoken of now as though it were somehow virtuous to resent the fact that others have more than we have.

All injustice that ever takes place springs from a previously existing injustice in the mind. As we have seen earlier, all sins of lust come from lustful thoughts. "He who looks after a woman to lust after her has already committed adultery with her in his heart." (*Matthew* 5:28). All sins of violence come from violence of the mind. "He who hates his brother is a murderer." (*1 John* 3:15). Similarly no one has committed a sin of injustice unless he has first had that envy and rancor in his mind. The real sin lies there.

The antidote to sins of thought lies in the practice of detachment from material things. Observe once again how the opening questions and answers of the Catechism are a pointer to the ideas we are now considering: "For what shall it profit a man if he gain the whole world and suffer the loss of his own soul?" (*Mark* 8:36; q7). We know that the purpose of this life is not material prosperity. The lesson we must learn in this material life is to disentangle ourselves from material things to come to those of eternity. The whole of life is, or should be, a process of detachment culminating in the supreme detachment of death. We should be disentangling ourselves all the time from the material world, which, please God, we shall have used as He meant us to use it, but without giving our hearts to it.

There is a difference between the modern sense of the word "poverty," and the virtue we may term "evangelical poverty," which is constantly counseled in the Gospels by our Blessed Lord Himself. Poverty as popularly understood is destitution, ignorance, dirt and disease—the life of Shanty Town. There is nothing Christian in that and we are urged not to cultivate it, but to do what we can to eradicate it.

Evangelical poverty, as understood in the light of nineteen centuries of Christian practice, means that whatever our material circumstances, whether easy or hard, we should not attach undue importance to material wellbeing. Be prepared to be deprived of it if Almighty God so wills, and in no circumstances commit sin to achieve or preserve it.

Poverty in the sense of destitution cannot be a virtue. Poverty in the sense of detachment always is—and plainly the greater the detachment the greater the virtue. We can give up things willingly and thereby gain great merit.

Consider St. Francis of Assisi, who is always held up as the example of evangelical poverty and is always referred to as the poor man of Assisi. Yet he was a product of a very highly civilized and sophisticated society, of which he had received all the cultural and educational benefits. Having benefited from the society of his time, he was doing a great and heroic thing when he stripped himself of all the material consequences of it and cultivated that complete detachment which expressed itself in an extremely ascetic and austere form of life. He could not and did not try to divest himself of the many advantages and benefits he had received.

It is impossible, our Blessed Lord tells us, to serve both God and Mammon. But in the easy categories which people so lightly make, talking of the rich and the poor, whether they mean nations or people, there is a profound unreality, because material wealth is a relative thing. Who is rich and who is poor? No one ever thinks he is rich enough, even if he is an oil magnate. Obviously there are very rich people. Equally obviously there are those on the borderline of starvation or beyond it. But there is no such thing as a norm from which departure is sinful. That meaningless concept underlies so much of the wicked and envious thought we have been talking about.

Throughout the ages standards have varied and they vary enormously among us today. What is affluence in one generation, country or age may be considered poverty in another. It is important to bear that in mind, because there is so much loose and wrong talk as though, in talking of those amenities which it is thought desirable that people should have or, worse, that they have a "right" to have, we were discussing Christian morality. When you come to analyze them you will see how relative those terms are against the whole background of human history. And you will therefore be free from the trap—into which so many people fall—of thinking that somehow a certain standard of living can be identified with Christian morality and Christian standards. It cannot be.

The Seventh and Tenth Commandments, which we have just been considering, are concerned with the application of justice to material possessions and with the envy of those who have them. The Eighth Commandment, to which we now come, is concerned again with the virtue of justice, in the matter of reputation and of our neighbor's right to the truth.

The Catechism says:

Q219 **The Eighth Commandment is, "Thou shalt not bear false witness against thy neighbor."**

That Commandment, like the others, has an extended meaning and covers two quite different though closely related transgressions. As here expressed, it is primarily concerned with our duty towards our neighbor, but it reflects that direct duty to Almighty God which we have looked at already in the Second Commandment, which forbids us to take God's name in vain.

Q220 **The Eighth Commandment forbids all false testimony, rash judgment and lies.**

Q221 **Calumny and detraction are forbidden by the Eighth Commandment, and also tale-bearing and any words which injure our neighbor's character.**

There is a difference between calumny and detraction. Calumny is saying what is untrue, to the disadvantage of our neighbor. Detraction is saying something which is true but which you have no business to say.

All these come under the sin of injustice because every man has a right to his character until he has publicly forfeited it. So it is perfectly possible for you to know something to the detriment of another man and yet be morally restrained from saying it because it is not generally known. Unless there is some reason requiring you to reveal it, you are committing a sin if you reveal something to his disadvantage which is known to you alone. Of course it is a much greater sin if what you are saying is untrue.

The Eighth Commandment tells us that we have committed an injustice if we tell our neighbor an untruth in matters which he has a right to know. And we have committed a very grave injustice if we destroy his character. So, by implication, this Commandment forbids taking God's name in vain. For the most harmful way in which we can destroy our neighbor's character is by taking an oath to his disadvantage. And we aggravate the sin by calling Almighty God to witness the truth of a lie.

If I have injured my neighbor by speaking ill of him, I am bound to make him satisfaction by restoring his good name as far as I can. Q222

As we saw in answer 217, when we repent, the intention of making restitution must be present. In material things it may be impossible to make restitution, but you must at least have the intention to do so: and the same applies to sins of injustice in speech. If what you have said is untrue, your duty is plain, though very painful. You have the duty of saying, "What I said to so-and-so's disadvantage is untrue and I repent of it." If what you have said is true, it is more difficult for you to make restitution, but you are bound to try in some way to compensate for the harm you have done at the very least by praying for him.

That completes our consideration of the moral law of Almighty God embodied in the Ten Commandments.

CHAPTER 22

The Commandments of the Church

WE ARE now starting on the last section of the Catechism with which I propose to deal. There are in fact three admirable sections after the end of this one. They deal with Virtues and Vices, the Christian's Rule of Life and the Christian's Daily Exercise. These are not primarily dogmatic and do not for that reason need the exposition which I have given to the earlier chapters, but none the less I recommend them strongly for your reading and practice.

The section on which we are now embarking is entitled, "The Commandments of the Church." This title and the fact that it follows immediately on the Commandments of God suggests a certain parallel and even parity between them. Our first concern must be to consider how completely different they are. The Commandments of God are a complete moral code, the observance of which is incumbent on all men. They are immutable because they are a reflection of the perfect and unchanging nature of Almighty God. A man who obeys the Commandments of Almighty God has fulfilled the whole purpose for which his Creator brought him into being. No man can knowingly and willingly disregard the Commandments of God and save his soul.

The Commandments of the Church, on the other hand, are a selection made from the whole body of Canon Law and are chosen out of that work as being those enactments of the Church which the Catholic layman is most likely to need to know in the conduct of his own life. Again, to point the contrast, there are no circumstances which will excuse a man from disregarding the Law of God. There are *many* circumstances which will excuse a man from not obeying the Commandments of the Church. For example, it can never be right to murder or to commit adultery. There may, on the other hand, be many circumstances in which a man may be excused from the obligation to hear Mass or to fast and abstain. This does not mean that the Commandments of the Church are not gravely binding in conscience. The idea that the Church has the power to bind in conscience derives from the concept, which we considered earlier, of the Church as a supreme and self-sufficient society in her own order, having power to legislate and to enforce that legislation by sanctions not only in matters relating to the moral law but also in matters of discipline, such as the number of Holy days of Obligation during the year. But when we come to consider the Commandments of the Church in detail it will be seen that they are largely concerned with particular applications of the Divine Law. The Law of God is, as we observed earlier, immutable; its applications can be changed and may be dispensed by the Church.

It will frequently be found, when people object—as they constantly do—to a particular example of this exercise of authority, that what they find repugnant is not so much the examples, as the idea that the Church has such authority at all They do not believe that the Church is a completely independent society in the spiritual order, as is the State in the temporal order, with all the powers necessary to guide men to their eternal salvation.

From this preamble the answer to Question 228 is plain:

> **We are bound to obey the Church, because Christ has said to the pastors of the Church, "He that heareth you, heareth Me; and he that despiseth you, despiseth Me."** (*Luke* 10:16) Q228

and plainly this may apply to matters of discipline in which we may find ourselves out of sympathy or in disagreement with what the Church commands. It should be stressed that we are speaking of matters of discipline and not of conscience. Should ecclesiastical authority ever require of us something repugnant to our conscience, our conscience takes precedence.

The Catechism now lists the chief Commandments of the Church:

> **The chief Commandments of the Church are:** Q229

1. **To keep holy the Sundays and Holy Days of Obligation by hearing Mass and resting from servile works.**
2. **To keep the days of fasting and abstinence appointed by the Church.**
3. **To go to Confession at least once a year.**
4. **To receive the Blessed Sacrament at least once a year, and that at Easter or thereabouts.**
5. **To contribute to the support of our pastors.**
6. **Not to marry within certain degrees of kindred, nor to solemnize marriage at the forbidden time.**

The Catechism says that the first Commandment of the Church is:

Q230 **To keep the Sundays and Holy Days of Obligation holy, by hearing Mass and resting from servile works.**

Here is a clear example of the Church laying down a particular application of the universal obligation resting on all men to worship Almighty God. It is the Church who tells her own children how they should fulfill this obligation by hearing Mass on Sundays and Holy Days of Obligation and by resting from servile works. The next answer,

Q231 **The Holy Days of Obligation observed in England and Wales are: Christmas Day, the Epiphany, the Ascension, Corpus Christi, Sts. Peter and Paul, the Assumption of our Lady, and All Saints,**

shows that the selection of days can vary from country to country. Even as between England and Wales, Scotland and Ireland the days of obligation vary. In France, I believe, they were reduced to four by the Concordat between Pope Pius VII and Napoleon I, including, significantly, the Assumption of our Blessed Lady on August 15, which happened to be Napoleon's birthday.

Q232 **Catholics are under a serious obligation to attend Mass on Sundays and Holy Days of Obligation unless prevented by other serious duties or by ill health.**

Parents, masters and mistresses are bound to provide that those under their charge shall hear Mass on Sundays and Holy Days of Obligation. Q233

Then the Catechism says:

The second Commandment of the Church is, "To keep the days of fasting and abstinence appointed by the Church." Q234

Here again we see a particular application of the Divine Law. No man, in view of the fact that our nature is fallen, can hope to save his soul without imposing certain restraints and disciplines on that fallen nature. As the Catechism observes, in a later chapter not covered in this commentary,

Our natural inclinations are prone to evil from our very childhood and, if not corrected by self-denial, will certainly carry us to Hell. Q344

The next five answers show the Church imposing what we may call a minimum and token self-denial, when she prescribes certain fixed days of fasting and abstinence:

Fasting days are days on which we are allowed to take only one full meal. Q235

The fasting days are Ash Wednesday and Good Friday. Q236

Days of abstinence are days on which we are forbidden to take flesh-meat. Q237

The days of abstinence in England and Wales are Ash Wednesday and Good Friday. Q238

Q239 **The Church commands us to fast and abstain so that we may mortify the flesh and satisfy God for our sins.**

The next five Catechism answers are concerned with the third and fourth Commandments of the Church:

Q240 **If we have been guilty of serious sin we should go to Confession as soon as possible, but never less than once a year.**

Q241 **Children are bound to go to Confession as soon as they have come to the use of reason, and are capable of serious sin.**

Q242 **Children are generally supposed to come to the use of reason about the age of seven years.**

Q243 **The fourth Commandment of the Church is, "To receive the Blessed Sacrament at least once a year, and that at Easter or thereabouts."**

Q244 **Christians are bound to receive the Blessed Sacrament as soon as they are capable of distinguishing the Body of Christ from ordinary bread, and are judged to be sufficiently instructed.**

Our Blessed Lord has given us the means for having our sins after Baptism forgiven and has given Himself to us in the Holy Eucharist to be the life and food of our souls. There must accordingly be an obligation upon us to make use of such means. The Church wisely imposes a minimal use, knowing that without such an obligation we might be in danger of neglecting these provisions altogether.

The fifth Commandment of the Church is, "To contribute to the support of our pastors." Q245

It is a duty to contribute to the support of religion according to our means, so that God may be duly honored and worshiped and the Kingdom of the Church extended. Q246

If, as we believe, the Church is incorporated in a visible, organized body here on earth, that body needs material means for its conduct, support and extension and particularly for the education and livelihood of its ministers.

The sixth Commandment of the Church is, "Not to marry within certain degrees of kindred, nor to solemnize marriage at the forbidden times." Q247

The times at which it is forbidden to marry with solemnity without special leave are from the first Sunday of Advent till after Christmas Day, and from Ash Wednesday till after Easter Sunday. Q248

This last Commandment of the Church carries us back to another concept which we have considered earlier—that matrimony, for all that it is a natural human contract, has been raised by our Blessed Lord to the dignity of a Sacrament for members of His own Body. Consequently the Church has the power to hedge it about with such provisions as she considers necessary to preserve its dignity.

Remember always that the Commandments of the Church are imposed on her members to lead them towards salvation. We should therefore be as grateful for their beneficial effects as we should be grateful for the material things of life which Almighty God has given us as the instruments with which, if we choose to sink our mind and will in His, we can build our road to the Kingdom of Heaven.

A proper concern for the material things of life is only elementary gratitude to the Creator and Giver of all good things. Only when there is a grateful appreciation of the excellence of God's gifts is there any value in the voluntary renunciation of them in order to achieve a closer union with their Giver.

The Catholic Church throughout the centuries gives us a constant object-lesson of this profound truth. There is no such defender of the sanctity and indissolubility of Christian marriage as the Church which holds up the ideal of voluntary celibacy to those who are called to it; no such defender of the rights of property as the Church which extols the ideal of voluntary poverty, no such defender of the dignity and freedom of the human will as the Church which preaches the ideal of voluntary obedience.

We should, therefore, be grateful to Almighty God that he has given us the Church and the World. We should be grateful to the Church for all that she teaches and for all that she asks of us, for her words are the words of our Blessed Lord Himself, whose Incarnation she continues until He comes again.

These expositions of the points of the Catholic Faith which I have given you have been dry and didactic in their tone. My concern has been to put before you the Truth unvarnished and unadorned, the Truth of God, the Truth of which the Church is the pillar and ground. But if you come to love that Truth as I do, if, please God, you come to love the Church who teaches the Truth, you will feel the wonder and the joy and the inspiration of which the Saints and fathers of the Church have written.

To convey to your mind the flavor of the inspiration which we experience in walking with God, let me end this commentary on the Catechism with Mgr. Robert Hugh Benson's vision of the Church, from his excellent book, *Christ in the Church:*

> For I see through her eyes the Eyes of God to shine, and through her lips I hear His words. In each of her hands as she raises them to bless, I see the wounds that dripped on Calvary, and her feet upon her Altar stairs are signed with the same marks as those which the Magdalene kissed. As she comforts me in the confessional I hear the voice that bade the sinner go and sin no more; and as she rebukes or pierces me with blame I shrink aside trembling with those who went out one by one, beginning with the eldest, till Jesus and the penitent were left alone. As she cries her invitation through the world I hear the same ringing claim as that which called, "Come unto Me and find rest to your souls"; as she drives those who profess to serve her from her service I see the same flame of wrath that scourged the changers of money from the temple courts.
>
> As I watch her in the midst of her people, applauded by the mob shouting always for the rising sun, I see the palm branches about her head, and the City and Kingdom of God, it would seem, scarcely a stone's throw away, yet across the valley of the Kedron and the garden of Gethsemane; and as I watch her pelted with mud, spurned, spat at and disgraced, I read in her eyes the message that we should weep not

for her but for ourselves and for our children, since she is immortal and we but mortal after all. As I look on her white body, dead and drained of blood, I smell once more the odor of the ointments and the trampled grass of that garden near to the place where He was crucified and hear the tramp of the soldiers who came to seal the stone and set the watch. And, at last, as I see her moving once again in the dawn light of each new day, or in the revelation of evening, as the sun of this or that dynasty rises and sets, I understand that He Who died has come forth once more with healing in His wings, to comfort those that mourn and to bind up the brokenhearted, and that His coming is not with observation but in the depth of night as His enemies slept and his lovers weep for sorrow.

Yet even as I see this I understand that Easter is but Bethlehem once again, that the cycle runs round again to its beginning and that the conflict is all to fight again; for they will not be persuaded; though One rises daily from the dead.

APPENDICES

Fundamentals and Accidentals

I WAS once asked to give a talk on "The Church I should like." This title had been chosen, I was told, in order to encourage speakers "to talk in wider terms than the bare essentials." This put me in something of a quandary because "the bare essentials" are what alone command my wholehearted acceptance and loyalty. More than that, they demand from me—and by God's grace receive—an act of divine faith. The accidentals, on the other hand, may attract or repel. They inescapably reflect the spirit of the age more or less faithfully (for there is often a time lag one way or the other) and they will attract or repel just so far as the spirit of the age attracts or repels.

We now expect to have things "as we like." It is part of the backwash of democracy that people should have the government they like, the legislation they like, the education they like. This pervasive tendency is powerfully played upon by advertising, mass media, market research and the rest. The housewife must have the goods she likes in the packet she likes. Our likes, which are the most irrational, the most irresponsible, the most fitful part of our being, are elevated into a principle. Fashion, which is the collective like of a period, is canonized. Departure from fashion becomes reprehensible. Only in such an age could one be asked to talk about "the Church I should like"

Have you ever considered that you might not have liked Jesus Christ our Lord; that His human nature was the product of a society, of a culture not our own; that a belief, by the gift of divine Faith, in His Godhead (and consequently an unqualified adoration and love of Him) would have been compatible with disliking His table manners, His method of conducting an argument, His treatment of His Blessed Mother? If we do not accept this possibility, there is something wrong with our understanding of the Incarnation, which is the central mystery of the Catholic faith. We are then thinking of our Blessed Lord in a Docetist way as though He were God playing at being a man, assuming the appearance of manhood, going through the motions of living and dying. We are not thinking, as we should, of the uncreated Word becoming a specific, identifiable man, as much conditioned in His human nature by His culture and environment as any of us by ours.

Now the Church is a mystery just as much as is the Incarnation. She is, in fact, that mystery continued until Christ comes again. We shall never come to terms with this mystery of the Church unless, in our consideration of her, we make a similar distinction to that which I suggest can properly be made about the person of our Blessed Lord. Just as in the Incarnation we make a distinction between the truth which we accept with a wholehearted act of faith and the accidental circumstances of culture and manner in which it comes to us, so with the Church we can accept her as our infallible guide in faith and morals and as our convenanted source of grace through her Sacraments and yet find the accidental and human channels through which she communicates her teaching and transmits her life distasteful to us. Yet while making this distinction we may not make a division. As in the Incarnation the two natures of our Blessed Lord—His divinity and His humanity—are inextricably united, so that all His actions are at once divine and human, so the Church, the spotless bride of Christ, lives and works through human channels as little perfect or attractive to other people as you or I may be.

It is necessary for us to appreciate how misleading may be the traditional distinction between the Church and the World. The antithesis which we set up between them is a false one. There is in fact no such dichotomy. It is rather like the traditional distinction between the Soul and the Body. In both cases the terms are perfectly acceptable so long as we do not think of two disparate entities brought together. In this life man is one single and indivisible being living ever on two planes at once, which are interdependent and constantly interacting on each other.

So with the Church and the World. They are not two separate, self-contained entities, facing one another. They are interpenetrating, interacting, since the same people belong to both. Every child of the Church is also the child of his own age, thinking its thoughts and influenced by the culture and environment which that age provides. The Church is constantly influencing the current scene not by exerting pressure on it from outside but because her members, who through their membership of her are citizens of the heavenly Jerusalem, are also at the same time actors on the contemporary stage.

I recall in this connection a remark made to me when I was a student in Rome in the heyday of Fascism: "Always remember that the next Pope but five is now a member of the Balil la" (the Mussolini Youth into which all Italian boys were enrolled). Of course he was. How could he not be? Just as at this moment the next Archbishop of Westminster but five is being indoctrinated in all the orthodoxies of the welfare state in a state school.

We cannot, if we would, jump out of our skins or escape the influence of our age. In more liberal times it was easier for some at least to contract out and to try to form (as they thought) pockets of more rational or Christian living. Such experiments are liable to be condemned by a collectivist age as a sort of escapism. They have much in common with the call of the desert and the cloister, states of life providentially designed for those whose vocation lies that way. Each of these is a voluntary society, but the Church is not and never can be. She is designed by the same Providence to be the one Ark of Salvation for all.

Once we have seen her in that light no likes or dislikes can affect our compelling duty to belong to her. She can never be selective in her membership (as can a religious order), nor can she be an ivory tower. Involvement (to use the current jargon) is not for her a virtue: it is inescapable. And so, in every age, we see her members entertaining, frequently adopting and even blessing, but always ultimately discarding, the current orthodoxies. This is a process which must be seen both as inescapable and as transient. It is the price we pay for the Incarnation. The mistake is ever to attach undue importance to the process and above all to imagine it final and enduring—to think that the Church has at last found the ideal material framework in which to express the unchanging truth. This is a temptation which assails equally, let us say, those who idealize the achievements of the thirteenth century and those who idealize the *aggiornamento* of today. The Church will work in and through a social or a political or even an ideological system as long as she can and then, when it appears to be strangling her or when she is in danger of being identified with it, she will shake herself free. Then the snapping of familiar ties may both bring much pain to her children and cause her to be regarded by others as the most unreliable of allies.

How many old-fashioned French Catholics, who had been brought up to believe in the union between the throne and the altar, must have felt cut adrift from their moorings when Leo XIII made his overtures to the Third Republic?

The swing between involvement and disentanglement is a constant if irregularly working pendulum. Pius XI, at the time when he was making concordats with the Dictators, is reputed to have said that he would make a bargain with the Devil himself if he could thereby serve the interests of the Church. Less than a century earlier Pius IX had declared that the Church had no need to come to terms with the nineteenth century. Neither the example of dissociation from, nor that of alliance with, the contemporary world may arouse much enthusiasm in a liberal Catholic today. They may serve to show how pragmatic the approach of the Church can be and to demonstrate an underlying consistency beneath superficial disparities. The process is one repeated again and again through the centuries, for in one form or another the Investiture controversy is always with us. There is always a price to pay for worldly support and worldly status and often the moment will come when the price is found too high.

The relics of discarded alliances are all about us and are plain to see. The territorial divisions of the Church, the parishes, the dioceses, the provinces, are a reflection of a feudal, a hierarchic conception of society. The promise of obedience which I made to my Bishop at my ordination, my hands between his, was feudal in form, concept and expression. Just so did a vassal swear fealty to his liege lord and become his man. The ceremonies at a pontifical High Mass, as we knew it till the other day, with the Bishop washing his hands and vesting at the throne, had a parallel in the Grand Levee of Louis XIV. The ritual of the papal court reflected and inspired the ceremonies of the national monarchies of Christendom. Many of our contemporaries now find these things embarrassing and we have become, like our age, collectivist and egalitarian. We are told by experts with a spirit very similar to that of Mr. Pugin and his followers (though with visual consequences vastly different from theirs) that only so and so may churches be ordered and ceremonies conducted. To the medievalizers of the last century the long chancel, the screen, the surpliced choir, the chant, appeared as essential to the spread of God's kingdom as ever the central altar, the stripped church, the vernacular liturgy, the Gelineau psalms, appear to their unwitting descendants today. Once again those who are caught up by a fashion are persuaded that a principle is at stake and that any deviation is morally reprehensible. The obvious difference between the modern liturgist and those of the 1840s is that today authority shares the outlook of the innovators and that this has imposed a moral obligation to accept the changes.

On a recent visit to Lourdes I was taken by an enthusiastic friend to a concelebrated High Mass in the underground basilica, which I had not previously seen. As we emerged he eagerly asked what impression the ceremony had made on me. "It reminds me," I replied, "of nothing so much as a Nazi rally." He was shocked until he appreciated that I was referring, of course, not to the content or the purpose of the ceremony itself but to its inessential trappings—the vast crowd, the raised central stage, the slow and impressive procession of half a dozen bishops and more than twenty priests advancing on the spot-lit altar.

The changes we have witnessed have come about not, as some might have us think, by direct inspiration of the Holy Spirit, nor yet, as some non-Catholic commentators seem to suggest, because of the fear that unless the Church can project a more contemporary image of herself she will lose ground. They have come about simply because those who direct the policy of the Church are themselves the products of an egalitarian and collectivist age. They think its thoughts and share its outlook. The changes to the accidentals which they have brought about are no more lasting than the adjustments to earlier orthodoxies made by their predecessors. Like other accidentals of the Church these changes will, as I suggested at the outset, attract or repel just so far as the spirit of the age attracts or repels.

The gift to believe in the Divine reality which is incarnate in those accidentals is one which God alone can give.

Extracts from Documents of the Second Vatican Council

1. Man, though made of body and soul, is a unity. Through his very bodily condition he sums in himself the elements of the material world. Through him they are thus brought to their highest perfection and can raise their voice in praise freely given to the Creator. (*Gaudium et Spes*, 14).

2. The dignity of man rests above all on the fact that he is called to communion with God. The invitation to converse with God is addressed to man as soon as he comes into being. For if man exists it is because God has created him through love, and through love continues to hold in existence. He cannot live fully according to truth unless he freely acknowledges that love and entrusts himself to his Creator. However, many of our contemporaries either do not at all perceive, or else explicitly reject, this intimate and vital bond of man to God. Atheism must therefore be regarded as one of the most serious problems of our time. (*Gaudium et Spes*, 19).

3. That which is truly freedom is a significant sign of the image of God in Man. For God willed that man should "be left in the hand of his own counsel" (*Ecclesiasticus* 15:14) so that he might of his own accord seek his creator and freely attain his full and blessed perfection by cleaving to him. Man's dignity therefore requires him to act out of conscious and free choice, as moved and drawn in a personal way from within, and not by blind impulses in himself or by mere external constraint. Man gains such dignity when, ridding himself of all slavery to the passions, he presses forward towards his goal by freely choosing what is good and, by his diligence and skill, effectively secures for himself the means suited to this end. Since human freedom has been weakened by sin, it is only by the help of God's grace that man can give his actions their full and proper relationship to God. Before the judgment-seat of God an account of his own life will be rendered to each one according as he has done either good or evil. (Cf. *2 Corinthians* 5:10; *Gaudium et Spes*, 17)

4. The Second Vatican Council sums up what we have said so far about revelation in these words: By divine revelation God wishes to manifest and communicate both Himself and the eternal decrees of His will concerning the salvation of mankind. He wishes, in other words, 'to share with us divine benefits which entirely surpass the powers of the human mind to understand." (Vatican I, *Dogmatic Constitution on the Catholic Faith*, c. 2). The sacred Synod professes that "God, the first principle and last end of all things, can be known with certainty from the created world by the natural light of

human reason." (Cf. *Romans* 1:20). The Synod teaches that it is to His revelation that we must attribute the fact "that those things which in themselves are not beyond the grasp of human reason can, in the present condition of the human race, be known by all men with ease, with firm certainty and without the contamination of error" (Vatican I, *loc. cit.*). (*Dei Verbum*, 6)

5. The "obedience of faith" (*Rom.* 16:26; cf. *Rom.* 1:5, *2 Cor.* 10:5–6) must be given to God as He reveals Himself. By faith man freely commits his entire self to God, making "the full submission of his intellect and will to God Who reveals" (Second Council of Orange, can. 7), and willingly assenting to the revelation, given by Him. Before this faith can be exercised, man must have the grace of God to move and assist him. He must have the interior assistance of the Holy Spirit, Who moves the heart and converts it to God, Who opens the eyes of the mind and "makes it easy for all to accept and believe the truth." (*Conc. cit.*, can. 7). The Holy Spirit constantly perfects faith by His gifts, so that revelation may be more and more profoundly understood. (*Dei Verbum*, 5).

6. The Tradition that comes from the Apostles makes progress in the Church with the help of the Holy Spirit. There is a growth in insight into the realities and words that are being passed on. This comes about in various ways. It comes through the contemplation and study of believers who "ponder these things in their hearts" (cf. *Luke* 2:19, 51). It comes from the intimate sense of spiritual realities which they experience. And it comes from the preaching of those who have received, along

with their right to succession to the episcopate, the sure charism of truth. Thus, as the centuries go by, the Church is always advancing towards the plenitude of divine truth, until eventually the words of God are fulfilled in her. (*Dei Verbum*, 8).

7. Although set by God in a state of rectitude, man was enticed by the Evil One and abused his freedom at the very start of history. He lifted himself up against God and sought to attain his goal apart from Him. Although men had known God, they did not glorify Him as God, but their senseless hearts were darkened. (Cf. *Rom.* 1:21–25). What revelation makes known to us is confirmed by our own experience. For when man looks into his own heart he finds that he is drawn towards what is wrong and sunk in many evils which cannot come from his good Creator. Often refusing to acknowledge God as his source, man has also upset the relationship which should link him to his last end; and at the same time he has broken the right order that should reign within himself as well as between himself and other men and all creatures. Man is therefore divided in himself and other men and all creatures. As a result, the whole life of man, both individual and social, shows itself to be a struggle, and a dramatic one, between good and evil, between light and darkness. Man finds that he is unable of himself to overcome the assaults of the evil successfully, so that everyone feels as though bound by chains. But the Lord Himself came to free and strengthen man, renewing him inwardly and casting out the "prince of this world" (cf. *John* 12:31), who held him in the bondage of sin. (Cf. *John* 8:34). For sin brought man to a lower

state, forcing him away from the completeness that is his to attain. Both the high calling and the deep misery which man experiences find their final explanation in the light of this revelation. (*Gaudium et Spes,* 13).

8. The Father of Mercies willed that the Incarnation should be preceded by assent on the part of the predestined mother so that just as a woman had a share in bringing about death, so also a woman should contribute to life. This is pre-eminently true of the Mother of Jesus, who gave to the world the Life that renews all things and who was enriched by God with gifts appropriate to such a role. It is no wonder, then, that it was customary for the Fathers to refer to the Mother of God as all-holy and free from every stain of sin, as though fashioned by the Holy Spirit and formed as a new creature. Enriched from the first instant of her conception with the splendor of an entirely unique holiness, the virgin of Nazareth is hailed by the heralding angel, by divine command, as "full of grace" (cf. *Luke* 1:28), and to the heavenly messenger she replies: "Behold the handmaid of the Lord: be it done unto me according to Thy word." (*Luke* 1:38). Thus the daughter of Adam, Mary, consenting to the word of God, became the mother of Jesus. Committing herself wholeheartedly and impeded by no sin to God's saving will, she devoted herself totally, as a handmaid of the Lord, to the person and work of her Son, under and with Him, serving the mystery of redemption, by the grace of Almighty God. Rightly, therefore, the Fathers see Mary not merely as passively engaged by God, but as freely cooperating in the work of man's Salvation through faith and obedience. (*Lumen Gentium*, 56).

9. Christ sent the Holy Spirit from the Father to exercise inwardly His saving influence and to promote the spread of the Church. Without doubt the Holy Spirit was at work in the world before Christ was glorified. On the day of Pentecost, however, He came down on the disciples that He might remain with them forever (cf. *John* 14:16); on that day the Church was openly displayed to the crowds and the spread of the Gospel among the nations through preaching was begun. Finally, on that day was foreshadowed the union of all peoples in the catholicity of the faith by means of the Church of the New Covenant, a Church which speaks every language, understands and embraces all tongues in charity and thus overcomes the dispersion of Babel. The "Acts of the Apostles" began with Pentecost, just as Christ was conceived in the Virgin Mary with the coming of the Holy Spirit and was moved to begin His ministry by the descent of the same Holy Spirit, Who came down upon Him while He was praying. Before freely laying down His life for the world, the Lord Jesus organized the apostolic ministry and promised to send the Holy Spirit, in such a way that both would be always and everywhere associated in the fulfillment of the work of salvation. Throughout the ages the Holy Spirit makes the entire Church "one in communion and ministry; and provides her with different hierarchical and charismatic gifts" (cf. *Lumen Gentium*, 4), giving life to ecclesiastical structures, being, as it were, their soul, and inspiring in the hearts of the faithful that same spirit of mission which impelled Christ Himself. (*Ad Gentes Divinitus*, 4).

10. The head of this Body is Christ. He is the image of the invisible God and in Him all things came into being. He is before all creatures and in Him all things hold together. He is the head of the Body which is the Church. He is the beginning, the first-born from the dead, that in all things He may hold the primacy. (Cf. *Colossians* 1:15–18). By the greatness of His power He rules heaven and earth and with His all-surpassing perfection and activity He fills the whole body with the riches of His glory. (Cf. *Ephesians* 1:18–23); *Lumen Gentium*, 7).

11. This is the sole Church of Christ which in the Creed we profess to be One, Holy, Catholic and Apostolic, which our Saviour, after His Resurrection, entrusted to Peter's Personal care, commissioning him and the other Apostles to extend and rule it, and which He raised up for all ages as "the pillar and ground of the truth." (*1 Timothy* 3:15). This church, constituted and organized as a society in the present world, subsists in the Catholic Church, which is governed by his successor Peter and by the bishops in communion with him. (*Lumen Gentium*, 8).

12. It would be quite wrong to say that the other Christian groupings in the world have no value. Ecumenism—a more friendly and charitable approach towards our separated brethren—is a growing force in the Church. The status and position of the Catholic Church and the other Christian groups is set out in the Decree on Ecumenism quoted in Extracts 13 and 26.

13. It is through the faithful preaching of the Gospel by the Apostles and their successors—the bishops with Peter's successor at their head—through their administering the Sacraments and through their governing in love, that Jesus Christ wishes His people to increase, under the action of the Holy Spirit, and He perfects its fellowship in unity, in the confession of one faith, in the common celebration of divine worship and in the fraternal harmony of the family of God. The Church, then, God's only flock, like a standard lifted on high for the nations to see it, ministers the Gospel of peace to all mankind as she makes her pilgrim way in hope towards her goal, the fatherland above. This is the sacred mystery of the unity of the Church, in Christ and through Christ, with the Holy Spirit inspiring her various functions. The highest examplar and source of this mystery is the unity, in the Trinity Persons, of one God, the Father and the Son in the Holy Spirit.

In this one and only Church of God from her very beginning there arose certain rifts, which the Apostle strongly censures as damnable. But in later centuries much more serious dissensions appeared and large communities become separated from full communion with the Catholic Church—for which, often enough, men of both sides were to blame. However, one cannot charge with the sin of the separation those who at present are born into these communities and in them are brought up in the faith of Christ, and the Catholic Church accepts them with respect and affection as brothers. For men who believe in Christ and have been properly baptized are put in some, though imperfect, communion with the Catholic Church. Without doubt, the dfferences that exist in varying degrees between them and the Catholic Church—either in doctrine and sometimes in discipline, or in matters concerning the structure of the Church—do indeed create many obstacles, sometimes serious ones, to full ecclesiastical communion. The ecumenical movement is striving to overcome these obstacles. But even in spite of them it remains true that all who have been justified by faith in baptism are incorporated into Christ; they therefore have a right to be called Christians and with good reason are accepted as brothers by the children of the Catholic Church.

Moreover, some, perhaps very many, of the most significant elements and endowments which together go to build up and give life to the Church herself can exist outside the visible boundaries of the Catholic Church: the written Word of God; the life of grace; faith, hope and charity, the other interior gifts of the Holy Spirit; as well as visible elements. All of these, which come from Christ and lead back to Him, belong by right to the one Church of Christ The brethren divided from us also carry out many liturgical actions of the Christian religion. In ways that vary according to the condition of each Church or community, these liturgical actions most certainly can truly engender a life of grace and can aptly give access to the communion of salvation.

It follows that the separated Churches and communities, though we believe they suffer from the defects already mentioned, have been by no means deprived of significance and importance in the mystery of salvation. For the Spirit of Christ has not refrained from using them as means of salvation which derive their efficacy from the very fullness of grace and truth entrusted to the Catholic Church. (*Unitatis Redintegratio*, 2–3).

14. The infallibility with which the Divine Redeemer wished to endow His Church in defining doctrine pertaining to faith and morals is coextensive with the deposit of revelation, which must be religiously guarded and firmly and fearlessly expounded. (*Lumen Gentium*, 25)

15. The infallibility promised to the Church is present in the body of bishops when, together with Peter's successor, they exercise the supreme teaching office. Now, the assent of the Church can never be lacking to such definitions on account of the same Holy Spirit's influence, through which Christ's whole flock is maintained in the unity of the faith and makes progress in it. (*Lumen Gentium*, 25).

16. The Roman Pontiff, Head of the college of bishops, enjoys infallibility of the Church in virtue of his office, when, as supreme Shepherd and Teacher of all the faithful, who confirms his brethren in the faith (cf. *Luke* 22:32), he proclaims in a personal decision a doctrine pertaining to faith or morals. For that reason his decisions are rightly said to be irreformable by their very nature and not by reason of the assent of the Church, in as much as they are made with the assistance of the Holy Spirit promised to him in the person of blessed Peter himself, and as a consequence they are in no need of the approval of others and do not admit of any appeal to another tribunal. For in such a case the Roman Pontiff does not utter a pronouncement as a private person, but rather does he expound and defend the teaching of the

Catholic faith as the supreme teacher of the Universal Church, in whom the charism of infallibility is present in a singular way. (*Lumen Gentium*, 25).

17. In full consciousness of the communion of the whole mystical body of Jesus Christ, the Church in her pilgrim members, from the very earliest days of the Christian religion, has honored with great respect the memory of the dead; and, "because it is a holy and wholesome thought to pray for the dead that they may be loosed from sins" (*2 Maccabees* 12:46), she offers her suffrages for them. The Church has always believed that the Apostles and Christ's martyrs, who gave the supreme witness of faith and charity by the shedding of their blood, are closely united with us in Christ; she has always venerated them, together with the Blessed Virgin Mary and the holy angels, with a special love, and has asked piously for the help of their intercession. Soon there were added others whom the outstanding practice of the Christian virtues and the wonderful graces of God recommended to the pious devotion and imitation of the faithful. . . , It is not merely by the tide of example that we cherish the memory of those in heaven, we seek, rather, that by this devotion to the exercise of fraternal charity the union of the whole Church in the Spirit may be strengthened. (Cf. *Ephesians* 4:1–6). Exactly as Christian communion between men on their earthly pilgrimage brings us close to Christ, so our community with the Saints joins us to Christ, from Whom as from its fountain and head issues all grace and the life of the people of God itself. (*Lumen Gentium*, 50).

18. It is most fitting that we love those friends and co-heirs of Jesus Christ who are also our brothers and outstanding benefactors, and that we give due thanks to God for them, "humbly invoking them, and having recourse to their prayers, their aid and their help in obtaining from God through His son, Jesus Christ our Lord, our only Redeemer and Saviour, the benefits we need." (Council of Trent). Every authentic witness of love, indeed, offered by us to those who are in heaven tends to and ends in Christ, "the Crown of all the saints" (*Roman Breviary*, Invitatory for the Feast of All Saints), and through Him in God, Who is wonderful in His saints and is glorified in them. (*Lumen Gentium*, 50).

19. The Virgin Mary, who at the message of the angel received the Word of God in her heart and in her body and gave Life to the world, is acknowledged and honored as being truly the Mother of God and of the Redeemer. Redeemed in a more exalted fashion by reason of the merits of her son and united to Him by a close and indissoluble tie, she is endowed with the high office and dignity of the Mother of the Son of God. Therefore she is also the beloved daughter of the Father and the temple of the Holy Spirit. Because of this gift of sublime grace she far surpasses all creatures, both in heaven and on earth. But, being of the race of Adam, she is at the same time also united to those who are to be saved; indeed "she is clearly the mother of the members of Christ . . . since she has by her charity joined in bringing about the birth of believers in the Church, who are members of its Head." (Cf. St. Augustine, *De S. Virginitate*, 6). She is therefore hailed as pre-eminent and as a wholly

unique member of the Church and as its type and outstanding model in faith and love. The Catholic Church, taught by the Holy Spirit, honors Mary with filial affection and devotion as its most beloved mother. (*Lumen Gentium*, 53).

20. Mary has by grace been exalted above all angels and men to a place second only to her Son, as the most holy mother of God, who was involved in the mysteries of Christ. She is rightly honored by a special cult in the Church. From the earliest times the Blessed Virgin is honored under the title of Mother of God, whose protection the faithful seek as they take refuge together in prayer in all their perils and needs. Accordingly, following the Council of Ephesus, there was a remarkable growth in the cult of the people of God towards Mary, in veneration and love, in invocation and imitation, according to her own prophetic words: "All generations shall call me blessed." (*Luke* 1:48). This cult, as it has always existed in the Church, for all its uniqueness, differs essentially from the cult of adoration which is offered equally to the Incarnate Word and to the Father and the Holy Spirit, and it is most favorable to it. The various forms of piety towards the Mother of God which the Church has approved within the limits of sound and orthodox doctrine, according to the dispositions and understanding of the faithful, ensure that while the mother is honored the Son through Whom all things have their being and in Whom it has pleased the Father that all fullness should dwell is rightly known, loved and glorified and His commandments are observed. The sacred synod teaches this Catholic doctrine advisedly and at the same

time admonishes all the sons of the church that the cult, especially the liturgical cult, of the Blessed Virgin be generously fostered, and that the practices and exercises of devotion towards her, recommended by the teaching authority of the Church in the course of centuries, be highly esteemed, and days regarding the cult images of Christ, the Blessed Virgin and the saints be religiously observed. (*Lumen Gentium*, 53).

21. The purpose of the Sacraments is to sanctify men, to build up the body of Christ and finally to give worship to God. Because the Sacraments are signs, they also instruct. They not only presuppose faith, but by words and objects they also nourish, strengthen and express it. That is why they are called "sacraments of faith." They do, indeed, confer grace; but, in addition, the very act of celebrating them disposes the faithful most effectively to receive this grace to their profit, to worship God duly and to practice charity. It is therefore of the greatest importance that the faithful should easily understand the sacramental signs and should eagerly frequent the Sacraments, which were instituted to nourish the Christian life. (*Sacrosanctum Concilium*, 59)

22. By baptism men are grafted into the Paschal mystery of Christ; they die with Him, are buried with Him and rise with Him They receive the spirit of adoption as sons "in which we cry, Abba, Father" (*Romans* 8:15) and thus become true adorers such as the Father seeks. (*Sacrosanctum Concilium*, 6).

23. The General Instruction on the Roman Missal, printed at the front of every new Missal, devotes a

whole chapter to The Importance and Dignity of the Eucharistic Celebration. These are the opening words of that chapter:

> The celebration of the Holy Mass, as an action of Christ and the people of God hierarchically ordered, is the center of the whole Christian life for the universal Church, for the local Church and for each and every one of the faithful. For in the Mass is the culminating action by which God sanctifies the world in Christ and men worship the Father as they adore Him through Christ, the Son of God. The mysteries of man's redemption are in some way made present throughout the course of the year by the celebration of Mass. All other sacred celebrations and the activities of the Christian life are related to the Mass; they spring forth from it and culminate in it.

24. The other Sacraments, and indeed all ecclesiastical ministries and works of the apostolate, are bound up with the Eucharist and are directed towards it. For in the most blessed Eucharist is contained the whole spiritual good of the Church, namely Christ Himself, our Pasch, the living bread which gives life to men through His flesh—that flesh which is given life and gives life through the Holy Spirit. Thus men are invited and led to offer themselves, their works and all creation with Christ. For this reason the Holy Eucharist appears as the source and the summit of all the preaching of the Gospel: catechumens are gradually led up to participation in the Eucharist, while the faithful who have already been consecrated in Baptism and Confirmation are fully

incorporated in the Body of Christ by the reception of the Eucharist. (*Presbyterorum Ordinis*, 5).

25. Pope Paul VI, in his Apostolic Constitution *Indulgentiarum Doctrina* (1967), sets out the nature and purpose of indulgences with great clarity:

> The taking away of the temporal punishment due to sins when their guilt has already been forgiven has been called specifically "indulgence." While it has something in common with other ways of eliminating the vestiges of sin, an indulgence is clearly different from them. In granting an indulgence, the Church uses her power as the Minister of Christ's redemption. She intervenes with her authority to dispense to the faithful provided they have the right disposition, the treasury of satisfaction which Christ and the saints won for the remission of temporal punishment. The authorities of the Church have two aims in granting indulgences. The first is to help the faithful to expiate their sins. The second is to encourage them to do works of piety, penitence and charity, particularly those which lead to growth in faith and which help the common good. Further, if the faithful offer indulgences by way of intercession for the dead they cultivate charity in an excellent way. While they raise their minds to heaven they bring a wiser order to the things of this world.

26. Our separated brethren, whether considered as individuals or as communities and Churches, are not blessed with that unity which Jesus Christ wished to bestow on all those to whom He has given new birth

into one body, and whom He has quickened to newness of life—that unity which the Holy Scriptures and the ancient Tradition of the Church proclaim. For it is through Christ's Catholic Church alone, which is the universal help towards salvation, that the fullness of the means of salvation can be obtained. It was to the Apostolic College alone, of which Peter is the head, that we believe our Lord entrusted all the blessings of the New Covenant, in order to establish on earth the one Body of Christ into which all those should be fully incorporated who belong in any way to the people of God. (*Unitatis Redintegratio*, 3).

27. Civil authority should consider it a sacred duty to acknowledge the true nature of marriage and the family, to protect and foster them, to safeguard public morality and to promote domestic well-being. The right of parents to procreate and educate children in the family must be safeguarded. (*Gaudium et Spes,* 52).

28. Property and other forms of private ownership of external goods contribute to the expression of personality and provide man with the opportunity of exercising his role in society and in the economy, it is very important, then, that the acquisition of some form of ownership of external goods by individuals and communities be fostered. Private property or some form of ownership of external goods assures a person a highly necessary sphere for the exercise of his personal and family autonomy and ought to be considered as an extension of human freedom. Lastly, in stimulating the exercise of responsibility, it constitutes one of the conditions for civil liberty. (*Gaudium et Spes*, 71).

29. Married love is uniquely expressed and perfected by the exercise of the acts proper to marriage. Hence the acts by which the intimate and chaste union of the spouses takes place are noble and honorable; the truly human performance of these acts fosters the self-giving they signify and enriches the spouses in joy and gratitude. (*Gaudium et Spes*, 49).

30. In questions of birth regulation the sons of the Church are forbidden to use methods disapproved of by the teaching authority of the Church in her interpretation of the divine law. (*Gaudium et Spes*, 51).

Afterword

THE FIRST privately published edition of *We Believe* appeared anonymously in 1983 and subsequently, to the author's great surprise, took a wider readership by storm, selling more than 15,000 copies before his death at the age of 97 in 1998. Alfred Gilbey was already a well-known priest, having been from 1932 to 1965 Chaplain to the Catholic Undergraduates of Cambridge University. The course of instructions he gave to enquirers into the Catholic Faith had, in A. N. Wilson's words, already "acquired a legendary status," and had been responsible for more than forty vocations to the priesthood and religious life. This book is modeled on Mgr. Gilbey's course, and edited using tape recordings of each instruction as it was being given. The success of We Believe may in part have been a *succ`es d'estime*, but exceeded all expectations and made Mgr. Gilbey a reluctant celebrity in his old age.

Alfred Gilbey was a priest of great charm, matched by the generosity of the gifts of his time and hospitality on the one hand and his capacity to enjoy the privileges conferred on him by inherited wealth and social station on the other. He was also devoted to the life of prayer. His Commentary on the Catechism of Christian Doctrine, as this work is subtitled, is based on a lifetime's reflection on the truths of the

Faith and, his many friends would wish to add, on the daily example he gave of the precepts of Faith, Hope and Charity. The late Basil Cardinal Hume O.S.B., O.M., revealed at Mgr. Gilbey's 90th birthday celebration that he had been the model of the Cardinal's own priesthood.

Though socially ecumenical, Mgr. Gilbey was theologically intransigent and belonged to a generation of Catholics who did not see it as part of their duty to strive to be the same as everyone else. He watched with ever-growing dismay as the religious artifacts and devotions beloved of generations and which, under the influence of a Spanish mother, had found a natural expression in a pious obedience to ecclesiastical authority, were swept away in a spirit of modernizing zeal from which, following his departure, Fisher House, the Catholic Chaplaincy in Cambridge, was itself not spared.

After the close of Paul VI's reforming pontificate, Rome began to express concern that liturgical innovation paid too little attention to the psychological consequences, invariably harmful, of replacing almost overnight a hallowed and reverent celebration of the rite of the Mass. The *Missa Normativa* did very little to help an older generation of Catholics, and a growing number of younger ones, to raise their hearts and minds to God. Mgr. Gilbey avoided the new rite of con-celebration and, as a Protonotary Apostolic, received a dispensation to celebrate privately, mainly for former members of his Cambridge flock, the old Latin Mass at the Jesuit church in Farm Street or in his chapel at the Travellers' Club.

It seemed to Alfred Gilbey that the Gospel was being pressed into the ideological mould (and even that the worship of the Church was being subordinated to the agenda, and bureaucratic modus operandi), of egalitarianism. Certainly in the 1980s, catechesis was being neglected by authority and even derided by the innovators as an outmoded and harmful form of authoritarianism. Quoting from Fr. Vincent McNabb O.P., Mgr. Gilbey insisted that "truth alone is worthy of our entire devotion" and revealed truth could be taught only didactically. The truths of the Faith needed to be not only memorized but learnt by heart and made the subject of prayer as they had been in the days of the old Penny Catechism. On this basis, and not by an appeal to feeling states—Mgr. Gilbey frequently remarked that our likes and dislikes were the least rational part of us—an instructed Catholic would have something on which to ponder for the rest of his life.

We Believe received no official encouragement from, and was probably an embarrassment to, the English and Welsh Bishops' Conference, a body collegially committed to the success of ecumenism. Mgr. Gilbey took great care, however, in the belief that his Commentary represented the official teaching of the Catholic Church, to request an imprimatur from the late Bishop of Salford: and, wherever appropriate, to support his text with extracts from the documents of the Second Vatican Council. We Believe is, of course, a work on a very different scale to the Catechism of the Catholic Church which was commended in 1992 by Pope John Paul II to the Universal Church, and is not intended to be a work of reference. Nevertheless, the reader feels that he has been able to form a relationship with the author rather than having been required to struggle to come to grips with a large number of formulations. Like the Catechism, however, Mgr. Gilbey's Commentary should be taken in small doses, and might even serve as an abridgement of it.

Anyone who knew Alfred Gilbey and can still picture him in his armchair in Fisher House will immediately have recognized and felt at home with the elegant precisions and gentle admonitions of his instructions. Of their orthodoxy there can be no doubt. Cardinal Hume graciously acknowledged that "a more comprehensive and reliable catechism would be hard to find."

Anyone who has read this book without having known the author will have been aware of the spirit of humility and integrity breathing through its pages. Mgr. Gilbey was endowed with remarkable gifts which were both pastoral and expository, and We Believe is an enduring legacy of his life and thought. Above all, Alfred Gilbey was guided by a conviction that, contrary to the collectivist spirit of the age, our Creator made us to be not equal to one another but, in virtue of our relationship to Him, unique; as awe-inspiring a thought, whenever we allow it to come into focus, as the author fully intended it to be in the pages of his book.

VICTOR WALNE
Easter 2003

CRITICAL REACTION TO THE ORIGINAL EDITION

Clear, straightforward and salutary. I look forward to reading and learning from *We Believe* again and again.

—Sir Alec Guinness, C.B.E.

Written with warm emotion and lucid intellect, *We Believe* presents a doctrine sufficiently complete and sufficiently rich in implication for the individual life as to make conversion possible.

—Roger Scruton, *The Times*

Monsignor Gilbey's is a voice reassuring us of the underlying permanence that sustains us all.

—Auberon Waugh, novelist

A welcome reassurance and service to the contemporary Church.

—Piers Paul Read, novelist

A clear and solid presentation of traditional Roman Catholicism.

—Rev. Brocard Sewell O. Carm.,
The Spectator

Elegant, thorough, uncompromising . . . the best presentation of Catholicism in the English language.

—Christopher Monckton,
The Salisbury Review

CRITICAL REACTION TO THE ORIGINAL EDITION

A carefully constructed presentation, written with grace and charm.

—Rt. Rev. Mervyn Stockwood,
Anglican Bishop of Southwark

Given its premises, the work can seldom be faulted.

—Rev. Richard Incledon,
The Times Literary Supplement

Monsignor Gilbey's Commentary is excellent: it really is hard to beat.

—Very Rev. Canon Francis J. Ripley, catechetist

We Believe is essential reading for teachers and parents and all who wish to recall the background and substance of their Faith.

—Major-General The Viscount Monckton of Brenchley C.B., D.L., *The Catholic Herald*

A book to be read often and treasured, for it is like food for those who hunger and water for those who thirst; it helps us renew our faith.

—John Cardinal O'Connor,
Archbishop of New York

At the same time traditional and contemporary, I warmly recommend this invaluable book.

—Most Rev. Kevin McNamara,
Archbishop of Dublin

TAN Books was founded in 1967 to preserve the spiritual, intellectual and liturgical traditions of the Catholic Church. At a critical moment in history TAN kept alive the great classics of the Faith and drew many to the Church. In 2008 TAN was acquired by Saint Benedict Press. Today TAN continues its mission to a new generation of readers.

From its earliest days TAN has published a range of booklets that teach and defend the Faith. Through partnerships with organizations, apostolates, and mission-minded individuals, well over 10 million TAN booklets have been distributed.

More recently, TAN has expanded its publishing with the launch of Catholic calendars and daily planners—as well as Bibles, fiction, and multimedia products through its sister imprints Catholic Courses (catholiccourses.com) and Saint Benedict Press (saintbenedictpress.com).

Today TAN publishes over 500 titles in the areas of theology, prayer, devotions, doctrine, Church history, and the lives of the saints. TAN books are published in multiple languages and found throughout the world in schools, parishes, bookstores and homes.

p 165 - p 166

As long as you are trying, there is hope / the moment you stop, Almighty God cannot help you because the process is a mutual or reciprocal one.

CPSIA information can be obtained
at www.ICGtesting.com
Printed in the USA
BVHW071407100720
583431BV00001B/29